On Swallows' Wings

A memoir of hope

Lesley Pendlebury

© Copyright Lesley Pendlebury, 2025

All rights reserved. No part of this publication may be reproduced, stored in or introduced into a retrieval system, or transmitted, in any form, or by any means (electronic, mechanical, photocopying recording or otherwise) without the prior written permission of the author.

This book is printed subject to the condition that it shall not, by way of trade or otherwise, be lent, resold, hired out, or otherwise circulated without the author's prior consent.

ISBN: 978-1-915548-20-7

Cover picture courtesy of Liz Huppert, stained glass artist
instagram.com/lizhuppertstainedglass

Disclaimer
This book is memoir. It reflects the author's present recollections of experiences over time. Some names and characteristics have been changed, some events have been compressed, and some dialogue has been recreated.

To My Mother

*"True hope is swift, and flies with swallows' wings.
Kings it makes gods, and meaner creatures kings."*

Richmond, from *Richard III* by William Shakespeare

PART ONE

1943–1983

1

KNIGHTON, RADNORSHIRE

1943–1945

If Only…

If only you could see the sheep that amble in the field beyond the grey stone wall. They graze, impervious to human gaze.

If only you could see the riverbank, the willow trees in yellow green, beyond them a dark mound from which the church spire rises. Its watchful presence is a sentinel, for all that passes in this place will be observed.

If only you could hear the silence as the rain descends. The sheep are huddled now. The humans have all vanished from the world of sight. It's comforting. It is a blanket of the night's compassion and its kindliness.

If only you could see the gentle hills that undulate for miles. They soothe me for I recognise that it is here that I belong. No one will praise the challenge of their modest heights. No one will understand the solace of the secret, nameless world that gave me love.

If only you could see a world where kindness was expected of us all, where each of us was joyful to accept what lay ahead.

If only you could see the small delights created for us then, for no materials were needed to provide the gifts that our imagination brought.

If only you could taste the knob of butter on my mother's knife – held out so that her child, in times of war, might taste this precious blend. Her radiant smile as she beheld the pleasure of the child that was myself.

If only you could see the darkness of the kitchen with its old black range – the five or six or seven of us squashed around the table at the centre of our lives.

If only you could see the leaves of Kinsley Wood – this magical extension to the drabness of our frugal wartime world.

If only you could see the things that I have seen, or felt the touch that soothed me as I grew. Who would you be? And would you understand the person or the soul that might be me?

The tolling bells are steady, and they punctuate the silence of the sleepy border town. The place where I was born. Activity's communal here, it seems. The going out, the coming in, are done, if possible, in unison and always at the proper time. And when folk are at home – especially when it rains – a sheet of silence falls across the valley. It's secret and it's safe. They know what life expects of them. It is the 1940s after all.

And though I'm only two, I somehow understand all this, if vaguely, in that trust-like way that children naturally absorb the way of life to which they are born.

One day I'll learn that wartime worlds are different from other worlds. That in the peace that was to come, most fathers would be at the heart of family life. That were it not for war, this sleepy town might not be home to me.

My father isn't here. He's fighting Germans so that Britain will be safe. My mother and my Aunty Florrie share the women's work of keeping house and minding little ones – in this case, sister Christine and myself. And Granny Taylor is in Heaven, Mummy says.

And, as it is, my grandad is the centre of my childhood world.

A slight, white-haired figure, Grandad lives in a wooden chair beside the old black range, with his reading glasses halfway down his nose.

He is there each morning when I slide down the stairs on my bottom as the pips go for eight o'clock. He is there when I run for a final cuddle before I go upstairs by candlelight and past the witch's hat to bed.

The bells announce the christening of a baby at St Edward's Church. It is the curate's baby. Thus, it is a day of note.

This day we're late.

"It wouldn't do to miss the vicar's greeting," Mummy says.

Her hair's been rolled round rags since breakfast time. On an occasion it, too, must behave. She's wearing her white frock. It has brown spots. It is 'for best'. It is the only dress of hers that I recall. Dresses are special. I'm sure of this. My dress is white as well.

We walk as quickly as we can up Station Road and pass the rounded wall beneath which flows the River Teme. There is no time to look for darting trout today. We've almost reached the row of shops where in the years to come a metal hoarding, blue and white, will still inform the passer-by that Mr Heywood's shop once sold the *News of the World*.

My mother holds my arm, determined that her family will be on time.

Chapter 1

I am reluctant. I pull back and stop. I feel her grip. It tightens on my arm. The heat engulfs me and my tummy hurts. I know I'm going to be sick and say so.

"No, Lesley. You are not," says Mummy firmly as she pulls once more. We stop again.

We start and, in the tussle, I am scared. There are steep steps down from the pavement edge. I think that I will fall.

I feel the furious ferocity that is the conflict of our wills. I drag behind. Mummy inhales slightly as she rearranges her face.

Her will prevails. The last bell rings as we arrive at church and hurry to our row. Anxiously propelled by Mummy, I scramble to the pew. Almost at once it happens. I am sick. The horrid mess smells of the dripping Mummy slathered on my toast before we left. I look down and I watch in horror as, slowly, and surely, the globs of pink run down my Sunday dress.

The journey home is faster. Mummy's tense with rage. I'm consumed by shame, tempered only by my sense of satisfaction that I was right.

And yet my small transgression would forever linger in the minds of those who graced the congregation on that day. For on the hassock, there remained a stain that could not be erased.

If only I had known, as I know now, that all the steps we take in life will show. Would I have taken greater care? Would I have understood that guilt and shame and loneliness might follow if I did not do the things that other people did or else would bid me do? Or if I did the things that shocked and caused the ones I loved to fear? Or that I'd face bewilderment until I could accept that being different might itself present a certainty – the reassurance that I could be me?

And if I'd known how far away that reassurance was, would I have faltered in my quest? A quest that was sometimes elusive and that I often could not see? If I had understood the pain and doubt that would surround my path – would I have tried to turn aside?

Or would I one day realise that every setback is as nothing when I measure it against the things I have? And understand that every slight might bring forth courage if I only have belief in me? That even stubbornness is not, perhaps, a fault, if what it seeks to do is cling to what I know is good and true? That all of childhood's visions and experience will linger on within the woman that I would become? And that, since there's no turning back in life, each one of us must harness all the love and beauty that we can, for only these sustain us when the past is gone?

And if I carry these within and seek to share them with the ones I meet along my path, might I find one day that the love I share shines back at me – that in acceptance of myself, I add to all the generosity that life has shown, the gift of peace?

2

HEMEL HEMPSTEAD – A STRANGE NEW WORLD

1946–1950

On my grandmother's dressing table, a white china swan sits, permanently poised to glide. By it stands a porcelain holder for the rings that Granny might not wear that day. Of these she has but two – a thick plain gold band and a second band, also gold but deeply carved. In years to come both will lie buried in the box that I will keep of discarded but once-loved trinkets. I will not wear this jewellery. The rings will be too small. The items will no longer be in fashion but will not be as yet antique. More importantly, these will not and never can be mine. Linked, for eternity, with those by whom they were once cherished, they are too precious to be thrown away.

Beyond the bedroom, to which entry is allowed on Granny's say so only, all is familiar to me though it's only weeks since we moved to this suburban semi in Hemel Hempstead. We have a granny here – a second grandad too. How can that be?

I'm only three but now it dawns on me that life will never be the same again. For no one told me that I'd one day have to leave my Knighton family behind. Or that I could not live forever with my Grandad Taylor, who I love so much. In future, Knighton would, for some, just be the place where I was born. And yet, to me, it was and would remain the only place where I would truly feel at home. But war, my Mummy says, is over now and three of us – she, sister Christine and myself – must join my father and his parents in this alien, unlovely world. A world in which my Grandad Hughes and Granny Hughes will be in charge.

Life's different here. There is a sense of neatness. The kitchen's orderly. The draining board is scrubbed and bleached to almost white. No crockery, no utensils are seen on it. The kitchen here is not like Knighton where it was the centre of the home. Here it is a place apart. We don't do things together in this world, except that Granny, sitting in the garden, sometimes lets me help to shell the peas.

Despite the cleanliness and order, Granny's never busy, so it seems to me. I never see her with a brush or mop. Perhaps she gets up early, with the elves, to make her household clean and tidy. I only see her sitting in her chair, like Grandad Taylor always did. But he was at the centre of our world, forever radiating certainty, and love. Here, Granny just looks on. Her face shows no expression as she simply gazes at the goings on around. And wrapped around her is an apron. It's a full-length, sleeveless overall of patterned cloth. It's always spotless, covering a long black skirt and high-necked blouse. One day I'll learn this is a uniform: a wartime style adopted by her generation and her class. This is her dress for every season and all times of day. Her bobbed silver hair is straight as a silken plumb line and, with her dark gimlet eyes, she might have been an arresting woman were it not for her sallow skin and her large and rather masculine nose. Together these belie all gentleness.

To Grandad Hughes she is, despite it all, quite beautiful enough – and I, in time, will come to understand that contrary to outward show, there is yet softness within this austere frame.

This second grandad looks quite different from my Knighton grandad who I miss so much. Beneath his thick and wavy hair, above his sunken laughing eyes, a crumpled face displays a prominent and permanent wen, or sebaceous cyst. A cheerful fellow, this new grandad does not seem to mind the constant orders Granny gives. He smiles, even at times when others don't. He has his tobacco pouch and his Rizla papers and thinks himself a lucky man, even though his coughs and wheezes still betray the impact of the poisoned gas so many soldiers inhaled in the trenches in the War to End All Wars.

Granny always has time for me. Sitting at her dining room table she is a tutor of dexterity: teaching me card games – Snap and Old Maid – which she plays with me again and again. Strip Jack Naked. Beat Your Neighbour Out of Doors. Best of all, she can transform the cards into houses with alternate tiers, vertical and horizontal. Try as I might, I cannot emulate this feat for, in my chubby fingers, the cards will never hold fast to the place where I would have them sit.

At three I have no sense of anything beyond our family life and yet the outside world will help to draw the path on which I walk. This is the 1940s. It is early post-war Britain. The bombing raids have wreaked destruction on so many homes. Overcrowding's no disaster in these days. It's just the way it is. Four of us squashed into the backroom of my father's parents' home means we are fortunate. So many families will not have a father home again. We have a roof beneath which we can sleep. All's well. And yet I know, from Mummy, this is not the way she'd have it be. It is not Knighton.

Knighton is the place where I was born. It was, for me, the land of early childhood and of Grandad Taylor too. And always hovering, with watchful gentleness, my Aunty Florrie shared with us her gifts of faith and feyness, of intelligence and love. So humble, yet this modest aunty always knew what it was right to do. Thus, without show and secretly, she'd send gifts to the fallen women of the town. That they would know that someone cared for them. So wise, she put God first, with family and friends not far behind. And yet, though self was always last to her, she brought a special magic to our childhood days. With her a woodland glade became a place where elves would dance. A hollow trunk, when filled with water after storms, became a "fairies' bath".

Knighton, a changeless town, which is, as Aunty was to write in years to come: "Sheltered by hills too gentle for renown".

It is and always will remain my spiritual home. Yet peace, in 1945 so welcome and the bringer of much joy, has threatened to obliterate my tranquil world. War over – and despite my mother's hopes – my father has refused the commission offered him. He's left the army and returned to Hertfordshire, where he was born. Where, after marriage, Mummy stayed until, with her first child expected, all agreed that she would be much safer if she spent the war years in her parents' home. Within a sleepy town, where war would seem a million years away. And thus, it was in Knighton that she gave birth, first to Christine, then to me. But all has changed now Daddy's back from war. For the first time, our family has four members in its daily life: Daddy, Mummy, sister Christine and myself. From now on, we will share our days, breathe the same air and sleep beneath the self-same roof.

And yet this perfect paradigm of family life has shattered all the comfort of the world that I have always known.

Back in Knighton, Grandad Taylor did his best to make this an exciting chapter in our lives. He told us we were going to live in 'Lemon Lemon' – as he called my father's home. At first, this sounded fun to me, for Grandad's stories always banished dullness, lightening apprehension with intrigue. But Mummy, strangely tense and tight of lip, has made us understand that Hemel Hempstead never can be home.

The joys we knew in Knighton are not here. Here is no Kinsley Wood with secret paths and magic glades. Here are no woodland creatures to befriend. Here is no Grandad Taylor sitting in his wooden chair, alert and watchful, ever loving. Live here we might, but Hemel Hempstead, though her husband's place of birth, cannot be Mummy's home and thus I'll never feel that it is really mine.

Always and forever, there will be a great divide. For Mummy, always and forever, this existence is to be a second-best.

And it is here, within this other world, that I first learn that things are sometimes not as we might have them be. And here, despite the superficial calm, lurks something that much later I will come to understand is hidden discord, latent discontent.

It is the first cloud in a sky of azure blue.

The Postman's Gift

The postman comes early to the drab suburban house, bringing, now and then, a rare excitement which, at four, I never really understand. On this day I watch, as Mummy, gasping silently and in some agitation, rips apart the envelope which plops upon the mat.

Mummy is transformed. The energy that she's suppressed beneath her dutiful if sometimes surly stance, breaks free at last. Nothing is said. She bundles me into my flannel coat and buttons my shoes, whilst Christine struggles to keep pace. Christine, my sister older by some eighteen months, who had been promised that I'd be a playmate just for her. So much would be expected of this firstborn child, her place in Mummy's arms – in life perhaps – usurped by me. And I must compensate for all the lost attention that this means. But I don't know this yet. I am immersed in my own world. And, when at last I understand, I realise it is too late.

Today, flinging open the front door, Mummy lets it be known that we are going to the factory where Daddy works.

This break in our routine unnerves me as it enervates. No one, I think, disturbs our Daddy when he is at work. Daddy, I know, has an important job. The paper mills and factory dominate this post-war town. *John Dickinson's* it is that now dictates the daily comings and the goings of the townsfolk here – their wage packets as well. Lines of men, in twos and threes, can be seen each weekday morning between seven and eight,

Chapter 2

walking past our house on the way to the factory. Though some return for a hasty lunch, most don't come back till teatime. In the absence of their menfolk, wives, children, parents live a separate life. Surely, I think, this postman's visit cannot change all that.

We scurry and we scramble after Mummy as she almost runs down Belmont Road. It dawns on me that something strange and unknown is afoot. We pass the baker's shop where Mummy always buys the patties that I love. We do not stop. Crossing Belswains Lane, we reach the Ash Path. This asphalt track takes us beside and then across the canal to the Apsley factory where Daddy works. Tiring, I hope that we might stop to see the ducks. We usually do. But Mummy, now impatient, shows no sign of slowing down. Sensing my hesitation, she grips my arm and firmly pulls me onwards.

Within minutes we reach the factory entrance. The great two-sided clock hangs over the doorway. Straight-backed and burly men in uniform stand guard. Surely, we can't enter here. I watch as Mummy, flustered and yet undeterred, appears to argue with the guards. She must, we hear her say, see Mr Alfred Hughes.

"He is my husband. It's important," Mummy says, the clarity of her Edwardian tones confounding those who think they are in charge.

Somehow, we are admitted. Chairs are found for us. No one speaks. Beyond a glass screen office workers carry out their daily tasks. We wait. I'm anxious though I'm not sure why. I try not to swing my legs. My tummy hurts. I wonder what will happen now.

Suddenly a door opens. Here is Daddy, white of face and with a worried look. He seems to be bewildered, just like me. Then, taking in the scene before him, he relaxes, and I feel the tension slip away.

His words come in a rush. "The kiddies! I thought something must have happened to them…"

"No. Look!" says Mummy as she plucks the letter from her bag and thrusts it into Daddy's face.

Our father's ashen face lights up in joy and disbelief. His smile dissolving Mummy's tensity, the guards, in turn, look friendly now.

The letter, it would seem, brings news for which my parents had not dared to hope. Their names have reached the top of the housing list.

Mummy is to have a home of her own.

Unbelonging – a First Glimpse

At almost seven I am bright and eager, happily immersed in school and fun. Our council house in Hobbs Hill Road is newly built, erected to receive the dispossessed from London's wartime blitz. And one or two, like us, selected from the local housing list.

In Belswains School, I am about to change my class – a move up to Miss Southwick's form, which Christine says is just the best class in the school. I am excited and I cannot wait. But then I learn that 'they' – the teachers – have another plan in mind.

I am so far ahead in intellect, they say, "We do not want to hold you back."

Thus, a decision had been made that I should move up not one class but two – and I will never be a pupil in Miss Southwick's class.

My dark brown hair, in bunches, is pulled back with Kirby grips. Yet, though my face is plain to see, it does not show the teachers how I feel. I always wear a placid look. I will not let them see the horror that I feel. I do not speak. I rarely answer back. I am pliant. I am a timid child.

Yet, running home, I feel the disappointment overcome my calm. I howl as I rush down Hobbs Hill Road, till Keith, the boy who lives next door, comes out and cuddles me. My mother hears the scene and pulls me back inside and tells me not to make a fuss.

Impatiently and, inexplicably to me, she chides, "Oh darling, that's enough of that. You'll be alright. You do not realise just what a lucky child you are."

But she is wrong for when I skip that year of school, I find myself with children older than myself. And even though I can keep pace with them in reading, sums, and history, they seem so grown up, so advanced in other ways. And different from me. And I, the smallest, cutest one, become the butt of jealousy, a thing I've not encountered in my life till now – for I have always been the one who pleased, whose actions are approved, and in these early years I have been sure of my identity and place. But now the sly remarks and barbs begin to pierce my soul and confidence. The jeers, the finger-pointing and the constant cry of "Teachers' Pet". I had not realised before but now I understand the crushing truth.

Not everyone will like me for myself.

Chapter 2

 I learn that in this life some humans will be cruel. And many more of them will be indifferent. And, to protect myself, I'll have to find a place to hide within the crowd.

 It is like Heaven has been found to be a lie.

3

THE WORLD OUTSIDE

1951–1958

First Love

I'm eight years old and he is nine. We're chosen for the summer fete at Belswains School. We're each to have a puppet that fits on our hands, just like a glove. We have to make them move and come alive. It should be fun and yet it seems so serious a task.

"Don't worry," says the boy with curly hair and freckles. "It will be OK. It is so easy. I can show you how."

Paul Watson is the boy who reassures. He lives two streets away. He's in my class. I think that he is nice though Mummy always says we should not talk to boys. Yet, when she sees the photograph I bring from school, she smiles. For there I am, her precious child, my hair tied back in bunches, solemn faced, my flowered dress a pinafore atop a short-sleeved vest. She does not comment, or perhaps she does not notice Paul so close as he and I stand side by side. Our puppets on our wrists are linked together as we separately face the camera's gaze.

And when the puppet show is over, Paul suggests that I might find it fun to travel with him on the milkman's float where, every day, he helps to take the milk around. I'm not sure what to think or say. I sense that Mummy may not want me to say yes. And yet I am so happy that he asks me – that I'm to be accepted in a world outside our home. And I have never travelled on a milk float, with its whirring sound that stops and starts and stops again. It whizzes through the silent streets. It wakes the world and greets the day. Most days it is the only vehicle that Hobbs Hill Road will see. For this is 1951 and nobody on this estate can yet afford to buy a car. And when the milk float stops, the milkman jumps down from the cart. He whistles as the silver crates are carried to the people's steps with milk – so porridge can be made, or proper tea, although that is a grown-ups' drink.

Chapter 3

It seems to me the milkman's life is real – a life more vital than the things we learn about in school.

And so, I go with Paul and, as I feel the breeze that's stirred by that same whirring, whizzing of the wheels of the float, I think I must be on my way to learn about excitement and adventure too – and life.

The half hour that we spend is gone almost before I understand it has begun. And suddenly I find myself outside my house again. And there is Mummy, stern of face and rather angry now.

I turn to Paul but have no words to say. I leap down from the milk float and I slink away.

Next day, quite chastened now that Mummy's made it clear that this behaviour will not do, I understand that outside school, I won't see Paul again. Nor feel the breeze and the excitement or the freedom that I tasted when I strayed from all the safety of our family's routine.

But somehow, I'm upset for Paul as well as for myself. I do not think that this is fair on him. He has been kind to me, and I don't want him to be sad. So, I decide to send a farewell note – a gift for him. I have an envelope (it's one that Daddy brought from work). I find a crayon and I write a note in red. I want to comfort Paul and so I take a ginger biscuit from the tin and though it's very slightly squashed I place it in the envelope. I take the bulging packet and I sit upon the lawn outside. And suddenly my eyes alight upon the clover creeping through the grass. It makes me think. If only I could find something so special that he'll understand that what he did was not just kind or friendly but important – well, at least it was for me. And with my mind alert and full of fairy tales, I vow that I will make this moment magical, especially for him. I pluck a three-leafed clover from the lawn – and then I pluck another one. And from the second I break off a single leaf. Indoors, I somehow glue it to the first.

Next day at school I pass my envelope to Paul. I tell myself that when he opens it, he'll find a memory of the heart that won't be nine until next year. Although he may not feel my loss or even notice it, there will be scrumptiousness to let him know I'm grateful for the kindness that he's shown. And if he looks with care, he'll find a four-leafed clover that will bring him luck throughout the years to come.

And maybe, when we're frail and aged and grey, perhaps the two of us – or even only one – will ponder and reflect as we look back. And then perhaps we'll marvel at how selfless is the vision and the purity of love – at eight years old.

A New Divide

A year has passed, and everything is different now. The days of puppet shows and fun have gone. Ahead of me is the Eleven-Plus. My teacher tells me that this is the most important thing for every child. I'm not eleven yet. I'm only nine so this seems strange to me, but everybody says I have to sit and pass this now, especially if I want to make the most of all the years that lie ahead.

I'm not quite sure of what will happen if I pass. I'm far too scared to think of what might happen if I fail. And yet I can't escape the gravity of this. I must work hard. I simply must not fail. I must not waste what I am told is my big chance in life.

At night I toss and turn, and when I sleep, the bad dreams come. I wake up screaming until Mummy comes and comforts me.

Months on, I sit the test and after that I have an interview with Mr Robinson, the Head of Hemel Hempstead Grammar School. Another girl called Paula's there as well. We sit and wait together in the secretary's room. The secretary gestures to a chair for me. It's at a desk. It has its back to her and to the other ladies there. I am so nervous that I do not realise that I'm supposed to turn it round to face her and the others in the room. The secretary laughs at me. Then, to console, she says that I and Paula came out top of all the ones who sat this test and that's why we are first to meet the Head.

And, within weeks, I learn that I have passed.

I am relieved but I am still unsure. I'd rather carry on at Belswains School. For though the boys have sometimes called me names, I've grown to like some pupils too. I worry what will happen to my friends, for Margaret Chennells, who I like so much, has been told that she has not passed. And nor has Paul.

I wonder if the teachers where I'm going will be kind the way Miss Campkin and Miss Tucker are. And at the Grammar School will there be fun?

I do not understand why everything must change. Why must the ones who pass be separated from the ones who don't? It worries me. Especially since the grown-ups say the ones who do not pass will have a life that will be so much worse than mine. It's so unfair. And I am devastated for though I know I may not like each child as much as I like Margaret – or even Paul – I've always thought of us as being all the same.

Chapter 3

I don't believe that other children can deserve a poorer, lesser life than me.

Panic

I am fifteen. For months I have been anxiously complaining to my mother of the panic that I feel in certain classrooms at Hemel Hempstead Grammar School. I think perhaps it is a phobia, though I am not sure what this word implies. I cannot tell her what might cause this stifling feeling that arouses every physical response I know and triggers each emotion too. When all I want is calm.

I know I want the world to blend in harmony. I long to be as one with everyone I meet. And when I sense that I am different or when the ones who taunt arouse a fear in me that I will always be apart and never can belong, then panic comes.

Panic is that overpowering feeling that narrows my airways as it shatters my control. Panic is the pulsation in my head. Panic forces my jaw to clench and my shoulders to stiffen. Panic causes my skin to tingle with tension as my lungs scream for air. Chaos. And, as my body falls apart, its fragments chorus: "Run. Hide. Escape. Don't let them see you as you splinter and disintegrate."

I'm very conscious of my body now. Its awkwardness dismays. Once it was compact, neat and pleasing, cute enough to guarantee that I'd be greeted with a smile. Yet suddenly I'm tall and gangling. My arms and legs don't know what they're supposed to do. And worst of all the rest of me is still a child. The onset of the puberty that Mummy insists every girl will have is late. I think that it will never come. My chest is flat. There's little flesh upon my bones. The other children in my class are more advanced. But then they're eighteen months ahead of me in age. They shriek at me.

"Look, here comes Olive Oyl."

It does not help that Mummy has dictated that my long hair must be cut. A short bob is, she says, appropriate now I am in my teens. The remnants of my thick and shiny mane lie flattened lifeless on my skull – a pinhead on a narrow beanpole frame. For now, I tower over Mummy who at just five feet is seven inches shorter than her child. This distance separates and makes me feel that I no longer fit within this family. The bathroom mirror is too low for me to see myself unless I stoop. I'm Gulliver. I don't belong – not here and not at school. Not anywhere.

This insecurity has grown as months have passed. At school I try to shrink into my desk. I almost never speak, for if I'm mute and if I do not move, perhaps no one will notice me. For, if they do, the boys will laugh and jeer.

I cannot talk of this. And when I'm asked by Mummy what is wrong, I simply say that I can't bear to be in class, at school.

And as anxiety and apprehension grow, my worried mother moans aloud, "Oh Lesley, you are just too sensitive to breathe."

Yet even Mummy, loving me despite her gruff exterior, begins to understand that something must be done. And thus, I find myself, with Mummy, in the Fernville Surgery, where Dr Phillips offers medicine and platitudes – and sometimes wisdom too.

This doctor is my mother's long revered GP. To her and many of those born in the Edwardian age, a doctor was and is a pillar of society. As such he is beyond the challenge of the ordinary folk, especially those brought up in small communities, where each one knows his place.

If anyone can help, it must be he. But Dr Phillips simply shrugs. He's heard such woes before. At first, he smiles faintly, with his eyebrows raised. And then he frowns, implying that he is accustomed to and rather tired of patients who complain of trivialities.

"Oh, is it this again?" he says, at last, impatiently.

"Help Lesley, please." My mother's tone is tense but abject as she voices the concerns that by now we share. "Sometimes my daughter's rigid with a fear I do not understand. Some days she's terrified to go to school. She tells me that she's frightened that she can't escape. Or that she'll draw attention to herself. I do not understand what's wrong."

Then, knowingly, the doctor tilts his head, his hands outstretched, palms up. At last, he deigns to say a word or two to quell my mother's fear.

"There's nothing wrong with her. Don't worry. It is just a passing thing. She will grow out of it."

But weeks on we return, and when at last the doctor sees the problem does not go away, he sighs and stares at me. Then, straightening the half-moon spectacles perched upon his nose, he takes his fountain pen and scribbles on a writing pad. He thrusts the note into my mother's hands and says, "Alright, if it will set your mind at rest, I think that this consultant is the man that Lesley ought to see."

Chapter 3

Weeks on, in West Herts Hospital, this more experienced doctor stares at me.

"Iberian Celt." He pauses then he speaks again. "Iberian Celt." His shaggy eyebrows raised, he whistles audibly.

It's not what I expect to hear. There follow words about my pale and dark-eyed countenance. And, when it's clear I do not understand, he talks to me about the wanderings of the Spanish Celts, washed up upon the shores of Wales so many years ago.

I try in vain to bring him to the point of why I'm here. "But I need help to understand what's wrong…"

But he dismisses this and simply echoes Dr Phillips' views. "Young lady, this won't last. You will grow out of this."

This wiser doctor barely listens as I haltingly explain what's wrong, while he, it seems, prefers to focus on the way I look, and all this signifies to him.

He is not interested in *me*.

And so we go away. And nothing's changed.

I'm on my own.

4

BEYOND THE FAMILY

1961–1962

Dick

In the distance the telephone rings. The unfamiliar cream instrument sits, isolated, on a white cupboard in the narrow hall of our West Valley Road bungalow. No chair is placed beside it, nor anywhere at all, for leisurely conversation is to be discouraged. Yet this prized possession has been longed for by my sister, Christine, and myself. And, encouraged by my mother's wish to clear the way for urgent communication with Aunty Florrie, Daddy has finally set aside his misgivings.

Today my mother pushes ajar the sitting room door. The features of her tiny face are strong, and her expression is stern beneath the harsh chestnut dye of her unbending perm. The call is for me.

"It's Dick," she says, her precise tones conveying her distaste.

Words are unnecessary. I know from her pursed lips and from her disapproving glance that the caller is my fiancé.

Dick is eighteen, as am I. Daddy, inwardly dismayed but hoping for the best, has given his reluctant permission to our union. And yet, in his and Mummy's eyes, I'm far too young to be engaged. Especially to Dick.

Dick, the adopted son of a scientist professor, is a school dropout, currently working as his father's driver and lab assistant. Despite his family background, he does not fit the image that Mummy has of a prospective son-in-law, if indeed she has one.

Dick's greased black locks, foreshadowing the "Fonz" of later years, condemned him when my mother first set eyes on him. In deference to my parents, his head is now close-shaven. But his swagger, the carefree way he picks me up from school in his blue Ford Anglia, his small retinue of hangers on – such things cannot be overlooked. And even I, who am quite sure that I'm in love with Dick, am slightly dubious of the tattoo he sports on his arm – my name, within a heart, in green and red.

Chapter 4

But for all that, I know that Dick has changed my life. Since he first saw me, walking in the cornfields on the way to Carole Drury's house, he has transformed me from the ugly duckling of my early teenage years to budding starlet on his arm, ready finally, I think, to make an entrance on the stage that I call life.

For life abundant is ahead I know. I long to see and one day to take part in this, the glorious, promised cavalcade. But first I have to find my place within the company. At eighteen years, I'm sure that this is what it means to settle down.

I am too young to understand that insecurity is natural at this age. I'm self-absorbed and think I am the only one who feels they don't belong. That it is only me who feels apart from life. That no one else knows panic when she does not feel included and at ease.

Yet, from the moment that I sat with Dick, huddled on the stairs at someone's party in a house in Ebberns Road, I have felt chosen, special, on my way to where I'm meant to be.

Wearing my white gingham Bardot dress, a cummerbund cinching my waist above the fullness of the skirt flounced out by petticoats, I nodded as Dick asked me if I'd be his "girl".

"I'd like that. Yes, I will," I'd whispered fervently.

It was late May, a month I'll always love. Life was enchanted then. At night, the silence when Dick walked me home was redolent with fragrance of the lilac and the philadelphus bloom. And all was innocence – a perfect hour within a night or two or forty that I can't forget. When nothing mattered other than our teenage souls – the miracle of life and our togetherness, the earth, the moment when we were at one with nature as a glow-worm flickered, lighting up our path. When all the panic and the restless throb of worldly care was stilled by God.

And reassured by Dick, my panics fade and just for now they almost disappear. For in his company, as once I was before my inner self was punctured by the barbs those schoolboys threw, I feel at peace and know that I at last belong.

And I feel close to all of humankind. In harmony with our Creator and His universe. But no one understands this, I reflect.

Hella

Except, I like to think, that maybe Hella understands.

Hella is my pen friend. She is German. At age thirteen our names were paired up for a school exchange. At Easter 1957 a coach drew up outside our Grammar School. It carried pupils from a school in Bielefeld. We hosting families crowded round to see the friend assigned to us. The numbers dwindled till, at last, our guest emerged.

And Hella stepped into my life.

The way she looked and dressed confirmed her foreignness. No English pupil would wear trousers in those days. Her hair was blonde and cropped. Her figure was athletic – quite unlike my own. But there was one thing that we shared. I stood entranced as here at last was someone just as tall as me. Perhaps a half inch taller even than myself, her back was straight. Her air was confident. I knew at once that she was destined to add new dimensions to my world.

And in the four years since that time, through visits and through letters, this is exactly what my friend has done. When I'm in Germany with her, I share a life that is unchanging, ordered and more prosperous than ours. A life where I'm absorbed by cultural differences and Hella's unfamiliar turn of phrase. Yet one where I am made to feel that I belong. And Hella's father, "Onkel Karl", insists all must be done to welcome me.

He makes it clear that he or she who is the family's guest is king.

But, best of all, my pen friend is quite definite. Though not unkind, she's always utterly emphatic and convinced that what she says is accurate. In Hella, all my adolescent insecurities can rest, propped up for now by all the certainty that she conveys – whether she feels it or not.

"It *must* be so", she'll say in her Teutonic tones. Or else she will aver emphatically "this *cannot* be".

Despite my friend's apparent confidence, her letters, just like mine, reveal a teenage angst. We tell of how we long to see each other once again – to talk, to share the anguish and excitement of our immaturity. And always there are things that I reveal to her alone. We keep our greatest secrets to ourselves until we meet again.

But, in the meantime, we do all we can to share the fads and pleasures of our different lives. No matter that, just years ago, our fathers were at war. We revel in the contrasts that we see. We're young and blessedly untainted by the enmity our nations were once taught to feel. Our parents saw beyond all that.

"Don't blame the ordinary folk for war," my father always said. "We had no choice in this. And nor did they."

Chapter 4

And Hella was and is a welcome guest within our home.

And thus, our lives are free to fill with trivial frivolities. We're fascinated by the different foods we eat. We wrap them up and send them to each other through the post. We share the music of the pop songs that we can't get off our minds.

And with these tiny offerings we, step by step, commit ourselves to friendship of a kind which will endure. And as we teeter on our separate paths to adulthood, we build a bridge to understanding and to unity.

The Bubble Bursts

But here, at home today, there's no such unity of thought. And, eager as I am to speak to Dick, I sigh and wish my parents welcomed him the way I always hoped they would. I trust in Dick and cannot understand the reservations that they clearly have.

But now the voice that's almost always cheerful and upbeat is not as I expect.

"I'm sorry, darling. I can't see you for a while. It's Mum. She's very poorly now." Dick's voice is flat and monotone.

A shock – but then I know Dick's mother has an illness that's incurable. It's multiple sclerosis. She's in a wheelchair now and things are getting worse.

"I feel so guilty, Lesley."

My sweetheart sounds so full of woe. My heart is touched.

"I should have spent more time with her. And now there's not long left. I need to put her first."

Immediately I share his guilt. His parents have complained about the time he spends with me. They are both elderly. They make it clear that they adopted him so he could care for them in their old age. That's what Dick says. And this is why, he says, he needs me just the way he does. Because, he says, I am the first to love him for himself.

And only weeks ago he'd begged me to elope. He could not wait, he said, till we were twenty-one. But I demurred and pushed him back.

"We can't build happiness on the unhappiness of others," I had primly said.

I would not push him back again.

Unhesitatingly I say, "I understand."

The conversation ends and I put down the phone. I do not tell my mother what was said. My private feelings are intense, and I don't want them to be changed by adult views. And so, I hug my secrets to myself.

Days pass, then weeks. I start to brood but I don't ring Dick and I do not hear from him. In 1961 the telephone is not an instrument for casual calls. It's rarely used and like a telegram its use is generally confined to pivotal or life-changing events – to bring news of the missing, or a birth or death.

I wait with patience till one day, when shopping in Kings Langley, I encounter Ted. I've met him once or twice for he is married to Dick's sister, Angela. In truth, he's never interested me before. Although he's only twenty-seven, he seems so old and so conventional. He always wears a suit – at weekends too. His light brown hair is short and parted at the side. Yet now I rush across to him. My voice is all concern.

"Please tell me. How is Mrs Wokes?" I ask almost imploringly, so anxious am I to receive some news.

He stares at me, apparently bemused by what I say.

"Why do you ask? What's it to you? She's fine," he says. "Well, just as fine as she will ever be."

"But I thought... and Dick said..." My voice trails off.

"Oh, Dick!" says Ted, impatiently, with not a little scorn. "We hardly see him now, not since he went to live with Jean."

I'm stunned. The bubble bursts. My world dissolves. I nod and somehow slink away.

I shrink within myself. I cannot eat. I hardly speak. And deep inside I see this as a punishment, but I'm not certain what it is that I've done wrong. My parents guess that it is over, yet I somehow cannot tell them what I've learned. And Mummy has no words to soothe the pain that must be obvious. She does not take me in her arms. Instead, to show me that she cares, she showers me with treats and makes me all the dishes that I used to love to eat. It does not help. The bright green colour of the peas I liked so much, will, from now on, remind me of the desolation of those days.

At Easter 1961 I go with Mummy on the Green Line Bus to Oxford Street. We buy a dress. It is a sheath of chequered brown and black. Its narrowness shows off the now too slender body that is me. And the assistant purrs at the sophistication that she thinks she sees. Yet, from the bus, all that I see, through Watford, Hendon and as far as Marble Arch,

Chapter 4

are dress shop windows full of bridal gowns of white. They seem to mock me. They will never be for me.

And though she's kind and loving, Mummy does not see the things I see. She cannot hide the feeling that I read as her relief. For now, my future will be back on track, she hopes. She thinks that she may get her daughter back again.

And yet perhaps there is no track both she and I can visualise. My understanding's limited by callowness and grief. The path ahead my mother sees is alien to me. And she will never understand the wonder of the moments that are gone, which, in their wake, have left me comfortless and lost.

5

CHARLES AND THE DEATH OF GRANDAD

1963–1966

Birmingham – Freshers' Week

He strides majestically through the sprawling crowd in Founders' Room – that meeting place where students throng with their coffee when they have absented themselves from their studies. They laugh, talk, and hold each other in casual embrace. Someone has painted a mural showing dancing figures, carefree rioters – the focus of our sixties student life. *Per ardua ad alta*: through hardship great heights are reached, our motto, is inscribed above the images. An irony, I presume.

My eyes cannot help but follow him. He is different. It's not the colour of his skin I first notice but his bearing: proud, imposing. He eschews the jeans and cords worn by the other men, men who in his presence are immediately revealed as the boy children they still are. His brown and cream sports jacket and his immaculate trousers elevate his presence. At his neck is a cravat.

I sense that he is aware of me and of the response in me that he provokes. I turn away, willing this to stop.

This man stands out amid the turmoil that is Birmingham in Freshers' Week – where I'm dismayed to find that almost all the first-year students are much younger than myself. The subdued period following Dick's departure from my life has left me out of time and step with my contemporaries, though now, at almost twenty-one, I find that I'm the one who is ahead in age.

Yet though I'm drawn to him, my interest is a passing one. For in this place there's so much to absorb. This university is not – as yet – the hub of academic learning I had thought that it would be.

The mêlée in the students' union building overwhelms. There is so much excitement, but there's apprehension too. Released from home and its constraints, new students vie and jockey for position as they try to make an impact here. They seem to me so shrill and raucous. Most are eager to avail themselves of all that is on offer here. And those who are not new are here to siphon off recruits – for this society or that. And some of them are smooth and more unscrupulous.

And now and then a predator will circle, seeking out the most naïve.

A Breath of Air

I'm here to study social sciences, for subjects such as politics and sociology appear more relevant to me than classics now. I want to understand why human beings act the way they do and why sometimes they push each other down. I hope one day to work to help society's oppressed.

The range of options is extensive, and I'm drawn to what is unconventional. My tutor tells me of a lecturer who he has found to be exciting, with a new approach. This lecturer has studied politics and government in Africa. He's spent much time in that great continent, so ancient and yet re-emergent now. This lecturer has things to say of the immensity of change and of the way in which old worlds are swept away.

And though it is so gentle that I'm unaware of it, a tiny breath of air drifts through my mind and soul, creating openness and space. As dimly I perceive that there might be no limit to my world.

At once my mind goes back to Charles, the tall and striking figure that I'd noticed at the start of Freshers' Week. I've only spoken to him once or twice. But he's the only African I know. I wonder if this course will be of interest to him. The things that I am here to study are familiar to Charles. But he is practical. He's here to study civil engineering. He plans to change his world by building roads and hospitals. He is not interested in thoughts or theories or dreams.

Yet my imagination links him to the things of which I learn. Thus, Charles exists within these lessons despite and indeed because of his absence. He gives context to the outline that our lecturer provides. His absence means that sometimes I can shape that context for myself.

When, as now and then we do, we chat quite casually over coffee, I realise how much I misunderstand. Charles tells me, as I speak, with hesitation, of the evils of the slave trade, that his ancestors were prolific sellers of slaves.

"I did not… know," I stammer in dismay. "It must have been… awful."

Yet instantly and firmly he responds. "No, Lesley, trade was good. My family are noble princes, and they led and prospered then."

I hear the pride in the projection of his voice. I see it in the thrust of his magnificent chest. I am shocked.

Yet my enthusiasm for my studies is undimmed by this encounter with reality. Although I am to write of socialism, it isn't just a narrow doctrine that engages me. I learn about the theory of symbiosis: the interweaving of colonial and post-colonial culture. I begin to understand and to absorb the joyful consciousness of Négritude, the affirmation of blackness and the heritage of Africa.

I embrace the beauty of diversity and the richness that it brings.

Knighton – the End of Childhood

I am in Knighton now. It is the vacation. I am glad, for I need time to complete my dissertation. I am glad, too, because I need to be with Grandad. He is gravely ill.

Grandad lies within the terraced cottage nestling in the lee of Kinsley Wood. To this house, some sixty years ago, he brought his shy Edwardian bride. Here, where their married life would start and end, their children first drew breath. Four children grew to adulthood. Of these, just two are living still. And Granny Taylor died some twenty years ago.

In 1965 it's Grandad's turn.

Now, in this place that's witnessed marriage, birth and death, Grandad is cared for by my mother and my aunt: his daughters and the daughter's daughter. He is eighty-nine and his heart is failing. I need to be close to him. His life is inextricable from mine. As it has been, always.

Surrounded by sadness, I escape the present day and let my thoughts drift back to childhood.

Life in our crowded railway cottage revolved around Grandad. Our every move was dictated and approved by him. But we, his grandchildren, were always loved. Grandad would tell countless stories about the people he encountered as a guard on the Swansea line. With every story he would open up new worlds for me and for my sister too.

It seemed to us that Grandad's place was firmly at the centre of our home. And yet, his books betrayed his principles and his desire to understand and change the outside world. He was a union man, a socialist. He worshipped at the pen of Hugo and of Shaw.

Chapter 5

From Grandad we learned about important things that happened in the land outside our sheltered home. We knew this was a different world where people might not always accept and love our Grandad just the way we did. Once Grandad had to go to the police station to explain things. It was, our mother said, because he read *The Daily Herald*.

His lovat green cardigan was always freshly washed. In later years, his newspaper was ironed by Aunty Florrie when he crumpled it.

From his chair Grandad set the rules by which the household ran.

"Close that blind," he would say, impatiently, as the first hint of dusk descended on the world outside.

But Grandad also knew how to enter our own childhood world. Behind our house the path up the rocks to Kinsley Wood was still visible from our window in the days before the foresters reached Knighton.

The woodland creatures held no fears for us for Grandad said that Little Susie Squirrel and Little Sammy Squirrel were our friends.

Beyond the grey stone wall which protected us from the River Teme, sheep grazed peacefully in the field between the river and the railway line, untroubled by the two or three trains which passed their way each day. And, further to the west, the gentle hills of the Frydd and the Garth rose serenely, giving shelter to our small community – and reassurance to our day.

No one could scold us when Grandad was around.

"Leave them alone," he'd say. "They'll grow up alright."

And now, in 1965, in Knighton once again, I *am* grown up. The wooden chair, where, in my childhood Grandad always lived, is empty now. Grandad does not live there anymore.

There has been a shift in Grandad's life. His bed has been brought downstairs, just as it was for my mother all those years ago when I was born. Then, it was so that my soon-to-be sister could run in and out and not be shut off from her mother at this time of change. Perhaps now it makes things easier for my mother and my aunt.

Grandad's departing is slow and gradual. But it is unmistakeable.

August this year brings a heatwave, too stifling for one who finds each breath an agony to take. I try to banish this thought. I sit in the bedroom upstairs with my books and my writing. Life goes on. We nurse as much as we are able, but not all the time. Sometimes two of the three of us take a walk in Kinsley Wood.

It is the year of the snakes which, propelled by the heat, have crawled down from the hills, searching for water. I seek them eagerly but with trepidation, just as I always rush to face the challenge of obstacles or innovations that I neither know nor understand. No one suggested to me then that some provocations are to be avoided. Some days we meet the snake catcher carrying a forked stick over his shoulder after a successful day. He has not shrunk from confrontation. I am utterly absorbed. Snakes, which I have always found repulsive, now serve as a distraction and relief.

Yet, all the time throughout our walks, I fear for what is happening at home, where Grandad lies. I understand that what we have to bear will be that much more painful if we are not there to witness it.

The day comes. I am upstairs, unable to study, staring into the mirror of the old brown wood mantel surround that Aunty has banished from the front room. I hear the latch on the entry gate. I hear the echo of footsteps. I hear Dr Garman's voice as he strides through the open door which we call 'front' although it is the only one we have and anyway it's at the back of the house. He attends to Grandad. I hear him call. He is the doctor of the town, commanding our respect and deference. We do as he instructs.

"Bring her down," he says, of me. "She must see death. It is a wonderful thing."

It is too late. Grandad has gone. My aunt's distress permeates the room: she is afraid that Grandad will have heard the doctor's words. Her Christian faith cannot assuage what she believes must be her father's fears.

That night her vivid dreams express her anguish.

"I dreamed about that hunting song – John Peel, you know the one," she says in tones that tell me that she's searching, desperate for comfort of a kind. "The one where the sound of his hounds awakens the dead – or was it the horns?"

Though I know nothing earthly can awake the dead, I don't reply. I feel nothing yet.

The family gathers to make preparation for the funeral to come. I try to push aside the truth I cannot bear to see. Until, just hours before the funeral, turning from Station Road to Wylcym Place, I almost collide with the graveyard workers carrying a bier for Grandad. I am shaken.

I remember nothing of the funeral itself. But of that day, I have a photograph. On the front steps, where all in our family have their pictures

Chapter 5

taken, I stand with my sister and our two cousins. Unsmiling, dressed in black, we stand, in eternal solemnity, as we contemplate not just the camera but the void ahead of us.

The past is gone and yet I vow I will not let it go.

Alone

As I start my third year of university, I try to chase away the emptiness by burying myself within the chaos of my student life. It does not help. The frenzied energy I find throughout the campus simply underlines the isolation and remoteness that I feel. I'm overwhelmed. There are too many choices, too few rules. I am unsuited to anarchy of any kind. I need an anchor if I am to have the confidence to float. Grandad has been my anchor. When, as not infrequently happened, I was upset, it was to Grandad that I fled. It was an easy journey, hitching from Birmingham to Knighton. Anxiety and panic never troubled me at times when I felt free as well as loved. In those days which preceded any awareness of violence and danger, I would hitch willingly. And when the lorry or the van pulled out of the suffocating suburbs, I breathed again.

I never said that I was coming. I knew that when I walked through the front door, I would be welcome.

Thus, it happens that, after one more upset, I hitch and make my way. And it is then, as I am put down from the first stage of my lift, that I remember: Grandad is not there now.

In Halesowen, on the grassy verge, I fling myself down and weep.

Into the Void

I want to avoid Birmingham now. It is too full of noise. It is disorderly and shrill. There is work for me to do and I no longer have the heart nor energy to play.

I am subdued. Yet, some familiar figures rise above what seems to me a sea of nothingness. And one of these is Charles. We are not close. We do not often speak. But in my grief his solid presence and his certainty are comforting. In Founders' Room he turns and stands beside me. He is composed and self-possessed.

The void that is left by Grandad's death is never to be filled. For everyone will now and always be a lesser man. And so is Charles, though his huge presence permeates the space in which I try to chase my thoughts away.

He is impassive though he chides me slightly when he learns that I retreat from social life to find a church where I can pray and let my sorrow flow.

"Lesley, you have things to do. It does not help to run. You have to live, not hide yourself," he says in measured tones. "In Africa we have a saying to remind us of the need for faith. 'The God who created the coconut will provide us with water'."

He tells me that his path has altered too. He's had a setback in his quest to graduate. He's not a member of this campus now. Life has brought him to a different setting where he will complete his studies. He is to live in Wales.

Charles rents a cottage in Rhydyfelin, in the valleys. It is quiet there, he tells me.

"The peace will do you good," he says, with certainty.

The calm of his demeanour and the power of his stature forestall doubt.

Days later I am in Cardiff. I take the Heads of the Valleys bus. I am tired when I reach the cottage he has rented, but it's still light. The cottage stands on the eastern slope above the valley. It is sparse but from the windows I look out. And, as at Knighton, when I look, I see the hills, there on the western slope of the valley just where they have always been.

I cling to the hills. The refuge that Charles offers is but fleeting, yet it sees me through. In years to come we'll write to one another now and then. From time to time, we'll meet – and yet our friendship is ephemeral. It's born of transient need and circumstance. For this short while, each of us will assuage the other's loneliness.

6

BETHLEM (1)

1968

A Life Half Full

And on the brink of adulthood, I am half formed. I have the strength that happy early childhood and acceptance give. But also, all the insecurity that adolescence brought.

And though I push them back, the panic and the phobia are constants now.

I try to rearrange my life around this inconvenient anxiety. And ten years on from that first time when, though she could do nothing, Mummy listened to my cry for help, I've built myself a life of sorts.

I've graduated in the Social Sciences. I love my work. My life's not settled but I've many friends. And yet I hover anxiously upon the edge of life's exciting core, unwilling or unable to believe I have the right or the ability to play the fullest part.

The subjects that I chose to study were the ones that don't demand a strict adherence to a rigorous regime; the ones where lecturers would be relaxed if my attendance faltered now and then. This meant I could avoid the classroom sessions if I felt I could not cope with that trapped feeling that they brought. Yet I have always understood that adult life would not indulge me in this way.

The friends I chose were undemanding too. They did not care if I would not accompany them to seminars or to the cinema. They were the ones who asked no questions and, perhaps, the ones who did not really have the time nor will to care for me.

Yet all of this imposes on me limitations that are harsh. I yearn for freedom to go where I choose in life, to sample all on offer in this brave new world. I long to work with those who find themselves adrift from life – the dispossessed or broken ones. And yet I can't ignore reality. I always understand that first I have to heal myself.

In Search of the Holy Grail

Thus, after university, I found work at the Tavistock, a clinic for research and the treatment of disordered minds. I was a PA and I hoped that I would undertake research. And here again I was indulged. I was excused from what was difficult for me.

"You need not be a part of any meeting. As long as you type up the minute taker's notes, so that you'll understand what was discussed," said Robert R when I disclosed my plight.

The social scientists seemed fascinated by the panics and the phobia that I revealed. The ones engaged in study were so keen to analyse and help me find a cure. They told me of new therapies that I might have. They gave me hope that I – like them – might one day find a role where I might help to make things better for the anxious and the sad.

And even when I left the Tavistock and went to work in industry, in personnel, I nursed the contacts that might one day lead me to a place where I'd be helped to heal.

And now, at last, I see a door through which, perhaps, it's possible for me to walk. That door is innovative therapy, which, I'm told, will rid me of this limiting, obsessive curse. I understand that, somehow, I will be desensitised, so that the places that I dread will gradually lose the terror that they hold for me. And so, I've willingly agreed to join a waiting list so that, one day, I also may be cured. I understand this may mean that for a week or so I must devote myself to this. And that this will be better done in hospital.

For such a life enhancing gift, it seems a tiny price to pay.

And here, on this clear February day, I'm on my way. The blue Cortina driven by my father navigates the unfamiliar roads and lanes. It's bound for Edenbridge, where Bethlem stands. This hospital has history. I'm humbled as I bring to mind the many who, in centuries gone by, were reviled, outcast and condemned as hopelessly insane. I tell myself that it is different now, for, in this present century, the sick may all aspire to find a cure.

My parents are tight-lipped. I don't know what they think or feel. We rarely share our inner fears and, if they nurse concerns, they keep them to themselves. They focus only on what is immediately in view.

"You should have turned off there," my mother chides.

"Alright, alright." My father tries to hide his anxious irritation, as he always does.

Chapter 6

By contrast, I am full of hope. Though timid, I am always optimistic, and today I'm sure I am about to find my Holy Grail.

We reach the place where I believe it can be found. I hold my breath. I am excited now. Ahead I see a red-brick house – a lodge that guards the entrance to the hospital. I'm eager and I rush ahead – I always do. My parents follow me inside. In my enthusiasm I don't sense the nervousness they feel.

Within this gatehouse is an office where a lady waits for us. She is officious, smartly dressed, and self-contained. She does not smile. She checks and finds my name – Miss Lesley Hughes. Her hands are full of papers and to these she adds a file I think must be my notes. Efficient as she clearly is, this load's too much for her. The papers almost fall. I leap to help.

"Oh, please," I say. "Let me. I'll carry my own notes."

Immediately she stops. She turns to me and stares. Caught in her withering and condescending look, I shrink, as I am meant to do. I feel a frisson that I do not understand and yet, somehow, I realise that here is not the script I thought to read.

She glares.

"Oh no! Not you. You must not do that. These are not for you to have," she says. Her scathing emphasis is on the 'You'.

And as I hear her harsh, derisive tone, I sense that all's not well. And suddenly I understand that I am suspect, for she's clothed me in the otherness that I will find pervades and dominates this hospital. She has already formed a view of what and who I am. I'm just another patient whose identity she does not care to see.

A thought forms in my mind. I try in vain to push it back. The thought is doubt. My headlong rush is halted now. Am I perhaps mistaken in my trust? With mounting fear, I understand that here, perhaps, it is irrelevant that I am me.

My parents leave. The optimism that burst from me on my journey's fading now. Enthusiasm disappears. Only timidity remains. My stern-faced escort indicates a path across the grass that stretches down the slope. Subdued and apprehensive now, I follow till we reach a low-slung, red-brick building in the hollow of the hill. Beneath its portico, between its stern, relentless lines, I see a mighty door of oak.

It opens now. Beyond it is a void. I walk towards it, and it swallows me.

A Place of Safety

The door slams. The key grates in the lock. I hear brisk footsteps fading down the corridor.

The nurse's words echo in my mind. They are to stay there, frozen, for some fifty years or more.

"Anneli!" she'd called.

I'd seen that she was smirking, as if she had, triumphantly, unpinned a hand grenade she longed to throw.

"Here's a new little playmate for you."

Furtively, for I am apprehensive now, I steal a glance in the direction that her words are tossed. The figure on the farther bed is clad in shabby black. Her manly clothes envelop her, obscuring both her dumpy frame and femininity. As she intends. Her mousey hair is scraped into a careless bun. Inelegant and formless strands escape.

In time, as months pass, I am to learn of her that, though she's volatile and violent, she's honourable. I come to understand that it's not she who is my enemy.

That time is not here yet.

I'm stunned. Why am I locked up here? And why with her? Who is she? What has she done that she's imprisoned here? This cannot be the place where I am meant to be.

My instinct is to flee. Escape! Briefly, a thought pervades my mind. I look around. It dies at once, impaled upon the crucifix that is the window bar.

Where am I? What will happen to me here?

Behind the iron door of hopelessness, I sit and wait for what I am now terrified to know. Time's frozen. So, it seems, am I. I do not stir from the bed where I crouch, unwilling to look around and place myself where I now do not want to be. There is no conversation. I don't recognise the stunned paralysis of my once mobile mind.

It's several hours, it seems to me, until, at last I can detect the scraping of the lock that means – perhaps – I'm not to be incarcerated here. A different nurse, stern-eyed, expressionless, stands at the open door.

"It's time for exercise. You'll walk outside. You may have twenty minutes. Just within the grounds."

She does not use my name. Her manner is impersonal and brusque. And yet it's clear that this command is aimed at me.

Chapter 6

Scrambling and dazed, I quickly walk along the silent corridor and turn at right angles into the passage that will lead me to the outer door.

Escape?

I stagger as the air envelops me and brings me for an instant back to life. Ahead the swards of green stretch upwards on an incline till I see no more. Somewhere beyond that grassy bank must be the gatehouse where I entered what I now know is a different world. A bright-faced girl with sparkling eyes of hope, I was so eager to embark upon the therapy I'd waited for these many months. A volatile but optimistic woman-child of twenty-five, on whom life seemed to smile at last, with work that I enjoyed and friends and sometimes fun. And yet not confident enough to shun advice received from, as I was assured, 'the ones who know'. Advice that only a brief spell within this 'marvellous place' which, they asserted, led the science in their psychiatric world, could rid me of the panic and obsessive fear that plagued my life. And now I'm in this place where I had thought that I would find a cure.

Was that young woman really me?

I turn to climb the hill but then I hesitate and suddenly I feel a hand that grips my arm.

A voice disrupts my frantic thoughts. "You're not safe here."

I twist around to face a scrawny man with oiled hair.

And, pointing to a figure skulking in the shadow of an oak, he says with firmness that I take as menace: "He's dangerous. He's here for rape. You should not be alone. Don't go that way."

Who is this man who seems to know so much? Perhaps he works here. Can this be? For all the nurses seem to wear a uniform of sorts. I feel the pounding of my heart. Somehow, I release the question that I know that I must ask.

"Are you a nurse?"

The answer, in his London voice, is curt. "No."

It is enough. My stomach tightens. I am almost sweating now. In horror, I recoil but cannot, dare not, pull away from him. So, side by side, we step away and walk in silence for what seems like half an hour or so, sometimes through bushes, then again on paths until, at last, we reach the entrance once again. I hesitate, for now, beyond the chaos of this day, I fear that there's no place of safety here, no corner of this world where danger does not lurk. *Where can I go?* A thought I cannot banish hovers in my brain.

And what might this man's illness be? Or what, perhaps, his crime?

And thus, in terror and in shock, I stumble up the steps until I reach the door. And then I free-fall, flailing, into the abyss where madness lies.

7

BETHLEM (2)

1968

Awakening

The remains of the first day are buried now. I cannot disinter them all. Somehow the day passes. No doctor sees me. There is no explanation of the curious and cruel world that claims me. I'm on my own. Back in the four-bed dorm, I shrink into my bed, ignoring the other occupants, shadowy figures, slumped and showing little sign of movement or of life. But, from my sideways sprawl, if I dare lift my eyes to look, I can see Anneli.

Somehow, I sleep and, waking, just for seconds, feel the joy that comes with dawn and with the promise of another day. Then, I remember. Horror overwhelms.

Anneli is awake. She crouches on the far side of her bed. She glances at me. For an instant there is something recognisable in those dead eyes. It's pity – surely not, I think, for me? And yet, it is.

Finally, she speaks. "It's not so bad, you know."

Her laconic Finnish accent hints at indifference to the drama and the tension that is all around. A mask, surely.

My breathing quietens, but not for long. The iron door that was so still and forbidding opens now. I see a young and bustling nurse. She's pretty. West Indian, I think. Her step is jaunty. In it I detect the rhythm of enthusiasm I myself once knew.

She has a job to do. Though I'm not ill, 'they' need a urine sample from me. She thrusts a clear receptacle into my hands. It has a white top. And there's no mistake, for on its label is my name – the name that no one seems to speak. There is no bathroom in this ward. No curtains either. I realise, with alarm, that I'm expected to produce this sample here, publicly, before the eyes of my three roommates. My body stiffens. It's less malleable than I. It will not follow orders that it does not like. This nurse is not unkind. She turns on taps to ease whatever blocks the flow she needs. In vain. My body does not answer to pretence. And when, at last, the nurse accepts I can't or won't comply, she turns away. Stiffly and silently, I leave the ward and hide myself within the bathroom in the corridor outside.

A tiny victory, perhaps, yet my humiliation is complete. My independence, my maturity, so longed for, so hard won, are shattered in a single day.

Errol (1)

The doctor's office is located in the space between the main ward and the outer door. Opposite is a telephone kiosk. On good days, patients may have access to this steppingstone from which they can reach out to those they used to know – the ones who still live in the normal world. On bad days, entry to this part of the building is barred. When there's trouble on the ward, the doors between it and the doctor's room are locked, no doubt affording escape for the important senior staff before a final closure of the outer portal.

Today I'm summoned here. It's been some days since my arrival in this new chaotic world. But, stunned as I still am and will remain, my heart stirs, faintly, for surely this is where it will begin – my journey back through therapy to perfect health. The reason why I'm here.

The consultation's brief. It is impersonal. The nameless doctors have their plan. They speak without a pause for breath, perhaps to bat away the questions hovering upon my lips. And suddenly I understand that little of this has to do with me. The doctors only say that "in the usual way", they must defer a final decision on my treatment.

"Nothing," they say, "will happen yet."

I am incredulous. For only now – when I have made the leap of faith – do they inform me that it is a prerequisite of any treatment for them to observe me and assess my suitability. It will, they say, be four weeks before their decision can be made.

I'm crushed. Briefly, my mind turns to the job that I have put on hold. I think about the happy Crouch End flat that was my home. The flat that housed three women on the cusp of adult life. Our life was filled with shared excitements as we ventured through those borderlands where childhood and maturity sometimes collide. A time and place where we

Chapter 7

don't move holistically to adulthood but sometimes face the conflicts and emotions natural to our changing and emergent selves. And even these have been much calmer now that Mikey's on the scene – this friend has been a stabilising factor in my life.

All this I'd left to follow my remorseless quest. I longed to rid myself of flaws I feared would ruin what might be a perfect life. And yet, the life, imperfect and abandoned, included happiness and kindness too. Now, darting through my mind there is a tiny thought I can't deflect.

What if my stubborn hope that my flaws could be cured was less than real?

I quickly brush the thought away. But it's a crushing moment and I am subdued. Defeated, I retreat, the angle of my head reflecting the downcast movement of my heart. I banish thought. Yet, as I pause, the outer door is opened. And thrusting through the gateway, here comes life. It's Errol.

Errol is a patient in the men's ward on the floor above. I recognise his slightly florid face and tousled hair. Each day, he brings the papers to our ward. His cheerful sociability, his Irish lilt, belie his status as someone who is assessed as sick.

He looks at me. His darting eyes – in just a flicker of those lids that shield the eyes that have seen all of this and more before – take in my stance, disconsolate, subdued.

"Cheer up," he says, in that so reassuring voice, the one that does not recognise defeat. "It's not so bad, you know."

And suddenly, in this encounter with this stranger on my road, I realise that I am not alone.

Rosamund

Lunch has finished. I have no appetite but even so there is just a trace of normality now we are together. The crowd in the dining room is dispersing, some with reluctance. A few are being rounded up by nurses to be escorted to the iron prefab halfway up the hill which houses the occupational therapy sessions. One or two are summoned by doctors – those faceless creatures that we rarely see, the power beyond what's visible. The numbers dwindle until, apart from me, just one remains. Behind me a voice barks.

"Hurry up, Rosamund, you can't stay here all day."

In front of me I see a slight figure, her half-hunched shoulders cloaked by unkempt hair of fine blonde silk. The baleful stare of her limpid grey eyes dominates her pinched cheeks and narrow lips. Her bones are almost visible beneath the ragged jeans and formless top. There's little colour in this place. Although we patients may wear what we like, the garb selected almost universally betrays the general mood. Black is now and then relieved but only by subdued shades of bone or mud.

The figure hesitates. Panic flickers through those lucid eyes. I shudder. For here before me is no woman, but a child. At most she's in her early teens.

Somehow the pathos of her mien restores my instinct and my voice. I grab a chocolate bar that lies, forgotten and still wrapped, beside the uncleared plates.

"Have this."

Rosamund starts and stares at me, though quickly her eyes retreat, fixing on the floor. Slowly her lips move. A sentence forms. Scared as she is, she answers me.

"I can't. I'm only allowed to eat apples."

She scuttles past me. I hear a door slam as she reaches the safety of her room.

As I turn the corner leading to the white-walled cell that's mine now that I've left the dormitory, I cannot bat away the questions that plague my mind. For the first time since my arrival, I forget myself and my own plight.

What is she doing in a place like this? No child should be locked up with madness. How can I help her?

Apples? My eye is drawn to the bowl of fruit on the locker by my bed. I take two apples, round and shiny like the cheeks of a Disney princess. I retrace my steps and knock on the door to Rosamund's room. She opens it and, with my hand outstretched, I make my offering.

"Take these – please, take them."

She hesitates, then snatches the fruit. Breath muffled, she mutters, almost inaudibly. "Thank you."

And, though we do not know it yet, we have taken our first step back to humanity – and freedom. Yet every step towards the future was a step that took me further from the past that I had known.

Chapter 7

Mr Lyons

A nurse knocks, peremptorily, on the door of my room. Her hands rest on her hips.

"You have a visitor – a Mr Lyons."

Within me I feel panic. My undoing.

"I can't." My voice falters but inside my head the words still ring.

I cannot – not like this. I simply cannot see him. For this man is my boss. Within the engineering firm, I help him in his role as Head of Personnel.

But this is surely in the past.

And, suddenly, nostalgia saturates my mind. I loved my job. I loved the atmosphere with people much less self-important than the academics in the institute where I'd worked before, the ones who'd been so keen that I should get a cure. The ones who had suggested that I place myself within this psychiatric tomb.

Mr Lyons had been jovial, benevolent, and kind – the things that clever people often fail to see that it is good to be. I was quite happy to be second in command; to know what was expected of me, rather than to think that everyone could have a theory that was their own. And in this job, I could not talk about my panic. Instinctively I knew that this employer might not understand. And anyway, I found that there was much for me to do. And helping Mr Lyons as he strove to run a calm and happy office, I discovered now and then I could forget the things that worried me.

The only contretemps we'd had was over that assistant that I thought that we should hire – an Asian lady, so astute and so composed and perfect for the vacant role. He'd looked askance at that. He knew that this would never do – in 1968. He said that though he lacked concerns himself, he did not think that she would 'blend' with others who the firm employed.

I vaguely understood that this was just a dressed-up lie.

I'd stood my ground and carried on, insisting that she was the best one for the job. He never faced me down. I think deep down he was aware that what I said was true. He did not challenge me. There was no need. He simply waited until illness kept me out of sight – and then, of course, he employed someone else.

The memories fade. The present floods back as I realise there will be one more 'someone else' – this time in place of me.

No, No! The voice within is shriller now. Almost hysterical. *I cannot see him, and I won't.*

I am indignant, and if I were a child, I'd stamp my foot. But anyhow, my stubbornness prevails – and overriding this is my embarrassment and shame.

The nurse, accepting her defeat, has shrugged, and backed away.

But then, impulsively, I hasten from my room and hover by the window, just to catch a secret, wistful glimpse. And there, beside the outer door, he sits. An ordinary man in business clothes, he is extraordinary here. He's out of place. He slumps across a bench. He shrinks down in his velvet-collared overcoat. His expression's almost hidden by the trilby that he's pulled across his face. Though even this cannot conceal discomfort and anxiety.

And suddenly I feel remorse. For all his faults, this man is kind. And he has come, unasked, to this forbidding place, to reach out to the struggling fellow human that is me.

And I have pushed him back.

Thus, thoughtlessness is added to the list of faults I find in me. I simply cannot get things right. And for the first time since I reached this place, I rush back, sobbing, to my room.

Dr Gonzales

Then, just when I'm about to give up hope, I'm told that I'm to see the doctor who is appointed to discuss my case with me. There is no warning. I stride anxiously towards the office. I am conscious of my energy flooding back, and, with it, surging panic. My nemesis. I try to check myself. I tell myself this is important. Much will depend on what may happen here.

Dr Gonzales is a short and swarthy man. Although he's young, he seems to lack the confidence of youth. He is not polished like the other doctors I have seen. Nor is he still. He fidgets in his chair, a fussy man. He tells me he is South American. I shrink a bit inside because immediately it's clear his English is not good. And yet it's so important that he understands me, my predicament and what I need. I clench my stomach, and my shoulders stiffen as I wait until he focuses on my concerns.

I wait, expecting that he'll ask exactly what my problems are – what causes the anxiety that has brought me to this place.

Chapter 7

I wait in vain. But suddenly his words are of the family – my own. He asks about my father, and he seems to want to know about the feelings that I have for him. There may be missing nuances. Without these, I consider that his questions are impertinent and crude. My father is affectionate, I say, though rarely in a physical or hugging way.

He asks if it was always thus.

I strain my thoughts. I try so hard to say the things I think he wants or needs to hear.

"He used to tickle me, when I was small," I say, remembering the games we played in perfect innocence.

His stare is hard. "You did not like it?"

I don't know what is in his mind but, truthfully, I say, "Mostly, I did. Not always, though."

And suddenly, to my alarm, he snarls. His agitation spills across the desk. He waves his arms and shouts at me.

"That's wicked. Children have to love their fathers. I am a father. This is the way it has to be."

He's spluttering now as Spanish words escape his lips, diluting his expressions and his clarity. In his incontinence, he spits.

I am aghast. What have I done? I try to speak and make things right. I love my father, and I know my problems aren't to do with him.

But Dr Gonzales is adamant. The interview is closed. The man in whom I'd put my faith now furiously waves me from the room. It's over now. He makes it clear he wants no further words from me.

Stunned, I slink back down the corridor. Dimly I realise that, somehow, in the mêlée of confusion and cross-purpose, I have razed another path to freedom and to health. But, so much worse, I know that in this maladroit exchange, my father is traduced – perhaps, unwittingly, by me. Somewhere, beyond these walls and far away, a cock crows. I hear it and I understand the shame is mine, for me to carry till the day I die. My father has done nothing that his character should be dissected here, his actions scrutinised, interrogated thus.

Whatever else they do to me, it can't be more unbearable than this. I have to put this right. I have to show my father for the man he is.

I call to mind an image from a photograph. It's Knighton and it's 1944. I see a father and his children on the grass beside the River Teme. They're caught by the unerring focus of the mother's loving eye. The father's skin is tanned, his white shirt open at the neck. He is relaxed.

There is no tension in the arm that folds the young child's body in its crook. The child's white embroidered dress has ridden up. This small malfunction is unheeded, and it matters not. The elder sister is oblivious. She threads a daisy chain. The father's eyes look steadfastly ahead with love, alighting on his wife. The Knighton sun breathes life eternal on a perfect summer day. I marvel at the light it brings me now.

And somehow time and pain dissolve. A blissful childhood is made whole again. For I am that young child, enfolded in her father's love. That childhood is mine. And if I wrap its strength around me like a silken shawl, I surely will survive.

The End of Hope

Days later I am back, waiting outside the doctor's office. This time the summons is expected, for it's now four weeks since I was told that I must be observed. I hardly dare to breathe. I tell myself there can't be any doubt the therapy will now begin. In hope of this new treatment, I have jettisoned the life I led. And yet, in horror I begin to understand that nothing now is as it used to be, that there's no certainty within the shifting dispositions of the people who are masters in this strange new world.

Inside the spartan room the senior consultant presides. He lacks identity. His hair recedes. That much I see. But even so he is anonymous. His horn-rimmed spectacles are faintly tinged. They shield him from too close a vision of my wretchedness. Worse, they confound my search for any lingering sign that here before me is a human being. To his left sits Dr Gonzales. He, at least, looks clearly alive. He fidgets. His face glowers, though I think I can perhaps detect a tiny trace of shame. He is embarrassed.

I know immediately that here is not the outcome I have sought. The words that issue from the lips of this consultant, erudite and dry, glance off my brain. And yet they have the force of bullets. I am felled. I have not passed the test they set.

"It is now clear to us," the senior doctor says. He spreads his arms to indicate that both the doctors are agreed on this. "You are not suitable for this – the therapy that we had hoped might help you with the difficulties you have. Your case is not one where we can desensitise. You can attend a class to help you to relax. There's occupational therapy. You seem to like the basketry. There is no more that we can do for you."

Chapter 7

Inside I flinch. I ask myself, *How can this be?* I've waited many months and given up so much to finally secure the glittering prize: the treatment that I'd hoped that they would offer me. Stunned, but still with some pretence at dignity, I rein in my despair. I say that I will leave the hospital today.

But they are not done yet. And, finally, come words that are to haunt me through the years to come.

"It's not for us to say… but, in our view, it is essential that you stay. You are depressed. We are concerned that, if you leave, you'll kill yourself."

And from the lips of those I thought would be my saviours, a curse falls.

I tell myself that, surely, they are wrong. I'm shocked to hear these doctors voice a thought I've never had myself. What could have made them think I might be vulnerable in that way? I'm not depressed – at least I've never seen myself that way. I've had my ups and downs of course, but it is life for which I yearn, not death. Yet now, within my mind the seeds of doubt and questioning are sown. I bury them at once. I can't afford to let them grow. My feelings, once intense and powerful, are now to be suppressed by medication they prescribe. It's not a sedative as such but something that they say will lift my subdued mood – a mood they choose to see as a depressive tendency. And it, they say, will stifle my anxiety as well.

I'm in despair. I cannot understand what's happening here. I don't have strength to challenge or to disregard the words of those I had entrusted with my care. I am too timid to reject the terrifying image they project. I shrink within myself. Cast down, I realise that I won't leave today.

Yet I am fearful for they seem to want to mask my feelings and concerns. Why don't they see that if they could just look at me the way I am – if only they would talk to me about the worries and anxieties I have – then maybe in the understanding of myself, they might yet help me with the difficulties I face? For in the chemical largesse they pour on me, they simply multiply the challenges that I must overcome. And though time stretches in this place, I understand that, overall, the doctors are but passing strangers in my life. And they can sign my discharge papers any time they wish. Whilst I will, for a lifetime, bear the scars that they inflict.

8

BETHLEM (3)

1968

An Anchor in the Sea of Horror

I leave the consulting room. I pass the telephone kiosk, and, for a moment, I pause. This is a place somehow beyond the rules that govern here. And here it is that, in the last four weeks, I've telephoned my boyfriend when I could. Mikey, a friend I'd met just weeks before my Bethlem stay commenced. An unflamboyant man with light brown hair that tumbles stubbornly around the outer edges of his face. An ordinary man, cheerful, uncomplicated. A man who's comfortable. A man who feels no need to try to shine. Despite his academic background he's content, for now, to earn a living working as a salesman in pharmaceuticals. He likes to dwell on the embarrassment that selling certain products causes him – discomfort that he covers telling jokes and drawing pictures to persuade me I should laugh at his ineptitude.

I'd met him at that party given by the Crowley Smiths. He'd fixed on me. And when he walked me home, he said to me I was, for him, the one who had stood out. A tiny compliment but it had been enough.

And in the weeks that followed we'd enjoyed a quiet friendship of a loving kind. At Alyn Bank – my Crouch End flat – I cooked an omelette, the height of culinary expertise for me. It was enough for him. We listened to the music that we liked. Simon and Garfunkel. *Layers of the Onion*, too.

And when he called to take me home from work, we kissed across a typewriter, and static electricity produced a kind of shock. We laughed, not knowing quite how many shocks the next few months would bring.

And he had quietly accepted all I planned. Whatever doubts he had, he kept them to himself. And yet his letters and the calls that we arranged were healing in a way that nothing else appeared to be.

He tries so hard to help me rationalise, to render this great hammer blow I feel from time to time, a fleeting glance, a tiny prick. He tells me, in his letters, to imagine that, although I am, somehow, a patient in intensive care, I am there just because it is a place where I may find the tools to get my "toenails cut". A little crude perhaps but also true. He draws cartoons for me and sends me books. And some of them are grandiose and dark, like Tolstoy's *Resurrection*, its hero so tormented by injustice that is all around. And others overflow with pithy comments, some of which he thinks appropriate for me to read and to absorb. He sends me *Archy and Mehitabel*, a satire in which animals and insects have the confidence to dominate their version of the world and in which some like warty bliggens, who's a toad, are egotistical and think the universe exists to serve their need.

And, visiting, he opens up the book and points me to the chapter that he thinks that I should read. Eyes fixed upon my face, he says with gentleness, "You, Lesley – you could take a lesson from that toad."

And thus, he speaks to me of my significance and bids me to continue to be me.

Ordinary Time

A curious feature of this strange and often hostile world is its ability, chameleon like, to change its colours for no reason – on a whim, it seems. Thus, there are times when all the doors are locked. No one can come. No one can go. Yet, just as we accept this as unyielding fact, capriciously, our freedom is restored. To all of us, regardless of our individual malaise.

At times like this we're free to walk around the manicured and well-kept lawns, to come and go for painting lessons or for crafts. As if this hospital is now a carefree summer camp.

And stranger still, on other days, we patients are permitted to depart these grounds and wander into town or where we wish. Sometimes we are escorted by our visitors. At other times we are cut free, to roam in groups or even on our own.

And in this atmosphere, my mother visits me. And on these days when rules are few, she can pretend that all is well. And so can I. We go in search of shops where dainty teas are served – a treat my mother would not countenance unless in company. And one day, we take Rosamund. She's blossoming a bit and in our company she feels relaxed. There are no apples for her here. And so, with hesitance and hope, we order chocolate cake. She takes a slice – and then a second one. And Mummy looks at me and smiles.

Such days exist, though they are rare. There is no pattern to this seemingly illogical largesse. Perhaps this is intentional, for, in confusion, we, the designated mad, are prone to cleave to what we think we know is sure and what won't change.

And what is sure is that we are no longer the people we once were. Within this cauldron, all the things we thought ourselves to be have been dissolved. We are to be remoulded in a form that we are not allowed to choose and don't yet understand. In this asylum, all identity has been usurped. Subdued by medication or erased by ECT, our former selves are now a nothingness.

And thus, in docile apprehension, though unchained, we nonetheless return. And pitiful as it may be, it seems that we are grateful for this tiny taste of liberty – this freedom that was once our own to squander as we chose. We bask in this momentary approval, in this fleeting time in which we're graciously allowed to be the selves we have become. We tell ourselves that no one really means us harm. It's not so bad, we say.

And thus, although it seems, perhaps, to others that we have the chance to flee, we can't and don't escape.

And yet... Jemima

The restless woman in the corner of the day room is tall and angular. A mop of straight fair hair falls forward in an unruly fringe, masking aquiline features. Her statuesque frame is contorted with anxiety. Even so, Jemima cannot hide the air of breeding that attaches to her manner.

The whispers tell me that she is a student of medicine, following in the footsteps of her doctor father. It seems that they are close. He visits often. That's unusual here. Perhaps his class or his profession provide privileges that others do not have – if privilege it is. I see him often, huddled with her in the harsh-lit corner of the day room, straining across the shabby wooden arms of the leatherette chairs that signal that we're in an institution now. I see him battling to reach the daughter he so clearly loves.

The urgency of his manner obscures the finer details of his outer dress. All that impresses is the fervour of his silhouette, crouched beside his daughter. His face is turned to her and thus, unwittingly, his anonymity is preserved. As he leans, his body screens Jemima's lately shabby, always classic, clothes. The cashmere that she wears above her pleated skirt is bobbled now. Her father's city suit is crumpled at the knees and at the elbows too. Apparel of which they once took the greatest care is now irrelevant. The desperation of their entwined pose will stay forever in my mind.

"Jemima, please…" Her father begs Jemima for some spoken word to show that she connects with him and understands that he is here.

Jemima has no words for him. She's silent. Her expression is now blank. I am reluctant witness to her father's misery.

The lack of privacy must be more daunting to those who once led cloistered lives. There are no secrets in this day room. For when there's trouble and when the outer doors are locked, the nurses like us to be where our actions can be scrutinised. Beyond the corner where Jemima sits, the day room's light enough, although the windows are too high to see the grounds outside. The wall the windows face is also glass, the better to ensure all movements can be checked. The rigid upright chairs are lined against the walls. There are no clustered seating areas for private talk. The corners are preferred for here there is some partial shelter from unwanted gaze. But otherwise, we face each other, all emotions visibly and cruelly exposed.

Jemima can give trouble to the nurses, so it seems. She can't or won't obey the orders that they give, for she is schizophrenic and, for her, the voices in her head are masters now. And they and only they can tell her what she knows that she must do. Sometimes she tries to flee. Perhaps this is at their command. Or else, perhaps, it is from them her instinct tells her she must run. But, either way, sometimes she tries to get away, and once – her private room mistakenly unlocked – she hurls herself beyond the outer door. Till, in her ragged nightdress, writhing in her anguish and despair, she's brought back to this place of safety once again.

In agony.

At length, her father makes to leave. Their corner of the day room's empty now. I think no more about Jemima and her woes. I try to banish thought. I need my focus and my energy to exist. If I exist, perhaps I am still me.

But suddenly Jemima reappears. She's not alone. She has a minder nurse. There are no chains and yet there might as well be. The pair of them are fiercely interlocked. The Caribbean nurse is stout. Impossibly, atop her head is ginger hair. She has an iron grip upon Jemima's arm, a match for her imperiousness. The nurse's look is surly and somehow this frightens me. I miss her usual warmth. All can't be well.

I see Jemima pushing, pulling. Her eyes descend, imploringly, upon my face, and suddenly I understand that it is me she seeks. I freeze. The nurse says nothing, but she tussles, though at last her struggle is in vain. Jemima's muttering and uttering. Her words do not yet reach my ears. They take a step back, almost falling, then Jemima pulls again and suddenly they are on top of me. It's ominous. I shudder, but a moment's silence can't prepare me for what is to come. Jemima speaks.

"You – you are next, my voices say. I've heard their plans. I need to warn you. Have a care." Her strangled voice is pleading now. "It is too late for me. They've got me now. They're coming for you next. Run. Run. Don't let them do to you what they have done to me."

Exhausted, she exhales and slumps upon the nurse's arm. The nurse has no expression, and she does not speak. There's nothing – no one – to assure me that I am not cursed.

What will become of me if I adopt the role she thrusts on me?

How has my life propelled me to this place? I am entirely alone. I feel quite powerless to resurrect the past and move towards the future of which once I dreamed. I question whether I can face a world like this. The words of the consultant haunt me still. *We are concerned… you'll kill yourself.* But surely not. Despite its panic and the sometimes-frightening recklessness of youth, my life has always known a place for joy – and even here and at this time, this is still true. Yet, nonetheless, I understand the doctor is important, and I cannot shrug his words away. I realise that all are vulnerable here – and some will not have strength enough and some have no desire to sustain the only life that's visible ahead.

Errol (2)

The bus from Croydon jolts unexpectedly as we approach the turning for Monks Orchard Road. My shopping done, I realise that it has taken longer than I thought it would. Standing ready to alight, I hurtle sideways, clinging to the pole. The bus is almost empty, and I have a clear view through the window at the side of the driver's cab. Beyond that I can see another bus. Now stationary and, at its rear, a gathering of people kneeling, some gesticulating wildly, others ominously still. My eyes follow the direction of their focus. I shudder. For, on the tarmac is a viscous pool of something I remember from an accident I witnessed many years ago. Its colour signals its identity. It's red – a sticky gut-wrenching red. I know at once. It is human blood.

Chapter 8

Shaken, I alight and walk for ten minutes back to the hospital entrance. I realise that I am late yet understand this does not matter anymore. Then, as I near my ward, I see a group of patients huddled by the outer door. One or two entwine in semblance of solidarity and strength. This is unusual for, at heart, we are all solitary folk and in this place all trust has vanished with our pain. Absorbed within the script of our own dramas, we ignore the sensitivity to others we might once have had. In fact, I'm wrong about this, but this is how it seems, for now.

The hum of chatter suddenly throws out a name I recognise, Errol. The kindly patient from the ward upstairs who brought out papers to the ward. What can this clutch of female gossip have to do with him? I feel myself recoil and yet I'm drawn. I understand they talk of one I know – and something that I've seen today.

"He jumped."

"He fell."

"It was an accident."

"Who pushed him?"

"Perhaps he'd had enough."

And suddenly I know – the reason matters not.

Errol is dead.

The stranger on the road has passed from view. And I have been the witness to his blood.

Summer

As months pass, other faces fade from view, though most in less dramatic ways. And others come to take their place.

Now, Rosamund is not the only teenage patient here, for Geraldine arrives. Her face is pinched. She's coltish, newly freed from childhood's cocoon. She's trying hard to make her mark. Her hair is naturally brown but has a Sassoon cut that's older than her years. She's just sixteen but stalks the passageways pretending confidence, dispensing knowing looks and information that she's eager to impart. She likes to talk about the cost of our accommodation here.

"It's utter wastefulness," she says, although this is no private sanatorium but has a cost which all, through tax, will bear.

She's apt to dwell upon the fate of others who are 'sick', like us. She likes to hold court, giving views on Sylvia Plath.

"*The Bell Jar* is," she says, "quite wonderful. At last, a writer who knows just how 'crazy' feels."

She's gratified to find an author whose identity, she feels, is just like hers.

And Josie, too, invades the subdued atmosphere. For Josie, with her careless frazzled hair and cigarette in hand, is restless. She is shrill. I see her pacing corridors where she hurls insults and profanities at all who pass her way.

"That stuck-up bloody bitch," she snidely says as poor Jemima utters her imperious commands.

And Anneli is just: "That fucking Finn".

I try to find peace where I can. I sprawl with Rosamund upon the lawn. It's early summer now and hot. The smell of new-mown grass reminds me of my school days when the groundsmen had just done their job. We talk now, Rosamund and I. And, piece by piece, she starts to tell me something of her life. And yet she does not talk about her animosity for nourishment, her fear of natural things which might well do her good. Instead, she shows me poems that she writes. The poems are less timid than her lips. They tell how she feels she is "buried in this tomb" and how, *perhaps* – that diffident and self-dismissing word – she, Rosamund, deserves much more than this of life.

I understand, and so, indeed, she does. Perhaps one day the sensitivity we share will help to ease the pain and awkwardness of others' insecurity. Thus, even these desultory chats improve our mood. We are not meant to live alone. And in these moments, we preserve the social skills we have and thus prepare ourselves for life beyond the hospital. The fragile friendships that we forge remind us that, diminished as we are, we are still 'us'. I cling to hope, for Rosamund and me, that there is more of life ahead of us.

ECT

Inside again, I fret and fumble in my anxious state, although I dress with care. I wear the Jaeger tartan dress I spied in Sloane Street so long ago. Its subtle hues of brown and grey reflect the sombre tones within this place. And yet the pleated A-shaped mini skirt from which my legs emerge so

Chapter 8

straight and slender somehow hints at youth and life. My square-toed patent shoes with shapes of caramel inset into the black remind me that, despite it all, I am myself.

Thus reinforced, I stifle my disquietude as best I can and pace the corridor between my room and the main exit where the kiosk is installed. I'm slightly early for the phone call I expect. I'm always apprehensive when I leave my room, and yet today I know that Mikey's going to ring. I can't resist the pull of the anticipated thrill and the so soothing voice that I will hear. And I have energised myself to look my best to match the tiny trace of hopefulness within.

I pass the alcove where these days Anneli is almost always to be found. I see her hunched over an enormous jigsaw. She finds this comforting. It is the only occupation that distracts her from her anger and fear. I do not understand from where those feelings come. But I can see that here, with what is no more than a simple pastime or a childish fad, is where she can forget about it all and feel at peace. On other days I see her wrangling, snarling at the nurses or at foul-mouthed Josie in the corridor she passes on the way to ECT – the corridor that's redolent with sweat and fear and anguish of the ones who're summoned to this fate. It is a fate from which I'm thankful to be spared but one that all have come to dread.

Perhaps, beyond the bluster and the surliness, she's just another frightened, wounded child.

I move the corners of my mouth so she can see the shadow of a smile. I trust her now. For me, somehow, she is a fixed point in this maelstrom of shifting characters and moods. Familiar now, almost, and yet not quite a friend.

I pass her by and, suddenly, ahead of me, the inner door bursts open. Tranquillity is shattered by the noisy presence of the lithe and loose-limbed woman that I see. She hurtles inwards and she thrusts herself into my path. It's Bridget, wavy auburn hair dishevelled from the breeze and by the effort of her haste. She's agitated and her youthful face is flushed. Two brothers trail behind. They can't keep pace with that young body or that overactive mind. They're here from Ireland to visit her. Their open faces show bewilderment and impotence. For Bridget is the youngest of their family brood. It is their duty to make sure she is alright. And this, it seems quite clear, they cannot do.

Already they have lost what scant attention she once offered them. For now, I realise in some alarm, her focus is on me.

She rushes at me, almost makes as if to knock me down, but somehow stops, just inches from my face. She wrings her hands in frenzy, then, quite suddenly, she clasps them, as in prayer. Her eyes beseech me as she gazes on my face, itself expressionless and calm with shock.

And somehow in my smooth and passive countenance, it's Holy Mary that she sees.

"Mother of God!" she cries, imploringly. "Please help me. Do not let them punish me. I beg you. Do not let them give me ECT again."

I cannot speak. She is so fervent and so sure of my identity. Is this another role in which I am to be submerged? Where I'm no longer to be me?

As suddenly as she burst in, she turns away, exhausted by her plaintive striving. She weeps for fear as she begins to understand her pleading is in vain. The piteous futility of her imaginings undoes me. I am powerless to help. Her brothers, surer now that Bridget's strength has gone, propel her backwards till they're out of sight.

My call forgotten and irrelevant, I too retreat. Back in my room the tartan dress is put away, with care and sadness, as I realise that in this other world, I do not write the script nor bring the characters to life. Perhaps, I think, I cannot even shape the actions of the character who once was me.

I take my simple nightgown from the drawer. I put it on and lie, emotionless, upon my bed.

I wait.

9

BETHLEM (4)

1968

The World Beyond

It's early June. A few days back we had a royal visitor – a patron, so I understand. And there we sat on our faux leather chairs, inside the day room where we gather when there is no other place to go. Where we line up to take the medication they dole out – the only treatment most of us will know. The room where we observe each other's peccadillos and each other's pain.

The Duchess did not see these things. Somehow, she only saw the stolid faces that we knew that we should make. She stooped a little, smiling graciously, as she approached the row of chairs and as she shook someone's hand. And then, in minutes, she was gone.

Today I'm drawn here by the sound. The day room's almost empty but, unusually, the television's on. I'm curious to know what other life they think is suitable for viewing here. But then I look. Inside I gasp, for there before me on the screen, I see not life, but a 'sarcophagus'. It's covered by a flag I recognise: the Stars and Stripes. *What can this be?* And, in increasing shock, I hear in solemn tones that Robert Kennedy is dead. Felled, in the land of the free, that glorious New World that reached out to the wretched of the earth. Slowly I ponder if this also is a myth, for I can see that there is no asylum there. And that there is no place of safety anywhere.

A solemn sound disturbs my thoughts. I hear a trumpet play. But here, to my bewilderment, I hear no funeral dirge. Beyond my shock, I hear the rasping tones of Louis Armstrong's voice: *And I think to myself, what a wonderful world.*

I can't recall from where this music came. Perhaps a radio played somewhere nearby. Coincidence. Perhaps it was a soundtrack quite intentionally juxtaposed to form ironic comment on the funeral scene. But these conflicting images laid bare the truth that violence and madness can be found in the most civilised society. For there, in the US, demonstrators fought for civil rights and to protest against a vicious war. And some would be the targets of the ones who did not welcome peace or change. Another Kennedy this time, just months since Martin Luther King was killed. Yet here, where those around me were now labelled sick, civility and common goodness very often pushed the baser instincts back. The scene was startling, and it triggered thought.

The Dawn of Compassion

I'm always apprehensive when I leave the safety of my white-walled cell. But, gradually, I come to understand that clinging to seclusion will not ease my plight. For, though remaining cloistered and alone, I may preserve a little of myself – I will not grow but I will surely fade. And after all, it was to learn to be my natural self, without anxiety, that I came to this place.

And so, each day I force myself to wander through the corridors, confronting all and anyone who comes my way. And each day, for a while, I eschew books and introverted thought and hesitantly take a battered chair within the day room where we languish in the absence of more purposeful pursuits. I understand that in this soulless room I will share inactivity, but also anguish and despair.

Within this atmosphere it's rare to hear the spoken word. No confidences are exchanged, no jokes are told. The language of this common room is silent pain.

I look around. The TV screen is still. The scenes that I imbibe are images of life and they are real.

Across the room I notice Rosamund. She squats upon the hard wood floor, her body partially obscured by trailing blankets and shawls. They are not hers. For there, despite the summer's heat, enfolded in this swelter is Jessie. The seasons are unnoticed, unremarked by her. She's eighty. She's confused and all days seem the same to her. And in her ampleness, she somehow merges with her chair whilst Rosamund takes comfort at her feet, half hidden, somehow sheltered in her skirts. A timid child not ready yet to face a world she does not understand.

I think that this would be a charming scene – perhaps – if it were somewhere else. A family scene in a suburban drawing room. But this is

Chapter 9

Bethlem. Silently I look and somehow understand that though we've forfeited the trappings of a home and family, we can perhaps still take some solace from the ones who share our present plight.

And sometimes, maybe, we can offer comfort too.

And to my left I see Diane. Diane has only recently arrived within our midst. The whispers – heard in discreet corners, in the hurry of the common bathroom, borne upon the air that passes quickly by – these whispers tell me that Diane has lost a child.

I contemplate her abject form. She sits, downcast, head lowered, swathed in shapeless garb as dark as night. She's motionless. There is no sign of life, except for tears that fall, relentless, soaking eyes and cheeks and clothes. I fear that she will drown before those tears subside. I do not need the whispers to explain her pose. Her woman's purpose unfulfilled, in her I see the agony of loss. I see defeat. Diane will sit this way forever, so it seems to me. Beyond her own once nascent hope.

Yet she is not alone for, at her feet, sits Josie – foul-mouthed Josie – Josie who, till now, I've only known as surly and insensitive. The crudest, most defiant of us all. Yet Josie is the one who kneels by Diane now. She shares the silence redolent with pain. Outstretched, her fingers linked with Diane's unresponsive hand, unbidden, she – that one in whom I only saw a termagant – absorbs the overflow of Diane's grief. No word is uttered yet this is a scene I can't forget. I think that she will sit this way forever if she's needed here. Beyond her own forgotten anger and her agony.

Each day, somewhere beyond these walls, in other places where they gather, two or three, I know the Benedictus prayer is said. And here in this drab room, it somehow reaches us.

Compassion breaks on all of us. And finally, the fog in which I'd been immersed begins to lift. For here, amidst the chaos and uncertainty is something that I recognise as valuable and true. Something authentic, solid, and so right, it is to me an anchor and a guide. A precious gift that will stay with me through the years to come.

Mummy

It's just an ordinary day – a run of the mill day for a family moving forward in this time of change and upward growth for most. In a Croydon boutique a mother and a daughter shop for clothes. As they have done before, in other places, other circumstances – and yet none like these.

I gaze into the cheval mirror. There I stand – that long-legged girl with dark brown high-piled hair. And clad in fashion's latest trend, I contemplate another me. For my reflection's bright with colour now – blue, red, and white. The woman in the mirror wears a coat dress, buttoned slightly to the side. Its primary colours thrust its wearer to the fore. She cannot hide.

The manager is unctuous. She almost claps her hands.

"How marvellous! I wish that I could wear that dress," she says.

Mummy smiles. She is delighted for she's heard those words before and thinks – perhaps – that she and I have moved to safer ground. She thinks – perhaps – that she might get her daughter back again.

I waver, as I always do when faced with any choice between the incandescent glittering of startling visibility and all the greater safety that obscurity might bring. From time to time, I'm tempted by the impact of a glorious shocking pink, but then, once bought, it hangs, redundant, in my wardrobe, extinguished by the soothing camouflage of earthly tones of green or beige.

And surely, in my present circumstances it won't help to draw attention to myself.

Yet even so, I hesitate – and, in that moment, Mummy signs the cheque. And, on the journey back to Bethlem, I clutch my purchase to me like the promise that it is. As the bus jolts round the corner of Monks Orchard Road, within me something stirs. I hear a voice inside me. It is insistent and I cannot silence it. The voice reminds me that I too had promise, once, that I might one day be something more than commonplace. Despite it all, my mother seems determined to believe that this is still the case.

I hear her and, although I cannot tell her how I feel, I vow, despite the trembling in my soul, that someday some time I will dare to shine.

Anneli

I close the door. My precious private space behind me now, I force myself to walk towards the day room and the strange, disturbing world that it contains. The world that I remind myself is normal now.

Yet, as I turn the corner, I immediately sense that there's a different tension on the ward today. And though as months have passed, I've grown accustomed to surprise and shocks, the general air of consternation that I feel is new.

Chapter 9

And soon enough I learn that Anneli has gone. She has not been discharged and she has not discharged herself. She simply isn't here. The jigsaw on the table in the alcove is untouched since yesterday. How can that be when she spends all the hours that she has in fitting things together as she tries to make a perfect whole? A whole, perhaps, that when complete, she hopes will make some sense of all the painful fragments that she knows as life.

Almost at once, I hear commotion up ahead. I see a nurse gesticulating, shouting, staring wildly at the inner door. And suddenly the one whose presence I had missed is back. For here is Anneli, hair tumbling, black clothes mud stained and dishevelled, panting slightly, with two other nurses almost running, chasing her. But once she passes through the door, she slumps. Her energy is futile now, for she is back – an inmate once again. And as she thrusts herself against a wall, as far as she can reach beyond the strangers that pursue, I realise that she's afraid.

I hear a murmur growing louder and more ominous. Yet, no one speaks.

I have no clue what this may be about but deep inside I also feel a rising of that same emotion – fear.

I stand immobile. I can't take my eyes away. But, in my sights, another, smaller figure looms. For, standing in the doorway of her room is Rosamund, who also gazes, panic stricken, on this scene. I will her to go back inside. I tell myself again – a child should not be locked up here. My arm instinctively reaches for her although I know that she's too far away from me to touch. But not so far that I can't see the terror on her face. We are somehow together, if apart. We neither move nor speak. We are both witnesses to something that we know we have no wish to see.

In front of us the door bursts open once again. Two men emerge. They wear white coats. In all, the nurses now are five. Their prey is Anneli. They have come well prepared to corner her, for in their hands I see each has a weapon which I take as a syringe. All motion slows. I cannot breathe – and Anneli herself is still. It's over now. She offers no resistance. They inject her anyway. And in her silent stupor, crumpled and defeated, she is dragged beyond our view.

The Whispers

The whispers screech around my head as suddenly the corridor is full of patients eager to make comment on the day's events.

"She ran away."

"Her girlfriend was unfaithful."

"I always knew she was the jealous type."

"They found her in a graveyard."

"She had a knife, you know."

"What will they do to her?"

"We won't be seeing her again."

"They'll lock her up forever now."

I've heard enough. I know the whispers cannot always tell me where truth lies. I only understand that Anneli is lost to us – and maybe to herself as well. I reach for Rosamund again. She darts towards me, and I take her hand – and then we run until we reach the sanctuary that is my room.

Aftermath

But now I realise that in this place, no sanctuary is safe from prying eyes or those who hold the keys. And just as Rosamund begins to calm, a nurse intrudes. This nurse is Julie, who is usually kind. Although her hair, once bright and permed, is faded now, she's fresh of face with rosy cheeks. She's comfortably stout. She has the air of someone who might look and feel at home behind a tea urn at a summer fete. I've never heard her raise her voice for she is almost always gentle in her ways.

But not today.

"I'm sorry, dear." She looks at Rosamund. "You can't stay here. It's not allowed. You must go back at once to your own room."

I try to intervene. "But she's upset…"

Nurse Julie tuts and pulls her shoulders back. I see that this is hard for her. "They say she must… this is against the rules."

I understand that this is not her whim. For Julie is the bearer of a message that she does not want to give.

And suddenly I realise that I am not like her and, even in my subdued state, I will stand up for those who cannot stand up for themselves. For what I know is right. For all my quietude I can't accept what's happening here. Within me is an unfamiliar knot that's growing tight and hard. It's anger and I know it will not be ignored.

Chapter 9

I hold my tongue. I understand that Julie's not to blame. And yet, inside, I seethe. How dare they treat a child this way. She is so vulnerable. She is exposed to things she should not see. And now they want to separate her from this slight comfort that is me.

As Julie leads her docile charge away, I vow that I will do my best to make this right – or, at least, easier for Rosamund to bear.

And here I see a tiny miracle of sorts. The fight I never showed to save myself is somehow still alive and shows itself when others are in need.

A Sense of Purpose

The drama that is Anneli's escape and her re-capture leaves a void in which all form has been dissolved. Rules that were once lax are under scrutiny, but not yet changed. One thing's for certain – Anneli has disappeared forever now. And in this new confusion unimagined things are possible if we but dare.

And thus, emboldened by my newfound anger, I too bring my fledgling courage to the fore. I walk with some determination to the office where the staff nurse is writing up her notes.

"Where has Anneli… gone?" I ask and I am told – to my surprise – where she may now be found.

My fears are realised, for Anneli, they say, is in Cane Hill. Inside I gasp, for other patients sometimes speak about Cane Hill. It is a prison, so they tell, and those in charge are sadists if their tales are true. Beside it, Bethlem is a leisure camp. Wherever truth may lie, it's clear that all who have been patients there are full of dread that one day they will be sent back.

And it is in Cane Hill that Anneli is now confined. She of the smouldering fire within that dour exterior – this solid, loyal 'almost friend' is now incarcerated there.

And, learning this, I face the sister once again. And somehow, I extract from her a confirmation of the hours when visitors will be admitted to Cane Hill.

That's all I need to know. It's afternoon. Too late to go today but there is much to do. I'll get the bus to Croydon and, when I return, I'll seek out Rosamund and tell her of my plan. I've bought a complicated jigsaw to be given as a farewell present from us both. We'll write a note – a ritual to comfort her and us. I plan to take it with me when I go myself, tomorrow. And Rosamund is slightly cheered. Her features, once so strained, begin to soften, with relief. She understands that, with this gift, our 'almost friend' will know that she is in our thoughts.

And, with an ease that is incredible, it happens as I plan. It's quite straightforward – just one change of bus. In Croydon, at the terminus, I change and, as directed by a passer-by, I take the Coulsdon bus.

I do not understand why I appear to have no nerves at all. I am not anxious for it's clear to me what I must do – as if I've finally alighted on a role that God approves.

In Coulsdon all I see at first are suburbs where the houses stand by tree-lined roads. And for an instant I imagine this is just another summer day in suburbia. I'm wrong, of course.

For suddenly ahead I see Cane Hill. An edifice built in Victorian times, designed to house the county's lunatics and its defective poor. It's grand. It boasts its power in solid wings with high arched windows that belie the prison that it is. It's vast and grandiose and bleak. Above the steps and central door, a tower looms. Engraved upon its face its year of birth – 1882. So solid, so forbidding and so menacing. I shudder slightly as I contemplate the fate of those who have sojourned here.

My steps don't falter as I walk the final distance from the gate.

A stern-faced man in uniform confronts me. Expressionless, like all the other gaolers I've known, he stretches out his arm and seeks to know my purpose here. I give my name.

"I've come to visit Anneli," I say. "Miss Vartinan, I mean."

My breathing seems to stop but something in my manner or my voice convinces him that he must let me pass.

He shows me to a room where those who visit wait and where, from time to time, a meeting might take place. It's sparsely furnished and anonymous. Yet, within less than half an hour, this space, so unremarkable, is witness to an unanticipated act of solidarity and faith.

Perhaps it's also witness to a faltering step towards emergent confidence and self-belief.

As Anneli appears I see her mousey unkempt hair. I note the circles underneath her eyes and, fleetingly, I wonder if she sees the look of pity in my own. She's trembling slightly, so I place the jigsaw on a table to the side. I nod and indicate the note that I have brought. She's silent but there's something in the flicker of her eyes that tells me that she understands, and that my journey was worthwhile. I shake her hand – a gesture of our comradeship and trust.

Chapter 9

At last, she speaks and in her flat laconic tone she says, "It's not so bad, you know."

Bella

And in the end, it is another patient who will hand to me the keys that lead me out of Bethlem.

Bella, tall, assertive, hair and heart both streaked with iron, is stimulating company. In late June, she accosts me outside the day room.

"Oh, I see you have *The Faber Book of Twentieth Century Verse*," she exclaims, plucking the book I carry from my hands.

Unlike the other patients I meet here, she's quick to tell me something of her life.

"I live in Ladbroke Grove. My husband is a doctor there. I've been a bit depressed – you know the way it is – but I'll be back home soon."

And in the next few days she talks to me about her interest in the arts and, later, of the social problems in the suburb where she lives. An enclave where most houses, once the homes of prosperous men, are now slum dwellings for the diverse ethnic groups who have few choices in the lives they lead.

I'm fascinated – and with Bella, I forget myself. I am intrigued to hear from her about the problems that my lecturers in Birmingham had talked about. And I'm surprised to hear these concerns on a woman's lips. A housewife's lips. In Bethlem. This seems remarkable to me. I look upon my friend with awe.

But Bella, clearly on the mend, is ready to return to life. And, in her upbeat frame of mind, she sees no reason why I should be left behind. I am her newfound friend, and she intends to quash the final obstacle to my release.

So, drawing me aside one day and pulling me into her room, she says, "Why don't you come and live with us?"

And, caught up in the glittering net that is her mind, I readily agree.

I know that I should weigh it up. But what is there to weigh? The room within the happy flat share I once knew is occupied by someone else. My job has gone, for Mr Lyons has a new assistant now. And even nice kind Mikey will, I'm sure, abandon me once he believes he safely can.

Thus, all I see is freedom and, finally, a strategy to leave this place. Impulsively and heedless of the consequences that may flow from any union of the lately volatile and vulnerable, I have no option but to take a chance.

And after sharply indrawn breath I speak the fateful words.

"That would be wonderful," I say.

And curious though it is, no one gainsays me. The doctors – those same stern-eyed didacts who'd instructed me that exit from this place might spell my end – now do not flinch. Within that room between the patients' quarters and the outside space I sit for one last time, remembering the sentence that they'd meted out to me four months ago.

I have not sat in this room since that time. And what, if anything, has changed? How am I feeling now? They cannot know. They do not ask. I realise that this is something they – the doctors – rarely do. I sit before the doctor who's disguised in spectacles – the one whose blandishments had influenced me to take up residence within this place of pain. I blurt out what I now intend to do. My plan evokes no murmur of response. I think – perhaps – I hear the words "I see" escape the doctor's lips. But nothing more is said. Nothing of substance. Nothing to guide – and nothing to express regret for what they have not offered me.

Such interest as the doctors had in me had vanished, perhaps around the time that he or they decided that I had no role to play in their research.

And only now, cocooned in Bella's confidence, can I acknowledge the extent of their indifference to me.

And so, we'll go away – and this time everything will change.

Reflection

And thus, in July 1968 I pass through Bethlem's gates one final time. It's five months since that February day when I arrived so full of eagerness. Behind me is a past I never thought to know. It's sobering and yet there is no chapter of our lives where hope and inspiration can't be found.

I contemplate the doctors who I thought would open doors for me within the house I came to see as unforgiving, inhumane, and sometimes bleak. I think of all the patients who at first I feared but who I grew to understand and sometimes love.

And which of these might help to heal and change my life? And who perhaps has qualities to which I might aspire? And was there kindness and compassion there, within this place that I believed would heal? And if so, within whom?

Chapter 9

And as for those I leave behind, I dare not think what lies ahead for some of them. And, if I live, I'll try to live for them as well as me. For here, within their world of violence and fear and pain, I've come to know compassion and endurance too.

And if it takes me fifty years or more, I'll honour them in memories and words. In these, their plight and fortitude and their humanity survive.

10

NOTTING HILL

July–August 1968

Ladbroke Grove

I never stopped to think how Bella's husband might accept the scheme she had proposed and put in place. For now, in Ladbroke Grove, I saw him only briefly, as he disappeared from view, drifting through the passages of their Victorian home. I only saw his well-worn jacket hanging loosely and ill-fitting from the back he turned on me: the guest he did not want to see. Busying himself, no doubt, with patients he was paid to cure. I never saw the line of humans, waiting hopefully or downcast, for their doctor to dispense a remedy. The rooms that housed the surgery were closed to us. I did not mind. I was just thankful for the box room that he had agreed – I thought – to lend to me. And yet I noticed that the doctor occupied a world at times apparently remote from that which housed his wife. And that, despite the many spacious rooms their home contained, I could not see that there was one that both might share.

But Bella, now at home and once again subordinate, was different. Caught up again in mundane tasks and other roles she had to play, she was not quite the lively, thought-provoking friend that I had known in times when all we had to do was pass the day from morn till night. Almost at once our plan unravelled.

And on the second day, the three of us – for Rosamund had also left the hospital – were gathered here together on what I hoped might be a carefree day. I longed to see a Rosamund who might be more relaxed. She was now living with her mother once again. Perhaps her eating problems were behind her now. Perhaps she had filled out a bit. It would be wonderful to have a day when we could focus on ourselves – our thoughts, our dreams.

But in the world beyond asylum, life is not like that. We had forgotten

Chapter 10

others must live busy, useful lives. And, in the real world, we had so much to learn about the way that we could fit and co-exist. Now Bella's husband swiftly prised her from our grasp. She came and went and gradually, each time that she returned, her husband's irritation and displeasure seeped into the room. And somehow it was clear – at least to Rosamund and me – we were intruders in this house and here was not the place where I could stay.

For Bella and for me, the truth was that we had no strength – as yet – to shelter anyone.

But Bella and her husband did not cast me to the winds. I like to think that Bella's husband had a hand in this, and that, reluctant as he might have been, he was responsible at heart, and not unkind.

And thus, it came to pass that I was summoned to his study where I met the man who had a plan for what might now befall the problem that was me. But Bella's husband was still stubbornly remote and neither he nor Bella would be with me in the study where the plan was to unfold. For, Pilate like, they'd washed their hands of me. The stranger said he was involved in the community and understood I was in search of work – and also of a home. He gave me an address in Notting Hill and said he had arranged for me to have a meeting there next day. He would not come with me but told me he was confident things would go well.

"You can't stay here. Please take this chance," he said. "The men you meet will help. I promise that they will."

And thus, he sought to rescue me and Bella from the consequences of our idealised mistake. And passed me on to others who, he said, would welcome the unsettled and displaced – the homeless ones – who now included me.

Denbigh Road

And so the next day, in another study, now in Denbigh Road, I sit and face the ones who will decide my fate. We meet, as Colin, Bella's friend, had proposed. "For mutual benefit," he'd said.

Behind an old, neglected antique desk, two men subject me to their scrutiny. Disturbing as it is to be inspected thus, I also look, and I observe the ones assessing me. The younger one is restless. Abundant ungroomed hair and casual dress suggest his status as a minister is less important to him than his work in the community to which he's called. The other man is solemn and urbane – the leader of the two, I think. But for all that, there is a warmth within his probing eyes. He speaks of putting right the evils of society – and yet I sense he cares about the individual too.

Vaguely I understand that these men are important in the vibrant quarter that is Notting Hill.

In time I will discover that, in 1968, I'm living in a place where liberals, mostly earnest and well-meaning, almost always white, have flocked to see if they can solve the problems of the immigrants, the ones, that is, who are black, and to obliterate the racist element that thrives within the slums – where 'Room to Let' adverts may specify 'No dogs. No Irish and No Blacks'. And these two men are part of that. To solve these things, they dedicate their lives. Yet though they do much good, they are not always thanked for that. The line between what was colonial and what seems now, to some, paternalistic, is quite fine.

But, just for now, they're only strangers to whom Bella's friend has turned on my behalf. And though they're busy with the poor, the ones exploited and reviled, they're generous and still find time to meet with me and offer me a job.

The pay is meagre but there is an offer of a home. They tell me of a hostel occupied by those who are prepared to dedicate their time to the community in Notting Hill. And, with the job, I am to have a room within this house. I can't decline the offer that they make. I'm flattered and intrigued and anyway there's no alternative. I'll do my best. I will not let them down.

And so, they take me in – a waif and stray of sorts – and even though it's far too soon, they seek to make of me a co-protestant who will help them fight the evils of the world, one who herself – like them – 'does good'. They do not see that, even though I am not broken, as those doctors prophesied that I would be, I am still vulnerable.

Pembridge Gardens

I stand before the so-called hostel where I am to live. Its name does not reflect the edifice I see. The building is Victorian, the style Italianate. Imposing Doric pillars top the steps up from the street. Three further storeys tower above.

It's not what I expect, yet I am changed as well. I hardly recognise the self that is uncaged; that climbs the steps and enters with alacrity. My face

Chapter 10

has rearranged itself. My eyes are eager and my breath indrawn, but from excitement now. I tell myself that fear is in the past. Whatever lies ahead, I will embrace. I am alive again and here within this building I will find the next unravelled skein that I must fashion into what will be my life.

Inside I'm greeted by a warden, Chris. He is a kindly, almost academic-looking man, whose modest pose contrasts with all the efforts he has made to vanquish homelessness – efforts that he will continue all his life. He shows me to a first-floor room. It's here, within this hostel, where I am to make my home. I may redecorate, he says.

He speaks about our common enterprise and tells me something of the ones with whom I am to share a lifestyle of a kind. It sounds implausible. For here there are so many colours, most of which extend beyond the spectrum of the life I've known till now. And here, beside the relatively familiar – the social worker and the lady from the church – are more exotic blends. Here dwells the leader of a steel band bringing rhythmic music to the streets. Here, too, resides a gifted demagogue, who claims the Speakers' Corner as his own and hopes to build an empire from the disenchanted mass. And in the basement works an expert in the race relations industry. He's James, a Trinidadian, a member of the Inter-Racial Council, one supposedly adept at melding all the different strands of cultural life within this place. Yet even he would one day, famously, declare of Notting Hill:

"Whatever community may be, this is not it."

Yet, just for now, the hostel's empty. The other occupants are out. It's left to me to form their images within my mind. I scarcely take this in. I can't afford, just yet, to let in truths that are uncomfortable, disturbing to the social mores that I have imbibed. I've got to make myself believe I can survive. It's true that I have learned the world is full of strange new lands that are in every way quite different from the world I've always known. So far, I've coped with this. I am still here, and I am ready now to live. But, even so, my instinct is to push the differences away and focus on what seems familiar to me.

And so, as Chris escorts me to his glass-doored cubbyhole, I feign an air of nonchalance. As if to say, however strange to me the other residents may be, I'll manage to fit in.

"For me, this is another fresh start, Chris. I'm used to these. This must be number ninety-nine at least."

Inside I cringe. The triteness of my words and their stupidity is so at odds with what I feel. Inside I'm scared – there is so much that's different. I try to bring the conversation back to the agenda that he set. And so, when Chris looks anxiously at my smooth hands and ladylike attire and wonders if I'll mind that I must lend a hand, I say, of course.

"I'll do the things you want me to. I'd love to decorate."

It's not expected that I do this on my own. For here, in Pembridge Gardens, we welcome other guests. These guests are Czechs, and they are fugitives. Dubček's Prague Spring has come and gone. It's barren summer now and we, the residents, have offered them a home. And in exchange they are to help us with our menial tasks. And unrealistic Chris declares that first they are to decorate my room.

"Of course, they will be glad to help, for, in their time of need, we've given them a lifeline and a base."

Yet those aflame with thoughts of revolution smashing down society are quite unlikely to conform to our domestic rules. However eagerly they commandeer my room, they will not see it as a place for manual work that does not serve their cause. They huddle round, squatting on the floor on which I've laid my precious orange sheepskin rug. I cringe. I want to ask them how they dare. The sanctuary I thought I'd found for me is taken over now. I almost cannot bear to look. This room is just a semblance of the safety that I seek. But even that appears elusive now. These fugitives, who rightly fear their land will be invaded soon, have no respect for what is, after all, another's home. The exiles argue in a language I don't understand. And when, from time to time, they notice me, they bark out orders. I must bring them newspapers or beer or tea. And I, for now the solitary female in this place, observe the trite convenience of this. And from now on I'll rue the readiness with which so many of the zealots who aspire to power political will use their single-mindedness to justify the less than civil treatment of the human beings in their wake.

And so, I leave my room to them and find myself a task that's more amenable to me. And, whilst I wait in hope and expectation that one day other female residents will appear, I quash misgivings by expending all the energy I have on cleaning, painting too. I join with others working in the ground-floor library. And here I find myself exposed. For several hours a day, the passers-by can see me if they look beyond once-shuttered windows, ones that now stand open to the street. I do not dress to suit the task in hand. I wear the only clothes that I have brought with me. So, in my pink and purple Marimekko dress, beneath a deep blue pinafore, I climb the ladders that the wardens bring. I focus on the ceiling rose and ornate plaster covings. And recreating beauty, I forget the question marks inside my head.

At times, I step outside and linger in the porch to get some air. My thoughts absorb me. I am heedless of the passers-by. And thus, I take no notice of the strangers who intrude upon this peaceful scene. Yet had I watched the silhouettes approaching from the southern corner of the street, I might have wondered who these two men were. I might have seen that one of them was tall and had a face that was lit up by curiosity and penetrating eyes. A face that was irregular in shape but somehow radiant, a face that could not hide a spirit out to conquer and to get the best from life. A face which some would find impossible to shun.

I might have seen the other walk, face lowered, shoulders hunched, within the shadow that the tall man made, as if to be condemned to cleave to his superior. And, had I looked, would I have seen him for the henchman that the tall man thought he was? Or would I have divined the stifled jealousy that lay behind the mask of loyalty?

If I had been attentive, just a touch inquisitive, I might perhaps have noticed that one – or maybe two – of these had trained his eyes on me and had me in his sights.

And, had I noticed, had I known what lay ahead, would I have run?

The Sometimes Sweet Familiar Past

I'm overcome. The strangeness and the pace are all too much. The scenes around my life are changing far too fast to be absorbed. I try to take things in my stride. I never shirk a challenge in which I can see a tiny bit of positivity. And yet, within me, my excitement's tinged with apprehension. Sometimes, even fear. It's less than two weeks since I passed through Bethlem's gates that final time. I've not returned to anything I knew before. I am dependant now on strangers. The misjudgement which was mine and Bella's shows me just how risky this can be. However warm its superficial welcome seems, the world in which I've come to live is alien, untested and unknown.

And so, because of that and, on a whim, I think I will postpone this next adventure for a week or two. I book a flight to Germany, where Hella lives. Hella who has been my confidante since 1957. The one who taught me that a stranger can become the closest friend; that worlds which used to be at war can, if they will, know harmony again. I need to feel again that solid strength that rises from the sweet familiar past.

But first, in preparation for my trip, my mother comes to London so that she and I can shop in Regent Street. I'm unprepared for all the crowds that jostle round. It's seven months since I have been exposed to mêlées of this kind. For, though I shopped in Croydon, when my mother visited, the streets were almost empty there. Bethlem removed me – not just from the things I feared but also from things with which I had always coped before. It's different now. It is a shock to feel the throng of human life. I struggle in the human mêlée, desperate for some space and air. My heartbeat rises and I fear that I will suffocate. And though the situation never threatened me in times gone by, I recognise that old familiar panic once again. The part of me that's so at odds with how I strive to be. The part that seems to hold no interest for the doctors of this world. The part of me that nobody, it seems, will cure.

Yet somehow, I survive and next day fly to Hanover.

I'm always slightly anxious when I fly above the European continent. Especially when the sky is clear. And on this day of harsh and unremitting sun, I long for clouds to form a safety net. When I was small, I used to think the clouds were there to stop the angels falling down. And now, perhaps, I think the clouds might catch the aircraft should it fall – as fall it seems to me it must – upon the patchwork quilt of villages below.

But soon I safely reach my journey's end. And there in the arrivals hall, I see my childhood friend. Her once cropped hair is blonder, longer now. Her mini skirt shows off those graceful, endless legs. Her arms stretch out and suddenly I feel the old familiar warmth of her embrace.

Next day, on Hella's parents' lawn I sit. We're painting empty bottles made of stone, gleaned from the Schnapps factory her father owns. The colour that we use is cobalt blue. I don't know why we're doing this except that Hella tells me this is how we are to spend our time. But I am soothed by her familiar tone, the certainty of her command, the fact that she brings order to my day. And here I don't recall the chaos of the past few months. The sun streams down upon the grass beside the swimming pool. I bask in a serenity that, just for now, the future has no power to disturb.

For here I feel myself restored, re-built. And thus, the past, familiar and beloved, will give me strength to face the strangeness of the life that lies ahead.

Chapter 10

Pembridge Gardens – The Dance

And now, in England once again, I sit, with warden Judy, in a crowded downstairs room in Notting Hill. This is the room of Seth, the demagogue. He's absent now. Thus Judy, tutting furiously, has done her best to tidy and disguise the signs of carefree bachelor life. The room is now a vestibule. At Pembridge Gardens it is party night. The beat of Ainsley's steel band permeates the house. The drums are grouped in the conservatory, which opens from the larger drawing room, itself transformed. The panelled timbers once so elegant now can't be seen for all the heaving throng of mainly Caribbean guests. I am on edge. The rhythm signals unfamiliarity – danger perhaps. Yet, lurking somewhere deep inside, suppressed by my timidity, from time to time I feel excitement too.

It is some months since last I had an opportunity to dance. But student parties weren't like this. Here are no awkward antics and no jerking hand jive that would masquerade as dance. For here the ones who crowd our home are lithe and limbering. Though most are uninvited, these visitors are polished, confident and in their element.

I shudder inwardly. I am a misfit here.

I perch, uncomfortably, upon Seth's bed, wondering how and when I can escape. When I'm alone, I love to let my body absorb and reflect the rhythm of the music that I play. But now, in public, I'm self-conscious, and I cannot bear my awkwardness to be exposed. My eyes are lowered but a sideways glance reveals that what I hoped might be a hideaway has been found out. And one by one, a slow but steady trickle of the hopeful ones who want to dance invades the room. And one by one, I turn them down.

"Thank you. But no," I say.

The atmosphere's polite. The would-be partners back away. But then, exactly when I think that I might slip away, my path is blocked. And from beneath my downcast eyes, I shyly look and understand there's one more partner to turn down.

"No thank you. I don't dance," I say.

He should retreat now – all the others have. But seconds pass – and I can see his tall shape has not moved. I do not look. But then he speaks.

"Oh, but why not?"

I'm stunned. Both by the question and the voice I hear. A voice that carries not just curiosity, but sureness overlaid with a benevolent amusement and a love of life. A voice that has the music of a siren as it rises with the question that it asks. A voice from which I know that I am for this moment somehow irresistible to him – and he to me. That here is someone who has all the answers that I need, someone who'll want me for the questions that I pose.

I recognise I cannot turn aside.

And so, words tumbling from my lips and heedless of the others listening beside, I explain how I feel. I tell this stranger of my shyness: how I will cower, safe beneath my carapace, when I can't bear the sunlight to expose the fragile and imperfect creature that is me.

"I cannot bear," I say in halting tones, "to be observed."

"Well then…" The stranger's words assure me that, despite the secrets that I've recklessly disclosed, he is beside me still. I steal a furtive glance. I see a face that shines, eclipsing features that might otherwise be commonplace. Huge eyes that dominate his Caribbean countenance. A head that's shaven now reveals a skull of curious, almost pointed shape. I take a breath. Who is this man?

"… 'ere's what we'll do," the stranger says. The missing 'h' confirms his Caribbean provenance. His speech is intimate. It draws me in, as he intends.

Towering above, he takes my hand. He pulls me from the bed and leads me from the anteroom. In seconds we are in the empty library which adjoins the room in which the party's held.

"No one will see you here," he soothes me as he pulls me close, then lets me ricochet away. Instinctively my body synchronises with the beat which echoes through dividing doors.

In minutes, a new world has opened up. My pulse is racing now. I almost dare to look. And in this momentary glimpse, I realise that maybe I have been quite wrong to think that miracles are only to be seen in all the wonders nature brings. The hills that undulate as far as eyes can see. The ever-changing yet unchanging trees. The mountain stream that flows anew with every spring. And in this evanescent moment I divine that, if we're fortunate and if we chance upon the place and circumstance that God ordains, we humans, too, may find ourselves in perfect and enduring harmony.

"But you are missing the experience," the stranger says. His eyes are cast towards the room where other dancers heave and sway. "Alone I cannot give you all that you should have." His shoulders shrug, as if he is nonplussed. And then he says, "But I can take you there."

Chapter 10

And so, together, arms around each other, we too join the throng. And suddenly I'm dancing just the way I've always done when I'm alone. This stranger has a gift I did not think that anyone would have. For he, I see, has all the power that it takes to set me free. And, without effort, in these fleeting minutes, this man sweeps away the barriers that sought to fetter me. This stranger understands – and shares the largesse of his confidence. He sees me, not just as I am, but as he knows and reassures me, I can be. Despite our unfamiliarity, there is no doubt. I am drawn to him, and, in his turn, he is excited and somehow entranced by what he sees – he wants, and he intends to foster and protect, the unsure fledgling woman that is me.

11

GLORIOUS LOVE

Three Words That Change My World

1969

January 1969 – it is my birthday. I spend it wondering what my twenty-seventh year will bring, knowing Johnny will be in it.

It has been just five months since we met at the Pembridge Gardens party – and four since Johnny moved to Connecticut to take up what he tells me is his scholarship. Four months during which I have lain longingly in bed remembering our days together. Days when I have anxiously scanned the morning post on the table in the hostel hall, looking for an airmail letter with its red, white, and blue edges. Weeks when I have walked on air around the streets of Notting Hill. I understand about air, for in it I have built a castle of a future fashioned on the handful of days of our togetherness.

In my journal I have written only that these were "the beautiful days".

Days when, wreathed in smiles, we tease each other playfully and gently mock ourselves too. Days when we cannot leave the miracle of our togetherness, pausing only for me to make some toast that Johnny, foreshadowing future sacrifice and with unintended prescience, describes as a burnt offering. Days when even the practical tasks that on my own defeat and depress, dissolve so easily in our united hands.

A splodge of white emulsion falls on the shining head of the man who has firmly placed himself at the centre of my world. "I will look like a dalmatian," Johnny says disdainfully as he wields his paintbrush.

It is now quite clear that the political exiles have no intention of helping to redecorate my room. But if the Czechs are heedless of my needs, Johnny surprises me by offering to complete their task.

"My Lesley shall be comfortable," he says in his mellifluous tone.

Comfort and I are strangers nowadays. My months in Bethlem separated us. The world within that place was harsh and full of jagged

Chapter 11

edges that cut and wound, creating scars to last a lifetime. Perhaps, I feel, with hesitation, it will be different now.

And it is then, just as I am indeed beginning to glimpse the comfort that he offers, that Johnny tells me he must leave me for a while.

"But it is only for a year," he says. He must take up his scholarship. He will be back. He will return. The future is before us.

It's a shock and yet, somehow, I still have faith that what he says will come about. Protected by the secret dream that Johnny engenders in me, I remain serene. Even autumn, as it comes, does not contain the melancholy that I usually sense in its falling leaves as they flutter to destruction on London's pavements cold and wet.

Our time together has been short, and yet I recognise that this relationship is unlike any other that I have known. It is not one that permits or needs analysis. I can't refer to its constituent parts for in our melding these do not exist beyond the fusion we create.

The letters Johnny writes perpetuate his existence. Their pages echo my memories as he writes about his joy in me. His sharing of his new experiences excites and delights. The smaller things of life that he describes – the things he eats, the outsize steak that's topped with coleslaw, the way the New York policemen speak – no more "Good evening, all" but more like "Buster, watch it or I'll run ya in". All this enchants.

The voice on the phone startles my comfortable torpor. A phone is not, as yet, a household thing. A transatlantic call is beyond my imagination. So unbelieving am I, it is only when Johnny describes the colour of a carpet sample I have sent him that I realise it is indeed he who talks to me. He speaks approvingly of my choice; he teases that only a confident woman would choose scarlet for her room.

Yet as December comes, I grow uneasy. Frank, the cheerful social worker who lives in the room next door, remarks upon the fact that Johnny has sent me a tape, a letter in his voice. I know nothing of this for it has vanished from the table in the hall where all our post is placed. Frank, who has recognised it by its weight and shape, is insistent.

"Most definitely it was there," he says.

I write immediately to tell Johnny what has happened. I am uncomfortable – why should anyone have taken something so clearly precious to me and of such little obvious value to anyone else?

Christmas comes and goes. There is still no letter, and my mood is pensive. And then, on my birthday, I am told that there is to be a party at the house where Johnny used to live. The house he still owns is now occupied by tenants and by my would-be host. The host is Stephen, and I am familiar with his name. For Johnny has been clear that he's a friend and tells me that if I ever need help, I should rely on him. I think I've seen him once or twice in Johnny's company.

Stephen insists. "You have to come. It is your birthday," he declares.

Despite my reluctance, I am intrigued. Surely Johnny's aura will still dominate a house where he has lived? I want to bathe in that reflected light. I decide to go. Carefully I choose the lime green minidress with cream brocade I wore that night when we first met. My preparation is with Johnny in my mind.

The journey is long. I take the Central Line, changing at Mile End, and when I reach my stop, I walk, past betting shops and ugly launderettes, for fifteen minutes until I find the street I need.

81 Primrose Avenue is a cottage in a grid of Victorian terraces. Unremarkable as it may be, it has a special meaning for me now, and always will. Inside, on the first floor, music invites me, though there is little room to dance. Couples jostle for space or, having given up, simply sprawl against the wall.

From a distance shorter than my arm, a man stumbles towards me. There's no room for him to make a proper approach and no way that I can turn aside. My would-be partner tells me that his name is Keith and that he has the flat downstairs. I inhale. Here it comes: the light that I expect. A smile forms on my eager face. I gaze at him: an ordinary man made glorious by association with the man I love.

I exhale. "So you know Johnny?" I say, as I tremble with excitement. There is one final moment of innocent joy.

Then he speaks. "Yes – and his wife," he says.

The lightbulb in my mind explodes. Darkness engulfs me.

There's a tiny crack in the darkness. Stephen bends over me as I crouch on the floor like a terror-stricken animal. I shake convulsively but no sound comes. I see nothing. I hear Stephen telling me that I can't go home "like this". He says that I must take his room tonight. I follow what I take as a command. The shaking stops. I am both passive and impassive. My past now changed forever, I discard my lime green dress. My petticoat is French blue lace. It lies stark against the smooth white tension of my skin that is bared, as if in preparation for an axe. It is an

Chapter 11

axe which has already fallen. Soon the wound will clearly show, but not quite yet.

I lay myself upon the bed. Sleep will not come tonight. Perhaps there will be no more sleep. Stephen comes. The child within me stretches out both arms. The child within me knows only that there's pain. But I am not a child for I am twenty-six. There is no mother here to soothe me now. There is only Stephen who, if human, is a stranger to me. My gesture is misread. I don't have words to set the story straight. Within my lover's house, a city's width from Notting Hill, he, Stephen, and this bed will shelter me for weeks. But I cannot know yet how false this proffered comfort is, for he has deeper secrets that will compound pain.

Next day my mind is closed. I can't afford to let in truth just now. I cannot know what else there is to come. Stephen goes out. I am alone. I wander through these rooms, which in my mind I once imbued with special grace. They're Johnny's still and yet, it seems, they are just rooms, and that's a consolation now. The furniture is pale and Scandinavian in style, its simplicity marred by incongruous cushions of shocking pink. On the mantelshelf are wooden antelopes. Each thing within this house belongs to and evokes the man I love.

I see another door and open it. It's crowded with what looks like junk except that, in the forefront, is a pram.

I gasp at what this means. This too is part of Johnny's life. I shut the door and stifle the siren in my brain. I cannot think about this now.

Thought disappears. I sleep, dress, eat. I write my journal. It says nothing of consequence though it notes there are no tears. Weeks pass. I manage the long tube ride to Notting Hill. I sit with Maggie in the basement kitchen. Maggie is Frank's girlfriend, and I wonder whether she has known the secrets that were kept from me. I learn that on the night of Stephen's party, Johnny telephoned. Later I learn that the missing tape contains the truths I did not know. I am never to discover what or who it was that caused its disappearance. Later Johnny will replace the tape. I have it still. In it he tells me the stark facts. There is so much I did not know. So much that was illusory. Even our memories are different. Our meeting at the dance, for me a moment of unimagined serendipity, was something, Johnny tells me, that was planned by him. He tells me that some weeks before, he'd spied me, lingering on the Pembridge Gardens porch. Approaching from the southern corner of the street, his eyes had alighted on me in my Marimekko dress, my stance uncertain and unsure.

And in that moment, he had vowed to find out who I was. He tells me that he did not want to love me and that he has struggled to reject that love. He cannot. He reminds me that, in life, it is important to acknowledge truth. Together, he says, we will go forward. He says that love and knowledge will protect me.

He sees no irony in the words he forms, but this new revelation is too late for me.

I look at Maggie. She's with Frank, a trusted member of the hostel's inner core.

"Why," I ask, "didn't you tell me?"

"I didn't know," she says in a voice that is unsure of what it needs to say. "I only found out when I learned who Stephen is."

Slowly, I sense with horror that a fuller reality is to come.

"Who is he?"

My words jerk and judder from my lips. I know that I must learn the answer, but instinct informs me that I do not want to hear it.

Maggie falters. But then, despite her clear reluctance, a sentence forms. Her words expose my present plight.

"Stephen," she says, "is Johnny's brother-in-law."

I inhale. I cannot comprehend this fresh betrayal. My professed protector is the brother of my lover's wife.

Like the vagabond I have become, I flee again to Primrose Avenue although there's nowhere now I want to be. But the anonymity of the underground gives temporary respite. No one knows me here. Emotion rarely shows upon the faces of these travellers. For this mass of strangers, life is put on hold. There is a curious relief in this today.

Back in Johnny's former home I seek my journal. I find it by a letter which has Stephen's name upon it. It is an airmail letter. The edges are white, red, and blue. It is open. I feel no shame as I begin to read it for this will surely be a trivial sin beside the rest. But then I realise. The writer is the wife of whom I did not know. Her words are all of me.

"I hijacked another of her letters today," she writes.

She quotes from it. I see my words of love, but they are damaged words, tossed into the anguish of this woman's heart, chewed, and spat out by her to her brother who, for now, she thinks the only one that she can trust.

Words that speak of love are powerful but power can also kill. That night I dream of her. On a stretcher. Dead. It is unbearable.

Chapter 11

The world that yesterday was vibrant, full of hope, is now a burnt-out shell within which lie the fragments of my dreams. But it is so much worse, for here are fragments of the dreams of others too. The splintered pieces mingle as they jostle to survive. It's hard to separate the guilty from the innocent. Deep down I realise that much of what I saw as perfect was a cruel sham. I struggle to accept this fact. My mind denies that I'm the victim that the facts suggest I am. It's not the way I want to see myself. I cannot bear to judge the ones I love. I shut out thought. And yet I wake with tears upon my eyes. They soak my pillow, and I think that I will drown before these tears subside. Meanwhile these tears create a wall beyond which none can reach me to insist on truths I am not ready to accept. No one can see or understand the nature of my anguish and despair. I cannot share it. Only I can one day face and move beyond the devastation that engulfs me now. And if they one day judge me for the actions that I take when I have no recourse to logic or to sensibility, I will have no defence. Forever shame and shock and disbelief will dwell within the shattered, tarnished person that is me.

12

BETWEEN THE WORLDS (1)

England

1969

Barbara (1)

Perhaps it was inevitable that all those tears, the catastrophic shock, would see me back in hospital again. But this time it is only for some days, not months. And here within the Maudsley, tears subside. I lift my eyes, and I see Barbara. A woman of my age, yet very different from me.

And though a hospital like this is less than likely to produce encounters of a solid and enduring kind, I'm drawn to Barbara for what seems to be her warmth and confidence and for her ordinary London ways. She is the antidote to my timidity and to the introspection in which now and then I'm mired. She is a reassuring balance to the strangeness of my life in recent months.

How white she is. Her skin is opalescent milk. And though my own despair is lagged so tight it can't escape, I feel her brightness. She seems merry. She is almost holding court. People are listening to her words and some of them are smiling back at her.

And when she urges me to take a walk with her, my heart flickers slightly, as if despite it all I am alive. From her response to me and mine to her, I understand that maybe life and I aren't finished yet. And suddenly I realise I must not hide myself within this sanctuary. I must believe that, somehow, I'll survive.

And I discharge myself.

And now, a bond begins to form and, in the years to come, Barbara and I will be unjudging comrades, accepting one another's weaknesses and sharing all the strengths we have. Her moods will vary more than mine. For pregnancy has triggered what will soon be labelled a bipolar malady. Thus, times will come when Barbara's manic energy is unrestrained and

Chapter 12

dangerous to all. And other times – and these she hates – when all is flat, and none can share the workings of her inner mind. There will be days when all the brightness she exudes can't push away the darkness that envelops her.

Yet, in the years to come, as she now welcomes me, I'll be her friend. And when the phone rings and I hear the monotone that has become her voice, I'll know that I must go to her. And though I have no money or vivacity to share, I'll travel desperately by train and bus, hoping I will be in time to reach her before the pills through which she seeks oblivion take effect.

At her bedside, I will breathe again as Barbara lifts her head.

"Oh, it's you," she'll whisper, her cracked lips forming the beginnings of a smile.

And she will find a place within my private universe – where every human nuance is accepted and every different being mine to love.

But just for now, she and her husband welcome me. Her husband thinks that company will do her good – especially if it's of the quiet kind, as mine is bound to be now that my life has turned to desert, and the palm fronds of my mind have closed around my inner core. For though I understand, if dimly, that I will survive, my wounds are deep and, to protect myself, I have to rest.

And so, I come to know their Streatham flat where in some months this friend will bear a child. And as milk spills from her now ample breasts, I cannot differentiate the luminescence of the liquid and the whiteness of her skin. She is a Milk Madonna, and we worship her as she deserves.

And in that perfect moment as her 'high' rests, exhausted on its gentle lower slope, and meets the rising curve of my own mood, comes equilibrium.

Resurrection

And with the kindness strangers often bring, I start to understand that maybe I can cope with some of all the daunting challenges that lie ahead. At other times I wonder how this can be so. Life is so changed and so am I. I scarcely recognise myself. I was a woman-child, almost an innocent. But I'm an adult now. And innocence has fled, together with the dreams.

I fear I don't have strength or skill to navigate the minefields of the remnants of what might have been. Yet I must try – and on the better days, I tell myself that all is well. I even try to resurrect the hopes and visions that I had. And superficially I'll ride the storm until, from time to time, I look inside of me – and then I crash.

When I can shut out thought, I manage well enough. Yet, though I'll visit to complete the work I undertook to do, I won't go back to live in Notting Hill. And nor will I return to Johnny's home.

I need somewhere to live. I need a job. And need is answered in most unexpected ways.

It's almost summer now. I'm out to resurrect my 'normal' life. Thus, now I find myself within a Piccadilly bureau that introduces youthful, rootless Londoners who seek a home to those who have a vacant room. And just as I spell out the things I need – a home to share with other women of my age – I hear a voice I know that I have heard before. I pause and listen.

"We're in Crouch End. Just by the church. It's quiet. It's a basement flat – and so it's cheap. We're looking for a third."

I turn. It is Deanna. She is gorgeous and gregarious and Greek; my flatmate from those long-lost days before I entered Bethlem's gates. It seems she has not left the flat we used to share. I gasp and she turns too. We stand and we embrace. It's settled. This is serendipity. We walk away. I'm going home.

The job I also find through a coincidence when I encounter Chin. Chin was a student in my year at Birmingham. We meet entirely by chance. And here, outside a Fleet Street jeweller, we chat and tell each other what has happened in our lives since we last met. He's working now at LSE in Educational Research. He's not a student. He is paid to devise projects that will test and shape the learning of the ones who want to educate.

And from the lips of quiet, gangling Chin, fall thoughtful words that shine an unsought practicality upon my path.

"There is a vacancy within the team that you might fill," he says. "If you don't mind some typing alongside the research that we need to do."

"Of course, I do not mind," I say.

And with these chance encounters, all's set fair. I can return to where I was before the traumas of the Bethlem age – and Notting Hill. It has been made so easy for me to pretend those fateful, devastating months did not exist.

And yet I can't.

Chapter 12

Reunion

For beyond this I have to forge a path within the normal, less forgiving world.

And in this world, despite the practicalities that I've arranged, so much is unresolved. For Johnny writes. He also sends another tape – and then another and another one.

And as I listen, I am shocked. The voice that spoke to me with laughter and delight is serious and sombre now. He talks about the marriage that he tells me is to end and how he's struggled with himself. And how he could not bring himself to break the news to me of his deceit – news that he believed might lead to loss and would in any case bring pain.

"I did not want to love you, but I do," he says, "and I am certain this will never change. I beg you to be patient till I fly to London in a month or two so I can help you understand. And we can plan the future that I know that we shall have."

His tone is solemn now. It almost seems his youth has vanished with the innocence he understands that I have lost because of him. The gravity I hear is strangely dissonant with all the passion and enchantment that we felt. And like a parent speaking to an errant child, he takes responsibility for all that has occurred and all the fleeting waywardness of my response in turning to the brother of his wife. He laments that his own deceit has led me to this foolishness we both regret. And this acceptance and the laying bare of all the problems that might lie ahead for us assure me – as elation never could – that I am precious in his sight.

I'm overwhelmed. I'm scared by the intensity that echoes what I feel inside. But I am mesmerised, and I can't run. I'm powerless as Johnny makes it clear he loves me, and he can and will return. And, even with the disappointment and misgivings that I have, I am excited and, despite myself, I am suffused with joy.

And one day, there he is, upon the steps down to my Crouch End flat. And all the shock and anguish suddenly dissolve within his arms and in the certainty of his embrace.

His visit is not long but it is all it takes to make me understand this is not over. We are not ready to surrender yet the nascent passion and the dream we share.

Yet dreams make way for practicalities as Johnny worries that the flat I occupy is cold and damp.

"This is not suitable," he says. "And even if you get a bedsit, darling, that won't do. I don't want you to be on your own at this unsettling time. Your parents care for you. Why don't you have a break and go back home to them?"

And when I tell him of the fleeting pain within my abdomen, he finds a private doctor who reassures us nothing serious is wrong. He tells me that my health is his concern and that he'll always fund such treatment as I need.

And then there is the next great stride to take. For Johnny wants me to experience the brave new world that is America. His marriage will soon end, he says, and I should have an opportunity to understand how life would be, if I were by his side.

In 1969 the world outside of Europe is unknown to me. The thought of travel to a distant continent both thrills and scares.

In any case I have no money for the fare. And I would like to say that conscience now intrudes.

But somehow both these issues are resolved or at least set aside. In 1969 all has changed in London now – and maybe in America as well. The social boundaries that once constrained our lives are swept away. And, for all that I may sometimes long for certainty, I too absorb a little of the spirit of the times.

We fledgling adults of the sixties greet each other with the message *Peace and Love*. Yet, freed from all the limitations that society imposed, we can't or won't anticipate the consequences there might be. We gratify our bodies and our minds as we reach out to claim the new experiences that we now think are ours to seize. We're hedonists. Not knowing of the heavy price that lies ahead for some of us, we tell each other that our love is free. Mankind in its entirety is ours to embrace – and just because we think we can, we launch ourselves beyond the path convention has mapped out for us.

And so it is that, notwithstanding all it threatens, my affair with Johnny seems to fit the zeitgeist now. What's noticed is that he is black and I am white, and while for some, this shocks, for others, it inspires. And in the plethora of such extreme reactions, it goes unremarked that Johnny has a wife – and child.

And the excitement and what seems to me the daring of our plans, subdue the qualms I have from time to time about their impact on the others in my lover's life.

Chapter 12

Now Roger, who's a would-be banker, buttoned up and prematurely grey, informs me of a charter flight to New York I might get. Though Roger also shared our Pembridge Gardens home, I see that I had underestimated him and that within his conventional reserve, there lurks a hidden unexpected depth and a romantic streak.

To my amazement, Roger says, "I'd like to pay your fare, so you and Johnny can be reunited there."

I am astonished at the ease with which I and my plans are thus enabled and approved. And so, I summon up the courage, or the recklessness, to make the transatlantic flight to the unknown.

13

BETWEEN THE WORLDS (2)

1969–1972

America

Aboard the crowded charter plane, I chatter with excitement to the journalist called Glenda sitting next to me. She's curious and my story tumbles out. She seems to be as thrilled as I.

"Follow your heart," she counsels. "This moment will not come again."

Hours on, I'm silent, lost in thought. I've sunk into anticipation of what lies ahead. And yet my reverie is shattered as we near the Eastern Coast. Through the loudspeaker system comes the pilot's voice. It's cultured and phlegmatic, but it brings alarming news.

"Ladies and Gentlemen, I'm sorry to announce that we are running out of fuel. We cannot fly to JFK. We're searching for the nearest point at which to land."

To my relief it is not long before we land in Bangor, Maine. Hours later, on another flight, I arrive in JFK's domestic terminal. The other passengers all drift away and suddenly I am alone. There are no ground staff, for at 3 am the building is deserted and closed up. And this is not where Johnny waits to meet me from my international flight.

There are no telephones and even if there were what number could I call? And all at once anxiety takes hold. For Johnny is the only person on this continent I know. And how is he to know that I am here? All I can do is wait. And, as I shiver in alarm, I wonder what my recklessness might bring.

But then I see a figure striding through the airport lounge. And now, at last, we're face to face again. As Johnny takes me in his arms, I tremble with relief and joy. And very soon we're on the highway as Johnny drives me to Connecticut, to Hartford and the city where he lives.

And after all, there is a welcome in this brave new world.

Chapter 13

And now I'm here, I'm swept away by all the new experiences that await – the affluence that is America. Its ambience, which in New England seems so insular and less friendly than the city life I've known at home. But I'm in love and this, at times, protects me from the harshness of the truth that in America in 1969 our inter-racial union startles and offends. And thus, I only notice what I choose to see. When we explore, I'm charmed by clapboard houses in Connecticut and by the cultural sensibilities that these New Englanders believe they have. And if I notice that some people that we meet display reserve, I tell myself that this is just the way they've always been.

If there are signs that our relationship may pose a problem here, I look the other way. And yet I can't escape the comment of a surly waitress as we dine. Her hands on hips, she looks from me to Johnny and lets out a sigh.

"Ah well… you are a big girl now. I guess you do exactly as you please."

And when I pay a visit to my mother's childhood friend whose marriage brought her here from England many years ago, she sadly looks at me and says, "But Lesley, you must understand – you're not in London now."

By contrast, when I visit a small agency to see what office work might be available were I to emigrate, I'm welcomed with alacrity. The manager seems thrilled to hear the story of romance that brings me here. And if I relocate, she's certain that an English secretary will not be hard to place, especially one with high-piled hair and elegantly dressed in Jaeger gabardine. The agent is so sure that I'll have bosses who will vie to have the cachet of my clear Edwardian tones.

And she explains the references that will aid my search for work and tells me that she will support my application for the visa that I'll need.

And just before I'm due to leave for England, Johnny drives me to a leafy suburb where he pulls into the drive of a white gabled house. And there in Cornwall Street before this clapboard residence he drops some keys into my lap.

I'm puzzled. I don't understand. "What's this? Why are we here?" I ask with hesitance.

And Johnny turns to me. "Darling." His gaze rests, lingering on my face as he declares in that mellifluous tone I love, "This is the house that I have bought for us. I have decided this shall be our home."

I'm shaken for it seems too soon to forge ahead as if the path in front of us is clear. I do not voice my thoughts because it's clear that a decision has been made. But anxiously, I wonder what will happen to his wife and child – to Emmeline and daughter Dee.

And yet I can't ignore the frisson of elation that I feel on seeing all that Johnny in the boldness of his generosity has done for me.

The house is empty and, as we explore, we cannot help but muse about what we would like to think might lie ahead. We speak of evenings when we'll sit together on the rustic porch. I hold my tongue when Johnny says we'll play Sinatra songs. I tell myself perhaps I'll learn to love them too. And Johnny speaks of how, in order to relax, an operetta is his choice. His favourites: *Iolanthe* or *The Pirates of Penzance*.

I marvel at the much that I have yet to learn about this man. I am amazed at what I see as incongruity. The man I know to be an activist in politics and, now and then, a rebel and a force for change, reveals a core that's solidly conventional. It's startling until I consider such a contradiction is an element we share. For deep inside my dutiful exterior, there lies an inner self which also strives to set aside the barriers that control and stifle life.

London

Back home in London I take stock. I am revived. And there in Hartford, Johnny's buoyant too. He is energised. I hear it in the words he writes and speaks. He's camping at the house in Cornwall Street. He is to see a lawyer now. And he and Emmeline begin to talk in civil terms about what is to come. He tells me that they have a pact to keep peace for their child. But neither wants to live like this.

He says that they agree on separation and eventual divorce – but then he hesitates. For he suspects that, though she's acquiescent now, when the time comes, she may well fight.

I'm deluged now by tapes and letters as we try to meld our separate existences. We share the projects that absorb our days. On flimsy airmail paper comes advice that's sound. It gives me confidence. The lists of figures that set out the cost of Johnny's plans for all of us don't draw my focus as his words have always done. Yet every dollar is a building brick that helps to form a path to take us where we want to be.

And now our letters start to reference other ones for whom we care. And this is sobering to me. And it is I who sometimes struggle now.

Besides the anguish and the guilt that come quite naturally, I feel deep

Chapter 13

shame that sometimes I am able to set these aside. How can I be so apathetic and indifferent to the fate of someone not much older than myself? Whose only slip has been to place her trust in this same person that I love?

Yet she's not solid in my sight and Johnny never makes her so. He talks about the barrenness within their home – how they both reach out to their child to give her all the love they cannot share between themselves. And yet he never speaks of her – of Emmeline, his wife. I don't know of her words, her mannerisms or her virtues or her faults. I don't know what she does all day – although he mentions one day that she needs a car. He speaks of all the practicalities her future holds. He never tells me how she feels.

And in this way – especially as I am three thousand miles away – I can sometimes ignore the fact that she is real.

So I apply my newfound positivity to what I need to do. For other flights will follow, funded any way we can. I want to share the load as best I can. It is my mission now to take on extra work of any kind to meet the cost. And those who care to understand my dream do all they can to help. The leader of our team at LSE requires a typist for his book. So, every Saturday I take a train to Croydon, then a bus. Within his study, brimming with eclectic books which line the walls of ochre red, I sit for hours as he dictates his latest masterpiece.

One day this scholar tells me that he's overworked. And delegates to me a column in a national magazine where he reviews research.

"I don't have time. You'll have to do the work for me."

The column is anonymous, of course. Yet even though it does not bear my name and even though it's money that I think I want, I can't resist a touch of pride that I'm a writer now.

And through these burgeoning opportunities I grow in certainty that I can flourish in America as well as here. For surely the New World will welcome me.

And as I bask in the reflected heat and light of love and positivity, all vestiges of caution shrivel till they fade from sight.

And deep within, I sense a steady rising of a feeling I have known before. It is determination. I will not accept that all that's past has been for naught.

Thus, here in England all I have to do is gather references and then persuade the embassy to issue a green card. This process is frustrating, and it will be long. But I am looking forward now and cutting free from recent memories of shock and loss. So certain am I now that there's a future for me in America, that when my research project ends, I simply take on temporary typing work.

Inside My Head

And if I do not weigh things up with all the caution that I should, perhaps that just reflects the desperation that I have to move from darkness into light. I cannot bear to think about the disappointments and betrayals I have known. I only know that hope is something that I must not lose. For, if, a year or two ago, I'd known what lay ahead of me, would I have had the courage and the confidence to live?

Thus, I suppress all superficial doubt, but deep inside I carry fear and sadness too. I don't admit to these but sometimes, when I'm on my own, they cast a fleeting shadow that I can't dismiss.

One day in Regents Park, I linger as I leave the mosque where now I have a typing job. And suddenly, ahead of me, I see a weeping willow tree of yellow green. I feel a pang. It is so like the Knighton trees that grace the riverbank that, as a child, I used to see across the field beyond the grey stone wall. And as I bring to mind the peaceful long-lost world that nurtured me, it seems to me this willow is an elegant reproach. It bids me mourn the carefree innocent that I once was. And, for an instant, pain and loss return, and I dissolve beneath this doleful verdant curtain made of tears.

14

TURNING POINT (1)

1972

Mr Fox

Somewhere behind the discreet Georgian façade of a Dorset Square townhouse is a solicitor who, my agency tells me, needs an extra secretary for today.

"Just for one day," Miss Chalmers says, with emphasis, as if I might not comprehend this unusual request.

Briefly, I wonder what the reason is. Perhaps today's boss plans a special event. Perhaps he's simply short of cash. And yet it's all the same to me. This work is no more than a stopgap. My future in America is still the focus of my life. Surely a visa will be granted to me soon.

I am shown to a first-floor room crowded with four desks jammed together without thought of ergonomics. It's not a dark room but the window overlooks a stairwell. This at once deprives it of all personality.

As I take a seat at the one unoccupied desk, a door opens. Here stands today's employer, the jacket of his grey-striped suit abandoned so that his pale blue shirt displays the leanness of his body and the vigour of his restless energy. His dark curls hint at waywardness, though today they have been trimmed and press against his head. I am surprised by his youth. I am twenty-eight and don't know much about the law or lawyers, but somehow, I don't expect a sole practitioner to be just a handful of years my senior, as he must be. But I learn at once that youth does not mean informality. I am to call him Mr Fox.

By 5 pm, I have completed the dictation that he gives. As I close my bag to leave, he hovers by my desk.

"You are not bad," he says. "You might as well stay till Friday."

When Friday comes, this invitation is extended.

Weeks pass.

Gradually I become familiar with this man and with the way his office works. Mr Fox is an early riser and, even though he goes first to the gym, he's always at the office by the time that I arrive at 8 am. I find him sifting through a mound of post piled high on the Victorian desk which occupies the centre of his office. Light streams through the Georgian windows, bouncing off the mahogany of the bookshelves that line the room. Classical music filters from an unseen source. Mr Fox is methodical. He takes a paper knife to each envelope, scanning the letter it contains before handing it to Marion. Marion is the chubby 16-year-old whose only function is to match the letters with the cardboard files she fetches from the safety of the attic where they are stored at night. These she arranges around the room, creating a border which unwittingly relieves the plainness of the carpet. Mr Fox works systematically as the day progresses. By lunchtime the border is no more.

To my surprise I come to love this morning ritual. It has a calm that's not expected in a business, even one steeped in tradition as the law undoubtedly is.

Mr Fox has clients as varied as the size and colours of the envelopes we sort. Their number includes film stars, a restaurateur or two, professional men and ordinary couples buying houses for the first and maybe only time. A self-ennobled viscount and his wife we call 'The Lady Anne' add so much superficial charm that I do not mind when one day I discover that their titles are not real.

For the first and only time, I feel the joy of waking with the realisation that today is Monday.

As my working weeks extend so, too, do my tasks. I am sent in taxis to the courts where I must issue writs or lodge important papers that the judge must have. If, as sometimes happens, Mr Fox cannot attend a conference with counsel, he delegates the task to me. On these occasions, I am not, of course, permitted to speak.

And, as I settle at my desk again, I can't resist a glance at those who work here too. This Georgian townhouse is the property of Mr Fox. And he has peopled it with those he likes to have at hand. His clients, entering from the street, are ushered in by Jane, a slender English rose with long straight hair. And, perched from time to time beside her when he's waiting for another job is Stephen with his freckled face and cheeky grin: the office boy who's been in trouble with the police.

One floor above, four secretaries share the crowded space adjacent to

Chapter 14

the room from which our boss dictates their every move. By day they're silent as they type assiduously. At 5 pm I watch them paint and redesign their faces, changing into leather outfits as they plunge into their social lives. And on the mezzanine is our occasional and elderly cashier, who likes to moan behind her boss's back but understands she's fortunate to have a job at all.

The second floor is sublet to another lawyer who's a sole practitioner. His secretary, Averil, is self-possessed, mature, and comfortably plump. Beyond her unflappable efficiency, she exudes a weary kindness. She's also black.

And on the topmost floor resides an old retainer of a sort, a Major who encountered my employer in his military days. To him these rooms are home: a grace and favour residence that Mr Fox dispenses in exchange for undemanding tasks like holding keys and keeping watch.

Perhaps it's just for old times' sake. I cannot know. But gradually I understand that some – and maybe most – of those who work with Mr Fox are misfits of a kind. I wonder if their presence here is due to Mr Fox's charity. Or if it somehow suits him that they are beholden to their boss.

Now, to accompany my slightly more important role, I have an office that I'm told will be my own. Except it's not. The vast Victorian desk is more than ample even for the ever-growing pile of papers that I have. And Mr Fox discerns that here is space that he can use to his advantage. Thus, he sublets half of my desk. And sometimes if it's morning, I will come across the young estate agent who rents the desktop that I had thought would be my own. And in the afternoons a cheery broker of insurance settles to consider all the calls he plans to make.

Neither, says Mr Fox, need know that he or she is not the only one to rent that desk.

Weeks pass and Mr Fox announces that he is to take a holiday. It will be on his yacht. There will be no method of communication with the office. It will be decades before such links are commonplace. The office will not, however, close. I am sent to buy a notebook divided into alphabetical sections. Here between these flimsy covers will be all the instructions I will have to care for clients and progress their cases whilst their trusted lawyer is away.

I have no choice in this. There is no time for apprehension here. I'll do my best – but, after all, it's just another job, I tell myself.

Despite this risk, the firm survives. My tenure is continually extended. My agency seeks other secretaries.

Shadows on the Path

I am absorbed. I relish every moment of my day. I give myself permission not to look ahead and I will not look back. I'm living in the present when I can, at least throughout my working day. If there are shadows on the path ahead, I do not want to see them now. For once, I am entirely focussed outwards, on the unexpected intrigue of this legal world.

And thus, I disregard the dull but now more constant pain I feel within my lower abdomen. This pain has been there since I cannot quite remember when. I pay it fleeting heed. I tell myself it's just another 'of those things'.

Bethlem, perhaps, has made a stoic of the troubled and impassioned girl that once was me. I do not have the confidence in others' expertise that once I had. I've learned there is no magic that will chase my ills away. And no one else can fix the life that's mine to nurture and to shape.

And as I've learned to manage panic, which, though less frequent, stalks me still, so will I learn to cope with pain.

Somehow this fortitude enables me. I cease to look for barriers on my path. And as I learn to cope, the fascination that I find with things beyond myself propels me to a place where, if I only paused to let in thought, I might surmise that I would thrive.

I cannot see this yet.

And, though each day I plant my feet more firmly in this new and fertile land, I can't release the hopes I've nurtured in the past few years.

The Nowhere Land of Hope

My hopes are fuelled by the tapes and telegrams that I continue to receive. Yet there are times when all my dogged stubbornness is needed as I'm shaken by events that I have not foreseen. I'm crushed to learn that our financial woes have meant there is no option but for Emmeline and Dee to move to Cornwall Street – the house I'd thought for just a few short weeks would be our home.

The lawyer cannot help. For in New England Johnny does not have grounds for divorce.

Chapter 14

Though Johnny changes jobs – he's working on an engineering project up in Buffalo – the money's simply not enough to fund the breakaway he planned. I'm devastated as my dreams are pushed aside for now. And I step back to heal the wounds I won't admit are serious. And yet I never think that I should walk away.

I put on hold the visa application that I made. And yet I do not cancel it.

The tapes continue, interspersed with telegrams and calls. The telegrams urge me to 'keep the faith'. 'Stay strong,' they say.

Then one day, when it's snowing in New England, Johnny phones to tell me Dee has had an accident. Her leg is broken and, with roads impassable, he has to carry her so she can get the help she needs. And something in his voice alerts my heart, for he is speaking in a tone of love and of concern that, until now, I'd only heard him use to speak of me.

And in this moment somehow it is clear to both of us that this young child comes first and always will.

And if this revelation has come late, I understand it's just the way that things should be. I know I'll never try to interfere with this.

And though we scarcely mention it, we understand that we, who'll always have each other's love, must wait until she's older and less vulnerable.

And from then on, in tapes and calls, much of our focus is on Dee. Her father is concerned that, living with the silent conflict that her parents do their utmost to suppress, she cannot grow to understand the possibility of healthy love between a woman and a man. Sometimes he tells me that he'd love to spirit her away to share the harmony that he believes that he and I will have. And yet he knows he cannot rescue her that way.

At times like this my lover leans on me. Just now and then he confides all the hopelessness that each of us encounters in our private time. He pleads with me to help him find a way to meld the lives most precious in his life.

"Help me, help me. Darling. Please."

But I don't know the way to help or, if I know, I do not want to see it yet. I am a fledgling adult and the wisdom that I need is many years ahead of me.

And even then – and even though I sigh and turn away – I know I can't abandon this one person who in that first moment of our meeting recognised me and embraced me as I am. Who saw what lay beneath the fragile charm and awkwardness. With whom I share a reciprocity of need, enchantment and of love.

And he, it seems, will not relinquish me.

And some weeks later, when we need each other most, my lover takes another plane and once again he's by my side.

Instantly, the present simply falls away as he commands. Though he expresses pride in all that I achieve, he's quick to draw me back into the world he knows. And so, he will not share the room I have. Instead, he insists that we stay with Seth – the demagogue I knew from Notting Hill. A man with whom I've always felt unease, a man who, though he stood on soapboxes and called for justice and equality, believed the female sex was there to service all his manly whims. A man who, since I would not stroke his pride or fetch his cigarettes, had no regard for me.

I'm overjoyed by my reunion with the man I love. But though we are together, there's no peaceful haven for us yet. That night the pain returns. I can't be ill, I tell myself. Not now, not here. Especially not in front of Seth.

Next day I struggle into Dorset Square and work. But, as I cross the road to court, I understand I can't ignore the agony. Somehow, I manage to complete the tasks I have, but in the afternoon the doctors diagnose acute inflammatory disease. And thus, I find myself in hospital.

Mercifully, I don't or maybe will not understand. I hear the furtive whispers that discuss the childlessness that may accompany the illness that I have. But I ignore them though I notice Johnny is subdued. I do not let myself anticipate what all of this may mean for me. I can't foresee how many times within the years ahead I will return to hospital. The pain subsides and that's enough for me. But precious time I'd planned to spend with Johnny has been cruelly usurped.

He's by my bedside every day for all the time the hospital allows. He pays a private doctor to advise. But dimly, through my pain, I recognise the overwhelming strain and desperation that he feels. Now he eschews the comfort of Seth's home. And, in my bedsit, Johnny lies alone upon my narrow couch, searching for the sleep that will not come. He tells me that each night he wraps himself within my cashmere dressing gown.

And, thus enfolded in the shadow of the closeness that my lover craves, Johnny weeps.

15

TURNING POINT (2)

1972–1973

And thus, the visit for which we so longed has vanished. And by the time that I am out of hospital, Johnny is no longer here.

But even now I'm not entirely alone. Though I need time to rest, my boss is practical and calm. So I can cut down on my travelling, he offers me a room in the hotel that he has bought. This also is in Dorset Square, so I am just across the road from work.

And yet again, although I am suspended in the nowhere land of hope, there is a hand that reaches out to steer me on my way. Thus, helped and reassured, I lose no time in turning to the papers on my desk. I have no reason to suppose this illness is anything beyond a short-term scare. And, thankfully, I set aside this inconvenient anxiety and tell myself it's just another thing with which I'll have to deal.

Finding Riverview – Chiswick

Beyond this grown-up world where trust is placed in me, I find that there are other shifts as well. Some friends of friends have begged me to take on a house that they have bought. It had seemed such a bargain and a sound investment, they believed. But once the house was bought, their energy and their imagination failed. The task of renovating and repair, the letting out and management, had seemed beyond their capability.

And now it seems they think that I might take it on.

Their quest at first seems hopeless. It's 1972. Chiswick is not yet desirable or gentrified, as it will one day be. An erstwhile fishing village by the Thames, this is a workers' quarter now. It offers little in the way of entertainment for the ones who are not old or else exhausted by their work. To a young woman, not yet tamed by domesticity, it seems remote. Away from Central London's action, who will visit me?

In any case, the only home for which I long is not in London. It is with Johnny in America. I cannot bind myself to any place where he is not a part of life.

"But it will be a base for you," my friends cajole.

"I'm not so sure. It's miles from all my friends," I murmur doubtfully.

"But this would be your home – and they could come and stay," is the riposte.

The thought of Johnny in a home that's mine – and therefore ours – lights up my mind. Thus, in the end, I grudgingly accept that I will take a look. And in so doing, though I do not know it yet and though I push the thought away, I find the place that I will call my home for twenty years or more.

Reluctantly I find myself at 'Riverview', a stone's throw from the enclave that was once a village clustered round the riverside: Strand on the Green.

Yards from the Thames, I view this house that I am asked to rent – the second of a terrace of Edwardian dwellings in a tree-lined street. Before me I see gabled houses, uniformly matched, distinguished only by the colour of their paint – unless the stained-glass panels in the doors have been replaced by something more in keeping with the times. I sigh. It's sad, I think, when beauty is discarded just because it represents the past.

This house has been disfigured by its casement windows, which obtrude against the elegance of sashes that adorn its neighbours' homes. And when I go inside, I see these windows are all swathed in double rows of satin, white on white. A spiritualist, I'm told, lived here most recently. And thus, I learn, these curtains have been hung to keep the evil spirits out.

The house is simply furnished in a motley of utility. Nothing fits. Nothing stands out. And yet, there is an aura which, despite my preconceived reluctance, draws me into this house.

I step down from the hall into a kitchen, of itself minute. Beyond the flagstone floor I see a door and open it – and understand that I have somehow chanced upon a magic world.

The garden's overgrown but it is a kaleidoscope of rampant blooms. A concrete cross was once a pristine path, though now its chiselled edges are usurped by spreading plants and leaves. And, as at Knighton, there's no lawn and every inch of space is crowded with the plants that somebody once loved. Here jostle ferns and scented stocks, and seedlings fight for

Chapter 15

space – and soil is scarcely visible. Yet, towering upwards, roses flourish, brandishing their bushy heads, on which, as in some children's fairy tale, hang vibrant clumps of yellow, white, and red. And in this wilderness, I see that nature has reclaimed the earth that somebody once tried to train and cultivate.

I recognise that here is somewhere that will claim me also as its own. And so it will.

There's solace in activity that takes the place of thought and doubt. In Chiswick I'm too busy to reflect on where my life is taking me.

At Riverview I sand the furniture and paint it white. I scour the shops for remnants from which curtains can be sewn. I place an ad and let two rooms – to Judy, who's a dental nurse, and Gina, who is new to London and excited by her move away from home. Thus, I will have at least two 'friends'. What's more, together we'll ensure the rent is paid.

And I explore the riverbank, and when the water's low, I tread the sometimes-flooded path. Strand on the Green was once a haunt of humble fishermen, but it has always been a place where handsomeness has been espoused. Imposing edifices flaunt their individual flair; their architecture and their history dominate the waterfront.

Beneath their gaze are tethered fishing craft, moored – as they were some hundred years ago – to wooden posts which rise above inflowing tides.

Around them, quietly serene, glide ducks and waterfowl, untroubled by the passers-by. They build their nests upon the tiny island, where, it's said, Cromwell once hid from Cavaliers.

And I am now beguiled. I am entranced by the undoubted charm I see. The blue plaques that I chance upon from time to time inform me that, within the confines of this place, artists and writers chose to make their home. Names such as Zoffany and Mitford echo in my mind and add to the enchantment that I feel.

I marvel at the way that God provides. He gives me shelter after all the turmoil of the last few years. Somewhere that, though unassuming, is secure. Somewhere as well where nature brings me back to life. A place where I can celebrate the modest progress that I make in life. Somewhere that will sustain me through the blows that are to come.

Though I don't know that yet.

Dorset Square – Watershed

One day, as I'm about to leave my desk for home, I'm summoned back into the presence of my boss. I quickly learn that Mr Fox has something on his mind. And, from his lips, a barrage of interrogation falls. He needs – he claims – to know about the people in my life and my ambitions for the future too. His aim is sure, and I am stunned. My answers are unguarded and in minutes he knows all he needs to know. My aspirations are laid bare as I reveal my plan to leave this country and to settle with my lover in what once was the New World.

"This will not happen," Mr Fox declares.

In his certainty my future is demolished.

He's adamant that my commitment is in doubt. I falter at the ruthlessness of his attack. Surely, I think, the dream I've harboured for so long cannot be prised away from me?

And sensing my discomfiture, he seizes the initiative.

"I have a better plan for you," he claims. "Stay here. I'll teach you to do all that a solicitor can do. You'll run my office. I'll have more time to see my family and to travel on my yacht."

I see a flaw in this. And, in an instant, I forget what's threatened here and challenge him.

"But why," I say, "should I do that? Surely if I can do all that I might as well retrain to be a qualified professional."

His riposte is derisive. I have no substance or ambition, he infers. To him I am a fickle fly-by-night. He tells me I don't have it in me to achieve what I suggest. I am – he hesitates but only for effect – precisely not the type to stick at things.

I'm angry now and all the indignation that I feel at his intrusive curiosity is channelled into my reply. I tell him that I am exactly what he thinks that I am not and that I will achieve the things he claims are out of reach. I'm cornered now. The more that he denies my worth, the more assertive my response. This is a reflex. It is not a choice.

And suddenly he tires of this undignified exchange.

"Alright," he counters. "I will take a chance. I'll give you articles so you can train. I'll pay your fees to study law."

I am too stunned to speak or gasp. What have we done? From this, there can be no return, I think.

I have no doubt this is a watershed, a turning point. The path I chose

Chapter 15

has veered away from where I thought that it would lead. Yet I am learning how to cope when dreams are challenged by reality. I simply block out what intrudes. Johnny and I must wait. I understand. But nothing can obliterate the future that we plan. And knowing this I set my dreams aside and face today head on.

And, as I wait to start my legal studies, I revel in the challenges that my employer sets. I have been set a task and somehow this enables me to have the confidence to welcome and enjoy the clients that I have.

One Sunday I receive a call from Lady Anne. She tells me that her husband's been arrested on a charge of fraud. He's at a Central London police station.

"I can't reach Mr Fox," she says. "Will you come, please. It's desperate."

I can't refuse. A friend drives me to Paddington where I'm allowed to see my client in a cell. And I am horrified to find him sitting on a concrete ledge – and that his glasses and his walking stick have been removed. Whatever he has done, he's elderly and frail. The basin and the lavatory are both some yards away. He will not reach them safely if he doesn't have his stick.

I remonstrate and tell them that I'll see that he's released. And, unsurprisingly, they laugh at me.

So, home again, I scan the Yellow Pages, and I ring up Nick – a barrister I vaguely think I've met somewhere before. He tells me that, although it's not his speciality, an application could be made for bail – if only we can find a duty judge. Within the hour we sit together in a judge's private chambers in the Inns of Court. The judge is affable and sanguine, unperturbed by our request. And, as he nods assent at Nick, he hands me chocolates from a box.

Civilities complete, I head to Paddington again. I clutch the precious piece of paper that will set my client free. Despite what seems to me like victory, the policemen at the station smirk.

"Too bad," they utter. "We can't let him out tonight. He's taken sleeping tablets. He'll be comatose till dawn."

Yet, even if my efforts don't entirely succeed, I am encouraged. Here is somewhere that I want to be – and here's a role I think I can fulfil.

And so begins this fresh new start in what seems now a lifetime of aborted plans. Behind me is a failed teenage romance, a job in personnel I loved and lost. A plan through which, I thought, in Bethlem they would cure the panic that thwarted my desire to embrace social work.

Yet now a college place is found for me. My first term's fees are paid upfront by Mr Fox. And every morning, in the early autumn mist, I walk the Chiswick river path to catch the bus to college at Lancaster Gate.

I find the studies dry and rather dull. I have to learn to focus narrowly. Here, learning is quite different from social sciences, where minds are taught they should expand and light upon new theories to resolve the question posed. It's challenging – and yet, if I can get through what to me is tedious, I can return to the diversity I have experienced in Dorset Square. Where there's an opportunity to help and to support the clients that I meet.

My first term ends. My mood is elevated, yet my joyful pleasure is short-lived. Anticipation is to be denied. There is a phone call and, abruptly, I am summoned back to Dorset Square.

The Georgian townhouse has not changed. Yet, as I enter, I can't quell a feeling of unease. And when I reach the offices, I know that I am right to be concerned. Most of the staff appear to be subdued. Our cashier, Mrs Abrams, weeps.

"What is it?" I question frantically, although I understand her answer will distress us both.

"He's dead," she says in monotone.

My shock is evident. I can't believe that Mr Fox is dead at thirty-eight. She will not tell me how or when he died.

It is a crushing blow to learn that one as young and vigorous as he can vanish from our lives in one short afternoon. The trauma is extended as I learn the sordid details of his death. He was found hanging from his children's swing. From photos it appeared that he had practised this, his final risk.

The details linger in my mind. I dream of them at night and, twice, I wake to find that, in my sleep I've woven round my neck the silken cord of my own dressing gown. The maroon cashmere robe I like to lay across my bed at night is now companion to the horror and revulsion that I feel.

I cannot understand. He seemed to have so much. And now his family are left to fend alone against publicity and spite and shame.

As shock subsides, the aftermath reveals my plight. This does not rank alongside all the trauma that his family must face, but still, it is disquieting. My training has been interrupted. I have no money and no job but, worse, as one who was a protégée of Mr Fox, I have to show that I was not caught up in any impropriety there might have been. A would-be lawyer

Chapter 15

must behave in such a way that inspires trust and confidence. The Law Society must consider if and how my training contract can proceed.

Whilst they investigate, I live from hand to mouth. I walk the four-mile trip to Acton, to an office which I hope will offer money for the unemployed. I walk in vain.

I learn to live on pudding rice enriched with honey or with jam. And sometimes on the food that others leave behind.

And Johnny helps me with the phone bills that I cannot pay.

Despite it all, I won't give up. My years of training are thus lean and tough. My illness does not vanish. Such is my gaunt and bleak appearance that even my tutor suggests that I give up my plans.

And when the pain returns, there's sickness too. It does not pass until, when I am overwhelmed by nausea, my doctor comes. And injects me. Few weeks go by when there is not at least one day like this. And now and then the doctor turns to me and says:

"I have no doubt, my dear, that hospital's the place where you should be."

Thus, days of energy are offset by debility and pain.

Yet silently and through some miracle, I'm learning faith and fortitude. And buried deep inside of me, a minute crumb of certainty begins to swell and threaten my anxiety and doubt. I scarcely feel it yet. But since catastrophe and I have met before, I've learned to hug my strength around me as disaster tries to pull me from the path I know that I must tread. I will not give up hope. I will survive.

16

LIFE AND LEARNING

1974

New York

It is spring 1974. After almost a year of upheaval and distress, I am to spend a month with Johnny.

I have left behind the desolation that followed death and disruption and the dreary offices in Mitre Court where the Law Society have placed me to complete my articles. Now that they accept my suitability for this profession, only my final exams stand between me and my admission to the Roll of Solicitors.

But I have never really thought that far. What mattered was that I did not give up. I was just glad to have a welcome in a world I'd thought was lost to me. I was content to revel in the warmth of Johnny's pride.

On hearing that the path to a professional future was now clear, he told me that he loved my perseverance and my fortitude – qualities once hidden by my anxiousness and my timidity.

"Hey darling!" On the tape I heard his smothered chuckle of delight. "My Lesley, you are stronger than I thought. Right on, sister!"

Yet somehow, we have never spoken of the implications for our future life. We always separated all the different sections of our lives. We simply focussed on whatever was before us at the time. The present never made us question what we both believed would lie ahead. However unrealistic and half-formed our future plans might seem, nothing could shake our inner certainty – our dream – that we would be together in the years to come.

And Mitre Court, the law and Chiswick are now briefly set aside. They've vanished from my consciousness.

In midtown Manhattan I stride, confidently, on my way to meet the man I love. As I near the Lexington Avenue subway, my violet Biba trench coat falls open to reveal the deep jade minidress beneath. My long dark

Chapter 16

hair is loose, echoing the sense of freedom that I absorb from this vibrant city. On my feet are soft, wedged pumps of ginger suede.

I have flown to my cocoon where Johnny waits for me. And here, despite the raucous clamour of New York and all the tenuous uncertainty of those beloved ties that bind me here, I am at peace.

I'll be back home in London soon enough. I'm thirty-one. I know the difference now between reality and what is simply stardust, flickering so seductively from the vastness of eternity.

Johnny works in New York now. This gives him distance from his daughter and his wife, who still live in Connecticut. Of course, he still spends time with them, especially Dee, but even so, a half and half existence enables all of them to have some space in which to breathe.

And I breathe freely too. For Johnny need not hide me now. My existence and his feelings are a fact. His mother sends a greeting to me. Though it's rather gruff and almost grudging, I am touched. I understand that she must be concerned. Yet with the message comes an iron that is lacking in the studio we share.

While Johnny works, I spend my days exploring this metropolis. I visit the museums. I am captivated by the social history of New York. I walk the streets with eagerness and open eyes. I am dazzled by the glitz of Broadway. I am left breathless by Manhattan's boastful buildings, by its opulence. I am deafened by the discord of its all-pervasive sounds. And then, as I walk on, I find myself in Harlem's streets of crowded tenements. Often incautious, I am still naïve, and I don't fully understand the danger lurking in these unquiet streets. I am drawn towards the children crowding on the steps that are the only outlet from the drabness of their indoor world. Some are restless and full of energy. Some look as if they still have hope. I know that many are already doomed. And, suddenly, my eye is caught by a Hispanic girl, perhaps some ten years old. Her chest thrusts forward and her smile is radiant as she surveys a world she thinks is hers. She wears a lilac top. It brings to mind the colour of a cardigan I wore and loved when I was just sixteen. I wonder what her future holds and whether she will even reach that age.

Reality has many faces and, however hard we dream, we can't escape them all.

And yet, beyond these new exotic images – the swaggering edifices sweeping to the sky, the teeming brownstones brimming with a nascent hope that soon will turn to loathing and despair – beyond all this, it's

Johnny and our naturalness that I will carry with me when we part. Despite the years of separation and the shocks, this man and I are travellers together on a path where, despite all apparent differences, we recognise that we belong.

One day there is a message from Connecticut. There is a problem, and it seems to concern Dee. Johnny is needed there, the message says. Hands firmly linked, we hurry to the bus station. We hold each other slightly longer than the other travellers expect. I notice that they stare at us. Then Johnny turns from me and boards the Greyhound bus. I've told him that of course he is to stay until all's well again and that I shall be quite fine on my own. And so I am. I buy some tubs of Dannon yogurt from the drug store on the street – and glossy magazines sold by the cheerful newsstand man who each day greets me like a long-lost friend. The magazines are full of Patty Hearst, an heiress who is kidnapped and held captive by some rebel group. America is fascinated. So am I. I barricade myself into the studio and settle with my law books and my magazines. I'm unperturbed. Lulled by the lingering aura of togetherness, I'm confident. I'll while away the waiting for the next few days.

But I've not long to wait for suddenly I hear the door. And though it's less than twenty-four hours since he left, Johnny is back again. The 'problem' was an artifice – a ruse by Emmeline to bring her husband to her side. And this deception troubles me for it suggests that Emmeline is not yet ready to accept her loss.

And I step back, though I do not acknowledge this. The truth is that the man I love has ties I can't and won't dissolve. I love him and I do not want to take away from him the things he has. I only want to bring him joy – and then, from time to time, to share the peace we know.

Now, as we chat across our coffee, all the tension from my distant London life dissolves. The trivial worries from my day-to-day routine all tumble out and melt away. And, as he listens, Johnny looks at me with eyes of such benevolence, I think perhaps I've seen the eyes of God himself.

And yet it seems that hesitance – or maybe cowardice – will pull me back to England's shores.

Too soon we're standing on the tarmac as my plane awaits. As Johnny holds me, I imbibe his aura – and the smell of him. I stretch my hands so that they linger on his skin and on his slightly foreign clothes. He's just an ordinary man. I stroke the ordinary jacket, shirt and trousers that

Chapter 16

encase the frame I've come to love. I elevate them to magnificence because they're his.

Our arms reach out. We hold each other in a last embrace. One day he'll tell me, in a letter, that he knew then we would never meet again.

I say his name. Within my soul the past will never die.

London and Hertfordshire

Back home in Riverview the present pushes dreams away. Each day I take the District Line. I alight at Temple, for it is here, within this Inn of Court, that I will pass my days. And beyond work, I have an extra mission now. Johnny has given me authority to manage the house at Primrose Avenue, where he once lived. It's filled with lodgers now and all their needs are mine to satisfy. I find this challenging and tiring too. There's little respite from my daily tasks, although one day, by chance, I manage to escape. My sister, Christine, asks me to make up a fourth. She and two friends are driving to the coast. Although I am exhausted, I agree. Despite myself, I join in with the beach football they play. I slip. One of the friends gives me his hand. He's Greek. He tells me that his name is George. It barely registers. The dull ache in my abdomen usurps attention now.

Next day, I see my doctor and he tells me there is nothing untoward. He reassures me that I'm well enough to travel to my parents' home.

That evening, I return to Hemel Hempstead and the bedroom of my teenage years. The doors that front the plywood wardrobe that my father built don't slide the way they should. But when I look inside, I find the still-loved outfits of my adolescent years and, pushed towards the back, a hula hoop. The kidney dressing table still displays its cretonne skirt of crimson red. The bevelled mirror is still here. It once beheld my teenage face – smooth and unmarked – a face on which no adult future was betrayed. And in this narrow bed I dreamed my adolescent dreams of pop stars, boys, and clothes.

I feel safe here. Yet in the early hours I waken. I am wracked with pain. This also is familiar now.

I call to Mummy, and I beg that she should call a doctor now. But Mummy says we have to wait. The doctor needs his sleep. He is important and he has a busy day ahead.

Finally, at nine o'clock, the doctor comes and tells me that there is no doubt. I need to be in hospital.

There, things go wrong. It's just my usual pain, the doctors say. They fail to notice my appendix also is inflamed – until it bursts.

There's panic now as nurses hurry round. The operation, they've been told, has failed. The wrongful diagnosis has delayed the action for too long. It's touch and go. It's less than likely that I will survive.

Fever engulfs me. The nurses use whatever means they can to cool me down. The images I see are vivid, but they quickly fade, along with dignity. There is a fan. Ice cubes are packed within a flannel that is striped with purple and with pink. It's mine. It's placed upon my head. Despite my agitation and my flailing, I absorb all this and tell myself this is absurd. I notice that the colours of the flannel don't quite match the maroon of the dressing gown in which my shivering body has been wrapped. How can I – febrile, fading, trapped within these blankets – catch the trivial details of this scene? And yet I do.

Somehow, I see all this. I also hear the whispers telling of my likely fate.

A final chance, I hear, at last. A doctor has returned. Vaguely, I understand there's something more that he can do – although I hear him warn that I must be prepared for pain. I try to think how bad the pain may be and what unspeakable procedure is to come. Yet, instantly I see I must abandon thought, for it's no good to me. The nurses flutter as I hear their indrawn breath. But all the same, I have no choice in this.

But on this day, I'm not alone. My father happens to be here. He could not know a duty visit might well bring him to a bed of death.

We are not close. Absences of war and work and duty robbed us of the camaraderie and fond affection that we might have had. Damned by our hesitance and inarticulateness, our lives are separate. It is too late to change this now. Yet in this fleeting moment of my life, I see at last what matters and is true.

For here, beyond the pain and the indignity – impassive, solid, and familiar – is my father. I marvel at his steadfastness. Beside my bed, he's speechless. So am I. And, in this present crisis, past and future disappear. We are together and I understand, somehow, that he is here to see that I will live. I realise, with some amazement, that he loves me. Whatever went before, whatever is to come, I'll never question that again.

And as we wait, our solidarity brings strength. I borrow from the weight that is his love. An hour on, they wheel me, unresisting, to a side room where a doctor does his best to free me from the poison that inhabits

Chapter 16

me. The anaesthetic's lost its potency and I will be exposed to pain that is acute. I clench my eyes against the harshness of the lights. I cannot see (though I can feel) the things he does, and he says nothing as he works. In silence, too, I count, as seconds, minutes pass. I am resolved I will not make a sound – and I do not. And finally, despite the agony, they wheel me back into the ward.

The trauma over, I am told that alcohol may stimulate me as it brings relief. The nurses settle me in bed. They offer sherry – Martell brandy too. My father clears his throat, uncertain, anxious. We do not touch. We rarely do. Yet, as I sip the brandy, I discern the relaxation of his strained but handsome face. He scans my countenance. I notice that his eyes are heavy, as from unshed tears. And, as these watering eyes catch mine, I realise that I am not to die today.

17

BEYOND THE PAST

1974

September – London

The surgery's behind me now. I need to put it in the past if I'm to thrive. And yet I feel so weak, so low – as if I will soon sink and fade into the earth from which we're told that we have come.

At Riverview, I do my best to heal myself and to recover from the illness I have had. And yet I do not heal. I cannot eat. My hair is falling from my skull. It beds itself into my carpet. It forms itself in matted clumps. It lies profuse and dense upon my comb. The pallor of my youthful flesh can't mask the contour of my bones. And from my abdomen protrudes a lurid and uneven scar. It's primitive. It pulls my skin together like some makeshift zip. It travels vertically from my navel, almost to my groin. I am defiled. A part of me is missing now. And yet I fear it is in vain. For pain is my companion still.

Despite all this, I cannot rest – there is so much to do. The woes of Johnny's tenants are now mine to hear. And one must be evicted when it's clear that she's a lady of the night and brings home strangers to disturb propriety. And when I tell her she must leave, she goes to court – and claims that her mistreatment is because she's black.

I am assaulted. I am pained by the injustice of her words – and yet the court decrees that I am guilty here not she.

That night, I lie cocooned within my narrow bed. As I reflect, I wonder why today's indignity affects me so. It's mean and petty when I contemplate the depth of the vicissitudes I've met before. Yet I am sinking into a despair I have not reached till now.

The day is drawing to its final hour. The deep blue velvet curtains sewn by me from remnants are closed against a sun that sets. There's no one home but me. Yet there's a new tape now – and Johnny's here to share his loving thoughts. What can he say to raise my spirit and to reassure me that I'm not alone?

Chapter 17

The tape recorder clicks. I hear the rhythm of the upbeat tones I know so well.

"And since you love Manhattan so, that's where we'll find a home." He pauses as if he recalls the confidences that we've shared about the life we sometimes dare to plan. We've talked so much about our hopes and dreams, but we have also talked about the limitations on our lives – the shadow of my likely infertility. Accepting all I am and all that I am not, he clarifies. "With children or without." He pauses and then, knowing all the things that touch my soul, he adds a final pledge. "And you shall have a garden of your own – another wilderness. You shall have all the plants you want."

My mind is crowded with the images of what, for us, might be a normal life. I think of all the separate plans we share for projects, books and films to highlight all the social issues that are at the forefront of our minds. And the discussions that we have. When we consider Nixon and impeachment and disgrace, Johnny is adamant that they should "lock him up and throw away the key". And yet he gently teases me for all the pity I express, since I consider Nixon, although risen to the heights of power, is just another damaged child.

Together we have everything that individually we lack. One day, perhaps, we'll make a little of the world a better place.

But 'one day' is not finite and it stretches ever further forward in a future that's uncertain – and perhaps unreal.

And Johnny seems to sense this too. The timbre of his voice is melancholic now. He says my presence haunts the studio – especially with the many bits and pieces that I left behind. And yet, he tells me that despite this he feels empty and alone, not knowing when or how we'll be together once again.

He pauses. Then the tape recorder clicks again and suddenly I hear those soothing tones. But they don't speak to me about today. The words I hear are timeless promises, suspended in the vastness of a universe I cannot always see. The man I love repeats his pledge.

"You are my hopes. You are my dreams. You are eternity," he says in that melodic tone that captivated me.

And suddenly I realise it's not enough. For though I'm brave and I'm prepared for pain, my strength is finite, and it won't sustain me till I reach eternity. I have to face the present and I must live now – with all the challenges that this existence brings. And even though I know that I'm a child of God and even though eternity is ours to share, this pledge condemns me to a life half-full, to isolation and, sometimes, despair.

Yet, even as this thought intrudes, I know that I have also made a pledge to him. I cannot break that pledge. I will not write and tell him that I want to live my life alone. I cannot – for without the man I love, I have no will to live.

And suddenly it seems so clear to me. The only answer for us both is this: that I must die. In this impetuous conviction there's no time or space for doubt. I am impelled beyond all thought of others that I love or who love me or even thought of God himself. And here to change my thought to action are the painkillers I need. Together with the pills that Bethlem once dictated I must take to have a chance of life.

As I ingest, peace comes. My worries fly away. I feel a sense of lightness, almost joy. And when I hear a key and understand a housemate has come home, I call her in, quite relishing the chat I think we'll have. And in what seems an instant, Christine too is by my side. My sister understands at once what's happening here. And as I drift into unconsciousness, I hear the siren of an ambulance.

Next day I wake up in a white-walled ward. A stern-faced sister gazes down at me. Despite her solemn countenance, I sense that her severity is mixed with kindness here.

"It is so hard to die the way you chose," she says deliberately, yet with concern, as if in this harsh moment she is speaking to her child. "And, if you try once more, I fear you'll simply find yourself in Bethlem once again."

My lips form no reply. Her words depress and stun. And yet I hear them, and I mark them and, exactly as this nurse intends, these words will linger in my consciousness throughout the years that are to come.

18

THE SAMARITAN

1974–1976

I am subdued. The guilt I feel at my destructive impulse saps my energy. I realise there is no straight and easy road towards the future for which once I hoped. The love I've always felt for life is, for this moment, hidden from me by my helplessness and self-disgust.

It's fortunate, perhaps, that I'm still frail, for now the task of clinging to this life exhausts me, leaving little energy for contemplation and despair.

And it is in this state that I encounter someone who will recognise the help I need. Someone who does not judge, but is prepared to share and, if he can, to shoulder all my woes.

His name is George. He's tall and burly with a waxen skin made even paler by his shock of blue-black hair. My eyes are drawn to his luxuriant moustache.

George is an unlikely Samaritan. His charcoal grey overcoat, buttoned, even in September, against the possibility of inclement weather, betrays his lack of ease and his mistrust of London's hospitality. Born in Larissa, Greece, he seems to be entirely focussed on his doctorate. Fluid Dynamics and Mechanical Engineering are his life. Only his homeland competes for the love his work inspires. Every waking hour is and always will be fixed upon these things.

And I forever am to ask myself: how did he ever notice me?

It happened at that near forgotten meeting on the beach when we – the four of us – played football – just a fleeting moment when a look, a casual move, persuaded him that here was something – someone – that he must pursue. No matter that I scarcely noticed him.

And when, within a week or so, I found myself in hospital, it seems that something made him want to visit me. Unwilling to reveal the invalid I had become, I quickly repelled such an intrusion. Yet he clasped my *'maybe when I'm better'* to him like a sacred promise.

A Kinder Chapter

A month or two has passed. I am not wholly better, yet I'm conscious of the promise that I must fulfil. Indifferent now to much, I keep my word and, as I take the hand that's offered me, I step into a kinder chapter of my life.

And when, inevitably, George asks me what has happened to me, and why I am reduced to just a fragment of the self that I once was, I tell him. For the first and only time, I recount everything: the horrors of the hospitals; the illnesses; the momentary crushing of all hope.

And, as I raise my head to look at him, I see that, silently, he weeps.

Somehow his questions and the sorrow that his tears reveal suggest that beside all the interest he has shown, this man is solid, steadfast, willing to commit. Thus, despite all the sadness of my past, he makes it clear he will not turn and run. He vows that he will bring me back to life. He thinks that if I cling to him, he'll take me from the edge of horror and despair and ground me in a safer world – and so I choose to be with him.

And, in response, George makes a plan and tells me how life will unfold from now. And thus, his student room in Kensington becomes a second home to me. The room itself is uniform and plain. And yet, beyond the window and against the winter sky, the tracings of the London plane trees grace our view, contrasting with our spartan world. And even in my forlorn state I marvel at what God creates. Each morning as I gaze upon these trees, I feel at first a flicker of amazement then a rising surge of joy. I'm mesmerised, for even skeletons have beauty if they're in their proper place and time. The fragile contours seek to reassure me that, however bleak our lives may sometimes seem, abundant spring will re-awaken if we only wait. And gently, and despite the desolation, healing comes.

I'm silent as George sets the programme of our lives. Illness has stolen time that should have been devoted to my studies. I have missed much. He tells me that I'm not alone and with his help I'll find my way again.

His mantra now is *study, eat, rest*. I have no energy to resist the commands he gives. Gradually, within the safety of his discipline, I come to feel secure.

And, after weeks have passed and now that I am almost calm, we talk again about the way things were before he came into my life. His eyes are dim with sadness, but they do not waver, for his mind's made up. He'll give me all the time and care he has. But now I must decide. For there to be a future, I must jettison the past.

There is a numbness in me now that blocks out pain. The situation's clearly grave. I have to bid the past farewell. I cannot bear to wipe out all the memories – and yet I do not have the strength to struggle anymore. Alone, I sit and write, one final time. I seal the edges of the envelope – red, white, and blue.

And there on Exhibition Road a postbox swallows up my future and my past.

And strangely now I'm shielded by oblivion. The words I write have vanished too. I'll never bring them back to mind. In years to come, I'll wonder whether – though I doubt that this is so – a hint of anger lies embedded in the tangle of the anguish and the love. And though I do not know it yet, this final message will have no reply. And nothing will relieve me of the guilt I feel. So much of our togetherness I've spent alone. In sorrow, I reflect that, even in our parting, I am not beside the man I love.

Learning to Live

But here in Kensington I cannot think of that. I have to focus now on learning how to live once more. George is a student too, but all he has, he shares with me. He cossets me. He tells me that I am a Queen, if only of his room.

His supervision is not only of my studies. He makes it clear that eating is important too. We do not leave the student dining room until the nourishment he can afford is gone. And when I tire, I rest upon his hard and narrow bed. When pain returns, he soothes my abdomen. When worry overwhelms, he holds me, and he tells me that he is a human tranquilliser – just for me.

Slowly I recover. Here, in the quietness of order, balance is restored. Grief and anger, passion even – all subside. One day a thought dawns. I could live here in this room with George forever. Though I am not in love, here, in this other womb, perhaps I'd find contentment of a kind.

But time does not stand still, and George's thoughts have moved beyond this present intermission in our lives. Despite the hours of work he has, he still finds time to contemplate a future he will help me build.

He labours to restore my shattered confidence. He brings a book of

IQ puzzles. Test after test I do at his request, until he shows me how consistent and correct are my results. There is no doubt, he says, that the exams are mine to pass with ease. Time comes when I believe he might be right. Perhaps.

When I'm convinced that I'm grotesque and shudder at the way my body is defiled, he takes a photograph. In it I am seated at his desk, my books spread out before me. He stands beside me, stooping slightly, with one arm around my shoulders. The other rests against my upper arm, as if he needs to make quite sure that I will stay upright. His gaze is solemn, and it speaks to me of his commitment and sincerity. He holds the photograph before my eyes. And then he tells me I am beautiful.

And gradually, step by step, he helps me leave the haven of his room. At first, on Sundays we will take a walk to Bayswater. He buys his copy of *Ta Nea*. Borrowing customs from those twice our age, we sip our coffee as we watch the world go by. Slowly and gently, we promenade beside the paintings hanging from the railings of Hyde Park. One day he buys one as a gift for me. It is of pressed wildflowers. It is to show, he says, that even fragile beauty can endure if it is treated well.

And now that I progress, he does not let me rest. He is insistent that I join him in the world beyond our tight, secluded life and, when the invitations come, there can be no excuse. No matter that I have but one plain dress that fits and covers my distended frame. Proud as he is, pride pales before the colour of his love.

And in the weeks that follow, what was first endurance turns to pleasure, now and then. The friends of his, who out of courtesy had once ignored my pitiful appearance, begin, at times, to show appreciation and respect. I'm welcomed at the dinner parties where debate is equal in importance to the food they serve. I have been reticent but now I feel a tiny trace of confidence. Just once or twice, I find a voice.

"Bravo, Lesley," chorus Anna and Apostolos – our hosts – as, with precision, I identify the flaw that voids the opposition's argument.

I see the satisfaction as it seeps across my lover's face. And in the years to come, though he may be no longer in my life, I still will feel the sunrays of his glance of pride.

In home life, too, there is a shift as I begin to shed a little of my passive role. I see that even George relaxes now. Concerns abate. When, after hours of study, he returns at night, he listens avidly to tales of how my day has been. He makes false protestation when I tell him of my woes.

Chapter 18

"Am I your worry bin?" he asks. By contrast all the anecdotes I tell are joy to him. "More. More," he cries.

I lead him to the world of books. We venture to the ballet and the theatre. We talk of studies, politics, of culture and, at times, we talk about ourselves. But here our conversations drift. Our words lie at a tangent to the focus of our lives. For George, the future's clear – an academic post in Athens and a stable married life. And, above all, he speaks about his longing for a son who'll bear his father's name. I study Greek in preparation for a future of which, fleetingly, I dream. Yet I'm ambivalent. I am unsure of where my life may lead. Sometimes I dare to think that there may be a common future for us both; at other times I think such hope is vain. Fecundity is not a subject we discuss. It's not an issue that my doctors have addressed. My illness has been dormant these past months. And yet inside I'm fearful that I cannot give him what he most desires. I call to mind the whispered talk of childlessness the doctors murmured in that hospital when Johnny visited so long ago. The talk I could not bear to hear – the truth I pushed away. And though I cannot, even now, give voice to this concern, I dimly realise how it may impact on this honourable man. And just in case – and to protect myself – I also find a city job where I'll be welcome when I'm qualified.

And in this way, we drift towards our studies' end. Two years have passed. There's balance now in our relationship. On George's face I see not just concern, as in those early days. Amusement, joy and pride are there as well. If, on occasion, he still feigns displeasure at my moods – when I am sad, exhorting me to "change face now"– on other days he roars with laughter at the rhymes that I create to banish all the stress that comes from work.

In years to come we'll look back on those days. And borrowing customs from our earlier lives, we'll stroll again beside the paintings in Hyde Park. And as he sips his coffee, I will listen with amazement as, all anguish banished from his mind, he tells me just how wonderful his memories are and just how perfect for him were our student days.

The Ferry

But now, in 1976, we've reached an ending of a kind. For, studies over, George must now return to Greece. And I am on the threshold of professional life. The future is uncertain, and the past has gone. And presently we drive together to the land where George was born. And though I'll travel with him for a while, I understand that what we've known won't come again.

Dawn breaks over the Adriatic Sea. Light filters through the comfort of the cloak of night. Here on the ferry, people stir. Beside me George is sleeping still. I let him be. The Pindus mountains are ahead. It's still a long and arduous drive until we reach his home.

The days I'll spend with him in Athens will be few. I must not dwell on that. I force myself to focus on the wonder of the breaking day and on the hopefulness that every dawn bestows.

But much is to unfold beyond this dawn. Ahead lies not just Greece but life. Our paths are destined to divide and there are tears to shed as part we must. Somewhere in this land of mists and myths reality awaits. However magical is its allure, I know it cannot be my home. In London my arms could console when love and family were far away. And yet, however genuine his feelings are, I know they won't survive within a future if I cannot give him what he needs. He tells me that he cannot contemplate an empty home. Sadness comes. I understand the barricades that barrenness has brought.

Behind us lies the past, both glorious and sad. Ahead lies all there is to come for each of us and all that I must face alone. I look around. I see there's only sea. No land in sight to fore or aft. The solid world I knew is shifting now. And yet the sea is tranquil and unmoved. I find it curious and marvellous. Though panic's been my ever-present nemesis, it's different now. For, like the sea, I am serene. I realise that, even as I contemplate its loss, the gift of love that has been lent has anchored me.

Becalmed yet calm, I know that I, at last, have recognised a strength within myself. Though lovers drift apart, the generosity of love remains.

I make a vow. Such love will be my guide.

19

BEYOND THE BARRIERS

1977

Oppenheimer's

It's 1977. I'm on my own in London now. A single, working woman, I am immersed in adult life. There's no one to protect or shield me and there is no panic behind which to hide – or, if there is, I'm learning how to fight it for my place in life.

I even have a title now.

Miss Lesley Hughes, Assistant Solicitor, Herbert Oppenheimer, Nathan & Vandyk.

I'm thirty-four. I'm conscious that by this stage many have achieved so much. Yet I am just a novice, starting out to make my way within professional life.

I recognise that, once again, I'm out of time. Within this proudly Jewish firm are partners not much older than myself. And some of them are women too. It's so much larger and less intimate than Dorset Square and yet I feel again that heady mix of apprehension and excitement and alacrity.

But month by month I grow accustomed to the tasks that are expected of me now that I am qualified. The partner to whom I'm assigned is small of stature, dark haired and urbane. His start in life was so much different from my own. He fled from Nazi Germany in 1939. He was just six years old. He does not speak to me of this but decades on I'll read about it in a newspaper.

Few of us care to flaunt the history that created us. Until we realise that without sharing this the lessons of our lives will be forever lost.

Meanwhile this partner's talent is to bring in work, and when he's absent, meeting other lawyers, contacts, clients too, it falls to me to deal with those who call and seek advice.

And in this way, I gradually find the roles to which I can adapt. I cannot banish all the lingering weaknesses I have. But, now and then, I start to understand that I may also have some strengths.

Thus, soon I'm also introduced to those who give us work. In banks and companies, I get to know the lawyers and the heads of personnel. And once or twice a mutual rapport is built, and I am asked to help in unexpected ways. I must attend an inquest to support the parents of a baby whose demise is unexplained. I'm chosen to befriend a secretary when her life is wrenched apart – first by her own admitted lapse in over-claiming benefits, then when her brother is convicted of the murder of the girl he loves. There's scant advice that anyone can give – and yet I understand that sometimes I can make a difference here.

The tomes of tort and contract law I had to memorise for my exams don't seem to have a place in this new world.

I am drawn in. I am intrigued.

A Brief History of Hope

But one year on from my acceptance in this firm, I'm conscious that my life will, even now, be strewn with painful challenges.

Just weeks ago, I found myself in hospital again. And there, in Crawley Hospital, the doctors made it clear that if I wished to regain health, I'd have to jettison my womb. I listened silently, remembering the hints and the concerns I'd heard so many times before. I'd never probed. I did not want to know a truth that I could not accept. I'd always vowed that one day I would hold a precious infant of my own. Deep down I knew my empty arms were purposeless. I understood the ache within my breasts betokened all my natural longing for the tender mouth through which I could pass on the wondrous gift of life. I had no child and yet I reassured myself this fate would change. For motherhood is woman's lot. I yearned for the fulfilment which would surely come. I'd keep my womb prepared at any cost.

I knew I could not countenance the violation they proposed.

Yet now, in 1977, it seems I can't ignore the shadow threatening to swallow up the latent longing that I have. The fears that went unspoken have been nonetheless an ever-present curb upon my hopes and plans. I can't commit to a relationship that's serious when even I don't know the truth about the illness that I have. I take myself in check. There has to be a way I can be helped.

Chapter 19

And I am fortunate. For even though there is no George to comfort and encourage me, the ones around me are solicitous. And Mr Summerfield, my boss, points out that my employers fund a private health insurance for me now. With kindness and concern, he tells me of a gynaecologist who specialises in the kind of problems that I have.

And now, weeks on, in an impersonal room within the Royal Northern Hospital, I sit with Mummy waiting for the test which will determine if my tubes are blocked. It's called an HSG – Hysterosalpingography.

We do not speak. We rarely say what's on our mind, but Mummy is tight-lipped and tense and so am I. I focus on her mackintosh of emerald green, its brightness so incongruous in this place of gloom. She's worn it to so many hospitals. It always flashed her presence to me as she waited at the door – the first in line for visiting. It signals love and loyalty and yet in times ahead I'll come to hate it for the memories that it evokes.

A nurse intrudes and ushers me into a theatre. In minutes I am lying propped up on a bed. A monitor has been positioned so I'll have a view of what is happening inside my abdomen. And Mr Fincham, balding, smooth, and almost genial, explains that we must hope to see injected dye run through my tubes.

He's practised, polished and a touch theatrical. His hands are raised as he exclaims: "Look here, young lady, look at this." He feigns amazement though he's clearly seen this sight before. "The flowing dye shows that there is no blockage in your tubes. How very wonderful, my dear."

I look. I hardly breathe. I cannot take it in. The pictures on the monitor are baffling to me, and yet I trust his mastery – the way that I've been taught to trust the pillars of society. Especially if they're men.

"Yes, wonderful – so wonderful," I stammer with some hesitance.

I tremble as I'm helped down from the bed. I leave the theatre. And suddenly I'm in a cubicle and Mummy's by my side again. I blurt out what I have just heard and instantly a flash of joy illuminates her tiny face. We're heedless of the squash within this box-like space. Our thoughts are focussed on the world that has been opened up for both of us. My mother contemplates the babies that will give her purpose once again. I feel relief and also gratitude that maybe I won't let her down.

As Mummy takes my gown, I tremble with emotion while I raise my patterned smock of copper rust and start to pull it on. But suddenly we're interrupted, and I flinch. The door is pushed ajar. I see the man in whom I put my trust. The face once so expansive is now troubled and perplexed.

He thrusts a photograph into my hands.

"I am so sorry. I was wrong. It seems that, after all, I cannot help."

I shudder with foreboding as my dress of copper rust falls, crumpled, to the floor. All comprehension vanishing, I stare at him. And Mr Fincham speaks again, in urgent tones suffused with gravity.

"I am so sorry, dear. I've had another look. The picture's clearer now. There is no doubt. Your tubes are blocked. I am afraid there's nothing I can do. There is a treatment now but limited to those in stable marriages. It's risky and expensive and the chances of success are small. No one will treat a girl like you. But, without treatment, it's unlikely that you ever will conceive."

As Mummy stiffens, I recoil. What does he mean by saying that although there might be hope for some, a 'girl like me' is deemed by him to be unworthy to conceive? His words will haunt me through the years to come. Defeated and appalled, I slump against the wall.

My mother does not speak – and nor do I. We do not have the words to verbalise the shattering of life and hope. Perhaps we think that unacknowledged grief will simply dissipate. It never does.

And separately we'll nurse this wound throughout the decades stretching out ahead. And we will never know the consolation that can come from grief that's shared. Our awkward reticence condemns us both to bear our pain alone.

Throughout the seventies we separately try to banish or at least suppress our grief. Yet grief brings understanding of a kind. Although I'm in my thirties now, to Mummy I am still her child. And even if the tides of life have sometimes left us stranded on two different shores, the bond between us is unchanged.

And gradually I understand that, far beyond the instant joy a newborn baby brings, it is a bond like this that is the greatest loss that I must face. This illness sweeps away a lifetime's natural moments of anxiety, concern and of unselfish love. I'll never have to show support through trivial anxieties I do not always understand. I'll never have to share those devastating days on which the blows of life rain down upon my child. My life is sterile – far beyond the reach of all the selfless hurt and worry that a mother must endure.

And grief enfolds me as I realise that I will never know the natural, never-ending, selfless love that Mummy knows because I am her child.

Chapter 19

And that I can't assuage her desolation as she understands this is a loss she cannot bear on my behalf. And that she'll never know the joy that is a daughter's daughter or a daughter's son.

And thus, our separate sorrow at our likely childlessness is overlaid with silent pity for the other's plight.

20

IN PLACE OF GRIEF

1977–1978

Yet though she cannot find the words to soothe me, Mummy shows her love in other ways. And Riverview provides a measure of salvation for us both. The garden wilderness I have no wish to tame is ours to tend and share. We nurture it. We revel in the vigour and profusion to which we give life. And often when I reach my home at night, I'll find that Mummy has been present, bringing gifts of cuttings to enhance the crowded space I love. And Daddy tills the soil the way he's always done in other gardens – Hemel Hempstead gardens, Knighton too – creating beauty for the family he loves.

For me there is the easy route of busyness. I plunge myself into my work and throw myself into a social ferment that seems ever present and enticing – though at times this too is challenging. I push my panic and anxiety away, but I'm a litigation lawyer now and every courtroom is a challenge to my fear of being trapped. There is no discreet exit if I panic here. A lawyer cannot leave the court without a formal bow to gain permission from the judge.

And social life so often overwhelms.

Despite my sadness and my panic, I am fascinated by the people that I meet. My work means that I must prepare for all the cases that may need to be decided by the court. Our clients come from every corner of the globe. There is no limit to the topics that my caseload may embrace. It satisfies my eagerness for learning and for life. I meet and work with businessmen and impresarios. They're keen that I should understand the work they do.

And yet the clients who will haunt my memory are those whose lives are broken by divorce and personal tragedy.

And gradually I come to understand that when I focus on my clients,

Chapter 20

taking on their burdens as my own, the frailties I have are overcome by my desire to understand and help.

Thus, work and my immersion in its social side extinguish solitude which might give space to introspection and to pain.

Though I don't recognise it, I'm still driven by the emptiness inside. I can't ignore the secret knowledge of my childlessness. It shapes and sometimes dominates the course of action that I take.

And thus, the men who vie to take me out to dinner – or who simply want to be my friend – are judged unconsciously by whether they can lift me from this desperate plight of barrenness. Or how I think they might react were they to learn of my predicament.

And thus, a Scandinavian businessman intrigues me with his knowledge of a Swiss physician who – he claims – can remedy the ill that London doctors cannot – will not – cure. An over-eager broker feigns a relative who has professional expertise. And if they use these wiles to gain my favour, who am I to remonstrate? For, deep inside, I know that I am also using them to gratify the wish that on my own I can't fulfil.

Around me glitters a kaleidoscope. I'm dazzled by competing shapes and images and possibilities. So many avenues down which it's possible to walk. So many men who seek my company, though all I long for is just one. It overwhelms me, though I tell myself I will get through this time. I must go on. I can't turn back. It is a part of what life has in store for me. A test, perhaps? Another test? I'm almost lost in this confusion, yet inside of me are pointers to which I – unconsciously – can cling. The natural instincts that were nurtured in my childhood will be mine until eternity. The simple ethos that we live to love and serve and try to do what we believe is right. And though it may take decades, I will find a way to use the sad experiences mixed with joy that life has given me. I'll find a way in which I can be useful and bring comfort and relief to those in need.

For, piece by piece, as the kaleidoscope restores its fractured segments to a kind of whole, I see that there are images which draw me to them, leading me to where I'm meant to be.

Jan

Her compact figure somehow dominates the room. This client is a dumpy woman – perhaps five feet tall. Her hair is cropped and dark with here and there a hint of grey. Her olive skin exudes her anger. Black eyes smoulder with suppressed ferocity. She's rigid with emotion that she knows she must control. And yet the tension of her stance – so still and outwardly submissive – informs me that quite soon she will explode.

Her name is Jan.

She is American. Her children have been kidnapped from her Californian home. Her former husband and the current wife Jan swears is evil have stolen them and brought them here to London – and away from her. She has no money. She's in need of legal aid. And I, a lawyer of some eighteen months, am asked to take her case. Their father has defied the laws that said his children should be with their mother, not with him. He has found work in London now. His children – ten and eight – are in his care. And in these days before reciprocal agreements have been reached, there's nothing to ensure these children will be restored to their mother as their national law decrees that they should be.

Their mother also is in London now. She's lodging in a cheap hotel. I think that reconciliation with the children will be easy, but it isn't so. The children, Ben and Judith, are now wards of court. And every action that involves them has to be approved – or not. An untrained civil servant will commence the necessary scrutiny. Her name's Miss Green. She's tall and unremarkable but clearly relishes the power that she has. At once I note with some concern that this official seems to be the disapproving kind.

"It is not right. These children must not be exposed to an emotional reunion in a hotel room," Miss Green pronounces with finality.

I flinch. I am incredulous. *What does it matter where or how such children may be reunited with an absent parent whom they love?*

I'm inexperienced and too naïve to understand I'm not supposed to have a point of view.

"You mean," I tentatively ask, "that if she had a home – or just a room within a house and not a hotel room, it might be possible for them to meet?"

"Ah well…" A frown creeps over Miss Green's face. She is, I sense, unused to those who deviate from all the narrow customs of a world in which she has a tiny measure of authority. She's on her guard but feels obliged to speak and claim the narrative again.

"That might be different. Perhaps."

"I have a home myself," I say, incautiously. "There's room for her and, if I take her in, will you allow a meeting to take place?"

Miss Green is silent, and she makes it clear that she will give us no more time today.

Chapter 20

Yet I persist and somehow my repeated offer finds its way into the courtroom where the judge is to decide the children's fate. And there, despite the stony looks and disbelieving gasps I hear from the abductor father and his wife, the judge decides that Jan can see her children once again. Provided that she stays with me.

And so, Jan comes to stay. For several weeks she is my guest and, in the years ahead, she'll sometimes stay with me for months. Like everyone, she has her ups and downs and there are, sometimes, scenes. Hysteria and anguish too. I'll come to see that no one is fault free. But for all that, she loves her kids, and they love her.

And suddenly my mind flies back to Hartford, to New England and to Dee. To Johnny's anguish and our selfish love – to Emmeline's despair, deceit and anger too. And how, for all the love professed for any child within a broken home, their interests are so rarely placed before their parents' needs.

And, knowing just how fallible we are, I understand that it is not for me to judge. And in the decades that still lie ahead, I'll do the best I can to reconcile and reunite – to see that children are not victims in their parents' war.

But here in 1977 I'm happy just to watch Jan's children grow. In years to come they will be lawyers too, and decades on, I'll have a card. At Christmas. From the USA. And, following the seasonal greeting, it will say: "Thank you for my mother. Ben."

House Guests

And Jan is not the only guest who stays with me and helps to fill my emptiness. Old friends are loyal visitors as well.

And Hella is among these, and I welcome her and all the certainty she represents. The certainty that life with her will not be boring and the reassurance she will always be herself. She loves my home.

"It has such charm," she states in such a way that I cannot believe that any other view is true.

But still, her husband, Dieter, thinks that it can be improved.

"How would you feel," she ventures, "if, while you work, we make a few small differences around the house? To help, of course."

I do not understand. I'm not unhappy as things are. But all the same I nod and simply say "OK."

That night at Chiswick Station, Hella meets me as I step from my commuter train. She is unique – no one can take their eyes off her. A tall, athletic creature with those endless legs now clad in purple shorts, below a purple vest. And, on her head, a headdress sporting two antennae topped with feathers that she'd noticed in some junk shop or emporium. She's waiting for me on the platform. I run to her, and I ignore the smugly suited fellow passengers, now all agog, alerted from their daily lethargy. And we embrace.

And when we arrive home, I realise that Dieter has removed a section of a wall between the kitchen and the dining room – he says, to make it easy when I want to serve my guests. I have no words, although I silently observe that other visitors don't feel compelled to change my home the way he does. Yet there's no outrage at this violation. For Hella is my dearest friend. And when I climb the stairs and see the bathroom, I find that it is here that she has made her mark. The hose that was just yesterday a humble shower attachment finds that today it is a painted snake.

A snake – just like the ones in Kinsley Wood. A symbol of the things that draw us into wildness from the safety of convention's narrow path.

Despite our many years of friendship, I ask myself, how does she know? How has she stumbled on this secret – that the serpent and the power of its hidden danger are a lodestone in my life?

Yet if the actions of my friends may seem to some unusual, I do not really care. I'm fortunate to have friends who I love and who love me. I'm joyful we accept each other just the way we are.

Interlude

Yet in between the visits that enrich my life, the sadness and despair return, despite the efforts that I make to push them back. At times, cocooned by the blue velvet curtains that have seen so much, I lie alone at night and grieve for what I'm almost certain now will never be. I tell myself it's good to recognise the feelings that exist. I have to find a place for them, so they no longer dominate. I make myself reflect upon the last few years and all the kindly benefactors who have touched upon my life. Their presence sometimes has been fleeting. They alone will not forestall catastrophes ahead. And yet they've shown me that there may be ways to move beyond my past. I am reminded that there may – perhaps – be hope.

Chapter 20

Barbara (2)

For others, I am sad to realise, this is not so. I think of Barbara, at her best the shining face of joy. For her, it's harder now. The structure of her life has crumbled, just as mine once did. The highs, the lows, the pattern I discern in her is now familiar, though every episode is more extreme. If her behaviour is bizarre, the social consequences are predictable. She is divorced. She loses the stability that once helped her to keep afloat. I'm unsurprised when, days after she moves to social housing, fire engulfs her home.

She takes another lover and decides that she will be a mother once again. In the midst of madness, she gives birth to life. Lara is born.

So infectious is her joy and her enthusiasm, even the social workers marvel. Before what looks – to some – like bravery, misgivings melt. Some consider that there may, perhaps, be hope.

But their hope does not last, nor does her joy. There follow other lovers and other moments of outrage. Her health is weakened for she has fits now. She is condemned – not just an outcast and bipolar but an epileptic too.

Yet Barbara has a gift. She knows, instinctively, where danger lurks. However weak and sick she is, she understands she must protect the children in her care. The labels that the doctors give can't hide the fact that she is love itself.

And one day, when she senses that catastrophe may lurk ahead, she knows what she must do. And thus, she scrambles with her children through the London suburbs in a desperate search for refuge and relief. She has no money, and this takes her several hours. But when she sees my Chiswick home, she knows her children will be safe.

We have shared so much. Perhaps, I think, the hope I have will see her through as well.

And soon the shadow of her silhouette appears beyond the stained-glass window of my door. I open it. Her situation is, I see, now grave. My query is unspoken but, in answer, she falls, fitting, to the floor. I am untaught yet, somehow, I know what to do and how to care for her. Gently I reassure her, and I cover her. I quickly make her safe. Matthew, her firstborn child, runs to the window, for he loves the overgrown garden that is bright with roses now. He has forgotten that, moments before, he was afraid. I have no cot for Lara. But, remembering my bible, I understand that something humbler will suffice. I take the lowest drawer from the bedroom chest. I line it with a towel. Gently, I lay Lara in it, and I place it at her mother's feet. On Barbara's pallid countenance, I see the slightest ripple, as a smile creeps across her face. And I smile too. Between us we can still find balance, as precious as it is elusive. I marvel at my Milk Madonna. Maimed as she is, she is still magnificent.

21

BEYOND THE TURNING POINT

1983

The first four decades of my life have passed and, in a sombre mood, I might reflect that fewer decades lie ahead of me. And yet I do not bring that thought to mind. I don't accept that things must always happen in an ordered way. I've always been so out of step – so far ahead in school, so far behind in settling down.

So slow, sometimes, to understand what life is all about.

Yet I have faith now that, however old I am, I'll live the life that I am meant to live.

The last three decades have been challenging. And even now, from time to time, the pelvic pain I've come to know returns. Anxiety still lurks inside, and latent grief can't always be suppressed.

And yet around me there are signs that I have reached and passed another turning point.

At Oppenheimer's, I have had the opportunity to grow. I've been exposed to worlds and cultures far beyond what I had known.

And sometimes there's a contribution I can make. I am excited that we number German lawyers on our staff. Our clients include German companies and businessmen. And memories flood back. I think about my childhood, when I was welcomed as a guest by Hella and her family. I seemed to fit in then, and now with clients such as these, I also feel at home. I recognise the sense of ordered certainty they have, and it seems that they appreciate my disciplined attentiveness. Most are paternalistic. It helps, perhaps, that I combine a natural deference with knowledge of those German phrases that they like to hear.

Thus, some of these will seek me out. Herr Schubert is just one. Tall, lean and gimlet-eyed, he sports a goatee beard of blond. He exudes calm and quiet confidence. No setback will deter him from the goal he thinks that he can reach.

He's from the shipping industry. He's charged with sorting out the chaos following the US imposition of a ban on the export of soybeans. So many worldwide deals unravelled in its wake. The litigation following this brief ban in 1973 has lasted years and will last many more. And with Herr Schubert's patronage I find myself in Hamburg learning from him what he thinks I need to know of how the shipping business works.

His colleagues gather round as, smilingly, he pours us Sekt.

"Welcome, Lesley, to our team. We'll help you and I'm sure together we can find success."

And side by side we'll sit in courts throughout the next decade, his arm so often draped around the chair on which I sit. A gesture others now and then misunderstand.

As he eschews the black that it's expected all will wear, his light grey suit identifies this man as one who cannot fully be accepted in this bastion of formality. As I am marked out by the cream silk pie crust blouse I wear beneath a purple knitted waistcoat and a flowing skirt of matching crepe.

I watch and notice how the ones to whom he pays so much are keen to sneer at him because he's not like them. Yet he will bring them cases that, for some, will make their name. I do not understand how they can reconcile their satisfaction at the opportunity he gives and the contempt they can't disguise because they know that he will lose each time.

I do not talk to him of this.

We recognise each other for the outliers that we are. And for a time, we relish solidarity that for us is rare. He is indulgent and he makes me feel that I'm important in his quest. I am the patient listener that he craves. I'll share each tiny victory on his path. I'll get to know the family he loves but has to leave behind so much. I'll be his chaste companion in those lonely moments when a case is lost.

And he will be my client for a dozen years or more. And each of us will count the other as a friend.

Yet other clients leave an impact of a different sort. More children find themselves on centre stage as parents die or choose to leave their home, with no thought given to those left behind. And families dissolve. I am filled with sorrow when I see that natural ties are damaged by a parent who once gave a pledge to love the other until death. And now and then I watch in horror as such ties are severed by a judge who maybe means well but who need not live with all the consequences his or her decision brings.

Chapter 21

And in the years to come, these casualties of love will haunt my dreams. And where I can I'll fight to bring a truce – perhaps a lasting peace.

But just for now I also think of me. To be a voice for others I must speak up on my own behalf. It's something that I've rarely done. Yet now at last I find the courage that I need to plan a future for myself.

As years have passed, I've watched as younger lawyers are promoted to the partnership. I've flourished here. I'm well rewarded in financial terms. But though I'm liked by clients, and I bring in work that I enjoy, there is no mention that within this elevated bond of partners there might be a place for me.

And one day I decide to ask why this is so.

My boss has not expected that I will confront him thus. He pauses and he stammers slightly, gesturing towards the conference phone as if he hopes that it will ring and rescue him from all the awkwardness of this. It does not ring and so he gives me platitudes and words he hopes will soothe. Yet, even so, for all his mutterings that socially we are not quite the same, I understand the only thing that matters is I do not have a future here.

That is, unless I am content to be a hireling all my life.

And I know now, with certainty, that this I will not be. I do not want to act a script that others write. I want to take all that I am and all that I have learned. And with it do the best I can – for me, but also for the ones I meet along the road.

And if they say I have ambition, they are wrong, for it is only that I have at last begun to recognise myself.

And, in another sphere and side by side with this incipient confidence, comes personal joy. My sister Christine marries, and, in 1980, her first child is born. It's thirty-seven years since Mummy held a baby of her blood. At last, she has a grandchild of her own.

I breathe a sigh of thankfulness and, as I cradle in my arms this tiny perfect gift, I cherish all the life and the delight she brings.

In months to come there'll be a second child, a second blessing bringing Mummy all the busyness and need she craves.

And I will be forever grateful to my sister and her daughters for the happiness they bring. That they deliver on the promises expected of a daughter but that I myself cannot fulfil. That they assuage my mother's grief.

And I give thanks that this child's birth dissolves the tension and the pressure that my childlessness has brought.

For my part, I have Riverview, which, with my sister's help, I've bought. And this will be an anchor in the decade that's ahead.

It's 1983. I'm forty years of age. Beyond the confines of professional life, new energy has swept away the sadness and the staleness of the past. Yet here, within my firm, I cannot see a way to move beyond what is familiar and routine. I am grateful for acceptance in this world. It brings me respite from an absence of stability. Yet I have grown accustomed to the shifting sands of challenges. I've learned that, though I've always craved an anchor in my life, it's when I'm cast adrift to face what is demanding and unknown that I have found new strengths. And now and then I've watched in disbelief and awe as, from the scattered ashes of my dreams, I've seen a tiny phoenix rise.

And now, on just another ordinary day, I sit within my box-like office, sifting through the papers that I need for court. And suddenly the telephone intrudes. I cannot know who's calling but I do not mind that I'm disturbed. I welcome it as I have always welcomed all that is unknown and lifts me from the triviality of what is all too soon routine. Something that I see as opportunity.

"Lesley."

I hear the smooth but slightly foreign voice – a voice that knows just when to pause for maximum effect. It's Alexander, and I wait, attentive now, for this sophisticated lawyer always interests me. He has the air of one who understands the way to mould and change the present just as history has rearranged the past from which he's come. He's lived in Munich and in Cape Town and America – and yet he won't forget his Baltic roots. Secure within a background of nobility, he's unafraid to challenge what's imposed on him.

We have been colleagues in this firm for several months and more. He understands I languish now, uncertain how to prosper my career. And for some reason it has pleased him to consider whether he can intervene.

"Lesley," he repeats in that harmonious but slightly halting voice. "I must be brief. Please listen to me. I have a name and number that you must take down."

I try to interrupt but Alexander will not hear me out. I listen carefully

Chapter 21

as he recites the information that he's sure I'll need. And on my notepad, I peruse the contact details that he says I should pursue.

"Just ring him, Lesley. This is my request. I think this man might offer you the future I believe that you deserve to have. And should he ask you if you'd like to meet and talk, please go."

The conversation finishes. The line goes dead. It's up to me to choose if I will follow the instruction Alexander gives. And, as my friend and colleague is aware will be the case, I am intrigued.

And I will not resist.

22

BUCKINGHAM STREET

1983

And thus encouraged, in a week or so, I find myself just moments from the River Thames within a cul-de-sac of terraced houses that have stood here for three hundred years or more.

It's peaceful. It is sheltered from the traffic of the thoroughfare that is the Strand. And to the south, I see the ancient Watergate where, centuries before, the riverboats would moor to bring their passengers to shore.

It's 1983. The river has receded now. The Watergate is stranded in the no man's land between the river and the street in which I stand. A strip of earth where grass and trees now grace the soil that once was busy waterway.

And here I pause, beside the entrance to the house where I must visit now. For somewhere in this building is a man who, I am told, is seeking someone who will bring a youthful balance to his team. And if he likes the image I present, then he may offer me a partnership within his legal firm.

This house has history. Beside the door I see a round blue plaque that signifies that Samuel Pepys, the famous diarist and writer, once dwelled within these walls. And other plaques on neighbouring walls inform me that this street has been a home to artists, actors and to many noted figures from the past.

I hesitate as I reflect upon what might have been the origins of those who prospered in this place. Did they know hardships in their lives? What force had driven them to strive and thrive?

I turn again towards the River Thames and all at once I contemplate that other river of my childhood days. In my first years, I lived a meadow's width from Knighton's River Teme, which flowed beneath the never-changing, ever-watchful gaze of Kinsley Wood.

The river of my childhood seemed to flow much faster than the Thames. Its waters sparkled as they bounced across the flattened stones

Chapter 22

towards the bridge in Station Road. Beneath the surface darting trout were clearly visible to passers-by. I loved to watch the pure translucent ripples of this fledgling river that, just days before, had been a tiny mountain stream. The waters rushed so eagerly towards the sea, impatient to be merged with destiny. Their urgent splashing brought a note of vigour to this sleepy border town. As if the river could not be content to accept everything must stay the way it was.

It was a rushing force that was alert, alive, and that looked longingly towards a future that it could not comprehend.

Unknowing that, in just a while, it would be swallowed up.

As, for a while, it seemed that I might be extinguished and engulfed.

For, like the river, my life also flows. I too am swept along by eagerness, though also by the changes other people sometimes think I should embrace. And now and then – and many more times than one person could expect – I find that, in the happenstance of life – or is it destiny? – I'm shifted to a place where I can grow, and I can realise the person that I'm meant to be.

It's many years since, as a child, I lived within the sleepy town where all was ordered and secure. My life is changed forever now. No yearning for the past will bring it back to me.

I've made so many missteps on the path that I was meant to tread. I've been impetuous. I've rushed to greet the opportunities I thought would rescue me. At times it's seemed as if I've lost my way. I've learned not everyone in life is kind. I've learned that things I choose to do won't always please the ones who care for me.

I've learned that life needs balance. And that though I need to show concern for others and respect their views and ways, I cannot let them trample on the person that I'm meant to be.

But I'm not here to muse about the past. For there are things ahead that I must do.

Within me eagerness and tension are entwined. I must suppress the nervousness I feel. I must not let irrational panic bring me down. I'm grateful that I've learned compassion on the road I've trod, but I will not forget that I have learned endurance too.

And now I need to enter this new chapter of my life. I must not linger on the threshold for, perhaps, beyond this door I'll find the anchor that I seek. A place where I will be sustained by certainty and by tradition, and yet a place where all my energy and curiosity will find a worthy role.

A time and place where I can use the quiet voice, that was once diffident and shy, to speak for others, with authority.

And somehow, I'm enabled and encouraged by the history of this place. Its continuity and its solidity engender strength. Those honoured here once made their way in life. Against whatever challenges they faced. And they endure.

And so will I.

PART TWO

1984–2024

23

MARRIAGE – ROBERT: A FLICKERING LIGHT

1984

Be yourself. Be yourself. If any words should be forced into children's consciousness, it should be these. And, if we are fortunate, we are indeed assured that we are fine, just as we are. But then we grow and, once beyond the family, doubt creeps in. For we are also taught that we must please.

And now begins a love that's like a flickering but sometimes overpowering light. Like flashes from those woodland trees we pass at speed, as in a train, it is now blinding, then in moments, gone.

At 41, I am beyond my youth. Impetuosity no longer separates me from the future that I planned. Beyond the lure of all that pulled my heart throughout the decades that have passed, I contemplate my life. And reason now intrudes – and will not be ignored.

And thus, from all the men who pass my way, one man stands out. Beyond the instant feeling that I have for him, I sense a possibility of comfort, for perhaps this man will help me balance all the needs I have. That, for the first time, I can choose a path that, whilst it draws me to it, does not bring dismay to others in my life.

His name is Robert, and I know at once that he will dominate the next years of my life.

And with this choice, I pride myself I have deployed my mind, not just my heart. For who could be more suitable than he? An accountant, solidly established in professional life, he is, I see at once, an anchor of a kind. He's unexceptional and that is wondrously exceptional to me. He happens to be middle-class and white. He is a self-made man. His southern English heritage will surely bring acceptance to the minds of those who have deplored the indiscriminate attachments of my heart.

His heavy spectacles disguise the eyes that seem to twinkle with benevolence as his conventional attire belies, at first, the vigour of his body, lean and fit. His hair is silken, sensuous and straight. He compels my gaze.

And though he is divorced, I see in this a freedom for us both. I will not curse him with my barrenness, for he already has a daughter and a son. And these, at twenty-one and eighteen years, are on the cusp of adulthood.

And yet three questions hover briefly in my consciousness.

Who is he? Do I know him? Does he know me?

I'm different from the Surrey matriarchs he used to know. Now that he's unattached, he wants to move beyond the confines of the life that's tethered him since early adulthood and fatherhood. He thinks that he's now free to shape his life exactly in accord with his desire. He feels released from the demands that others make. Yet even so, he has no wish to live his life alone.

In me he sees an 'other worldliness' that sometimes falters in a life of mundane power. In me he sees fragility – a gentleness he, wrongly, thinks implies complaisance and docility.

He cannot know the stubbornness and strength of will that lie beneath my outer grace.

And he will tell me that he is bewitched.

And for my part I am relieved and reassured that this man offers more than suitability. With Robert, I am instantly at ease, as if I've known him so much longer than the months that I can count upon the fingers of one hand. His humour lulls me as his vigilance attracts. And buried deep within me is a fading image of the knight that childhood dreaming promised me. That dashing being who would rescue me from all the perils that I have been taught I can't negotiate alone. And though my dreams are tempered by the realism I've absorbed throughout the past decades, I will not yet relinquish them.

I cannot know the errant ways and casual ruthlessness that lie beneath the charm.

And thus, I also am beguiled.

And so, the questions that the two of us might have are swept away as what we thought was unattainable drifts into view.

For though it's clear that this is not the all-consuming passion that comes just once in life, I sense that here before me is a kind of love.

And on an evening when this most reliable of men is late in fetching me to take me out to dine, we both dissolve in shared relief. He perhaps that I have waited patiently for him and I because I feared, if fleetingly, he might not be the person I hoped he would be.

Chapter 23

Thus, plans abandoned, we sit side by side but silently within the dark blue Jaguar that hides from all who ride in it the danger that its speed may court. Now Robert drives me to his home in Camberwell. A temporary residence for one who will not be a bachelor for long. And there, before an oil painting as yet unhung, we kneel together and embrace. The air is redolent with urgent but unspoken thought. Until a voice breaks through.

"Now, will you marry me?"

And in an instant comes the answer, "Yes."

And to my shock and disbelief it is the second voice that's his.

Next morning, I am overwhelmed by what I've brought about. For I had made a promise to myself that I would think with care before I took some action that would change my life. A promise now made worthless by my recklessness.

I am bewildered too. Throughout the months that I have known him, Robert has urged caution on himself. His thought has always been that it was still too soon for him to wed again.

Confused, I speculate. How is it that five words of mine have changed all that? For he is not a passive man, nor one that anyone can dominate.

I question what might be the reason for this change of heart. Is it the reassuring status marriage brings? Or is it me?

He moves within the higher tiers of banking and finance. Perhaps he needs a partner for those banquets and those foreign trips. Perhaps our marriage is a way to soothe the wound inflicted by his first wife's faithlessness. For she, it seems, has triumphed now. A wedding to her lover is arranged.

I cannot know.

Wherever truth may lie, his pledge is not to be revisited, although I tell him that I'll understand if he needs time to reconsider and reflect. I long to marry him but instinct tells me that our time together is too short for certainty. And though I'm loath to push him back, I force myself to speak.

"We do not have to marry yet. If you would like more time…" I start to say.

His response is to arrange a special licence. I am not strong enough to step aside. We will marry within days.

My family is overwhelmed by the emotion of the hour. They are reluctant to attend the wedding that has been so hastily arranged.

But on a clear November day, I marry Robert in the presence of his children and his mother and the registrar.

I have a photograph in which, his arms around me, Robert gazes at me so protectively. My hand rests on the book where I have signed my name. The name that is the same as his. This photograph will reassure me, but it's true that pictures can mislead.

Outside again I stand on cobbled stones. An old Victorian lamppost leans a little in the shelter of an ancient tree. The tracings of the leafless branches form a blackened cobweb that hangs proud against a winter firmament. Beneath the sombre sky I am oblivious to earthly pain. I wave my flowers. In my exuberance, all hesitation disappears. I explode with jubilance. This scene will be forever filled with fleeting but remembered joy.

Swiftly and smoothly the dark blue Jaguar drives us to Swansea. Catherine, Robert's daughter, is a student here. We are to share this precious time with her. How curious – and yet I tell myself all will be well.

And finally, the evening comes. We are at last alone. I dress myself in voile and lace – a flowing robe I've chosen and have kept aside until my wedding night. And though we are not strangers to the union that binds us both as man and wife, I'm mesmerised. For in my husband's arms and in the words he speaks with softness that is rare for him, I recognise a tenderness in him that he has never shown before.

And for this unexpected sensitivity and for the depth in him that few will see, I tell myself that I will walk beside him come what may. In years to come my husband rarely will reveal this inner grace. And yet, for its existence, I'll forgive him much.

Next morning as we take our breakfast, Robert's sensibility has fled and now the testing of our marriage is to start. For Robert's mood today is boisterous. He wants the world to know of his prowess. Beating his fists against his chest, he greets the waitress with a wink.

"I'm on my honeymoon. I've just had my wedding night. I need a second helping to recover and to build me up again."

I flinch and turn my head away.

When evening comes, there is a student dance that Cath attends. To my surprise we keep her company. The DJ takes requests. Robert is in fine form. He leaps to the floor and tells the crowd that he is newly wed. His song choice? *Yesterday*. The audience titters as the crooner sings: *Yesterday, all my troubles seemed so far away...*

I freeze.

I'm shocked at his uncouthness and his brazenness. But so much worse

Chapter 23

than this, it's hard to reconcile his cruel choice of song with all the sensitivity that he has fleetingly revealed.

Who is this man? What have I done?

Christmas Day

Yet if there are regrets, they are not visible throughout the weeks to come. We don't admit to any qualm. The month till Christmas passes in a haze of shops and parties as I am introduced around. My husband's friends look at us, stunned.

"You didn't have to marry her," one says in disbelief.

A response from me is neither welcome nor expected.

This is Robert's world.

Do I exist?

Our first Christmas Day lies close ahead. It will be just the two of us, my husband says. Yet when the day dawns, Robert, ever restless, always active, will not leave his bed. There are no signs of the malaise he claims defeats him now. What ails him is unclear. I sense the threat of yesteryear that has my husband in its grip.

I am to spend this precious day alone.

Rebuffed, I busy myself. I cook for mouths that I know will not eat. I answer calls from family and friends. Brightly, I excuse my husband's absence by recounting things that I imagine he might do on Christmas Day at home – if only he would just take part.

I browse through rented videos we chose together. Alone now and unthinking, I pick one to fill the quiet of the empty room. *Gandhi*. It distracts. I watch it through not once, but twice, as hours pass. Upstairs Robert is silent still.

On Boxing Day, we have a visit from my husband's son. Jamie is eighteen and shy and lacking all the poise his father and his sister show. But suddenly, all malaise gone, Robert is revived. He tells us that the bank for which he works has designated an apartment for our use. And this, he says, his son must see. And I must visit too.

I don the midnight blue suede coat that is my husband's gift. He smiles, approving both my elegance and his largesse. Thus, bonhomie restored, he shepherds us through town. His arms around us both, we stroll down Pall Mall towards St James's Street and to the panelled rooms that are to be our London base.

An onlooker might suppose we are a happy family with joy and life ahead.

Stables Lodge

It is almost spring. Robert's insatiable energy has found a palliative. The London apartment alone will not suffice. We must now find a home. It's Surrey where my husband wants to live again. The pages of *Country Life* take on new meaning for me. Weekends are consumed as the dark blue Jaguar re-visits country lanes that Robert, as a bachelor reborn, forsook. In this shire, no agent will remain unvisited by him.

I am dazzled. Yet a dichotomy is clear. For while I am entranced by period homes and sometimes by converted barns, Robert holds modernity and ease before him like a spiritual guide. And yet…

"There is this house we really ought to see," he announces. It is, he says, a rare and special property. He makes it clear that it is not to his taste and yet I see he relishes the prestige that surrounds the prominence with which its sale is heralded. This house has all the cachet that its history bestows. Perhaps my husband wants to show that even this he can attain. Perhaps he simply sees that I will love this house. Wherever truth may lie, he tells me we will go and look.

A young woman stands at the iron entrance gate to Stables Lodge. Over the gate an ancient lantern hangs and trembles, slightly, in a sudden gust. The agent ignores her folder of papers.

"You will find nothing ordinary in this place," she says. "The enchantment starts here."

Indeed, it does. Pink-washed walls enclose these former stables that once housed horses from the great manorial Sutton Place. As we step inside, I notice nothing smart or modern. Brought from the manor house itself, a Tudor fireplace dominates the living room.

"This once belonged to Catherine of Aragon," the agent says.

A sloping conservatory in glass and iron, still elegant despite some lack of care, shelters a rudimentary kitchen. An afterthought.

But from here our eyes are drawn outwards over the extensive grounds.

Trees and shrubs punctuate the vast expanse of grass. Within feet, rabbits frolic. This is their world, not ours. This is no house with garden

Chapter 23

as appurtenance. It is a whole new world within which someone once carved out a space in which to dwell awhile.

Upstairs a bedroom leads onto a wrought iron balcony, from which, clinging to the outer wall, a spiral staircase twists and plunges to the ground outside. At its foot, I see again the spot where rabbits play.

Who ascends here? Who escapes? From whom? And why? A myriad of fairy stories tumble through my mind.

In this dreamers' land of whimsy, comfort and efficiency are of scant concern. For here it is charm and nature which are king. I know at once that here I can find home. I have no words and yet my face informs my husband this is so.

But Robert?

Dazzled and dazed, I catch myself. I hear my husband say we want to buy.

"Ah well," the agent says. "Then you must make a bid. The bids are to be sealed."

The dark blue Jaguar moves quietly away. Little is said. I am amazed by Robert's impetuosity.

Shyly I question him. "Why?"

"I saw your face."

This is the only explanation he will give. Yet happiness is what I want to see in Robert, and I cannot live with sacrifice. There's comfort for me in the presence of sealed bids for I need never know how low the bid will be that Robert, on reflection, will decide to make.

Yet when the bids are opened, it is his bid, precise and accurate, that tops all the rest. I am uncertain what to feel. Is it for me my husband has done this? Or is it just to demonstrate his power?

The spell is lifted soon enough. A few weeks on Robert announces that he has withdrawn his bid.

There is no discussion.

24

AN ADULT LIFE

1985

Beyond this new, untested world of marriage, professional life proceeds as I had hoped.

I am excited by the offer of a partnership that follows from my visit to Buckingham Street. The entrance to the house where Samuel Pepys once lived has led me to a suite of dreary rooms within which is a practice anchored in the past. I have an assignation with the senior partner, Mr S. All hope of any future for this firm will rest upon the foresight and ambition of one man. And even that ambition is, I see at once, constrained by languor and a predilection for a cultured and unhurried life.

Sound as his business acumen may be, this man is too unfocussed to transform this firm into the thriving enterprise that it might be. His history has made him slow to risk the comfort with which he surrounds himself. Like other European lawyers I have met in my career, he was displaced by war. Though more than forty years have passed since as a child he was uprooted from his home in the Sudetenland, his instinct is to rein in his ambition if it threatens the security he's worked so hard to build. The gentle Surrey suburbs have replaced his pre-war home. Within his tile hung residence, he's now content to relish domesticity. His children flourish at expensive schools. He's rightly proud of what he has achieved. It is enough for him.

And who can blame or criticise? For which of us will not seek quietude beyond the struggles and the hardship that we have endured?

But then I realise he also wants prestige.

It's his inclusion in the salons of the Garrick and the National Liberal Club of which he is most proud. Acceptance in what he believes to be society's higher echelons is what it takes to satisfy the cultural dissonance he sometimes feels.

And maybe from ideals or else to reinforce the point that he has landed safely on this other shore, he helps to form an Anglo-German

Chapter 24

group where lawyers from two countries that were once at war unite to foster reconciliation and prosperity. And tellingly, he counts himself a leader of the English section of the group.

He designates his firm as niche. It boasts a special Anglo-German clientele. He and his junior partners specialise in non-contentious work in commerce and in property. There's no one who can deal with matters that must be decided by the courts. Perhaps, I think, my background will be helpful here.

He's courteous and, as I enter, rises from a Queen Anne chair that has a velvet padded back of olive green. In times to come, I'll learn about the habit that he has of leaning back, legs stretched across his antique desk. Then with his hands entwined and clasped behind his head, he will dictate his correspondence as he lolls against his chair. But I can't know about that yet. Today he simply stares at me and offers me his hand.

He is a tall, imposing man, perhaps two decades older than myself. The stern impression that he gives is slightly softened by the fading colour of his salt and pepper hair. He sports a neat moustache. I notice that, although his mouth adopts a slightly twisted smile, he wears an air that speaks of faint disdain. I sense that, though he's affable as well as suave, he will expect to be obeyed.

But just for now he's charm itself – perhaps because my quiet manner does not threaten him. He seems attracted to the image I present but voices a concern that I am young enough to still have children if I choose. It's clear he feels that pregnancy might restrict the time and the commitment I can offer him.

My gentle smile conceals the pain of which I do not speak.

"That will not be an issue," I declare.

And in the months that follow, we meet from time to time. And I am now the one who has to weigh up all that I might risk in leaving work that's satisfying and secure to follow the uncertainty a partnership might bring.

And though I cannot quite believe what may be taking place, I understand that here before me now lies adulthood.

A New Beginning

It helps that Robert is beside me now, and I have gained in confidence – at least within the world that is beyond our home, for there, as showcased by him, I can make him proud.

My husband showers me with gifts of clothes which he prefers to those that I already have. Thus, suitably attired, I go with him to banquets and on foreign trips. And in return he makes it clear that he will stand beside me in my dealings in the legal world. And, if he needs to, he will fight with Mr S on my behalf. For everything I am and that I may achieve in image and in status will, he thinks, reflect on him.

Thus, he suggests that I accept the partnership that Mr S has offered me. If I work hard and can attract a clientele, this partnership will anchor me to the success that my career might bring. And money need not be an issue now. My salary is to be meagre, though I can expect to share the income earned from clients that I introduce. It is a risk for me and one I might not dare to take alone. Thus, Robert's generosity and his support propel me to a height I had not thought that I could reach. I am to be forever grateful for my husband's gift. And yet...

How strange it is that he salutes my independence and success in my professional sphere yet craves my strict allegiance in our private life. How curious that my gentle deference in marriage and in love is so increasingly at odds with who I am at work.

And very early in this new unpractised role as partner in this firm, I am encouraged by the loyalty my clients also show. On my first day, I'm visited by members of the legal team belonging to an intercontinental bank.

And within minutes they have offered a retainer to my firm.

Germany – the First Cut

Within a week there is a call from Germany. Herr Schubert, who has been my client for a year or two, now summons me to join him at some meetings in the shipping world. Almost at once I find myself in Hamburg once again. Paternalistic and conventional, Herr Schubert is delighted with my news. My partnership will make it easier for him to transfer work to my new firm. My marriage marks for him stability and gravitas. He is glad to think that I am settled. He and his business need not lose me now.

And with the distance this trip brings, I ponder on the marriage I have made. I am caught up in joy, buoyed up by the elation that my status as a new wife brings. I am relieved that all the expectations that were placed on me so many years ago are now fulfilled. And I am overjoyed to feel this marriage is much more than just a superficial shell constructed to protect

Chapter 24

me from convention's scorn for those who disregard the social patterns it prescribes.

Thoughts of my husband dominate and will not be suppressed. And yet, despite my superficial happiness, uneasy thoughts can't be dismissed.

It's sobering as I consider that this union must last a lifetime through.

I dimly realise how much I have to learn about the man that I have chosen as a partner in my life. And while I try to push away each jarring incident that threatens to disrupt my quietue, I cannot help but be disturbed by their intrusion in the settled life I'd hoped to find.

I sit within my comfortable room in Hamburg's premier hotel and muse upon the shift my life has seen. Yet, even as I try to focus on the happier times that married life has brought, I am distracted by a sudden fear that's inexplicable.

And though my husband has not given cause for me to doubt his faithfulness, I'm overwhelmed by sudden certainty that, at this moment, though it's only months since we were wed, my husband Robert is in someone else's arms.

And in the face of this uneasiness, I am compelled to telephone my husband, who will surely reassure me that this fantasy is some aberrant dream. I'm certain he will laugh with me at the perverseness of my thoughts.

Yet when he hears of my concern, my husband does not laugh. Instead, there is a pause I don't expect. And with each lengthening second, my heart shrinks. Then finally my husband breaks the silence that now frightens me. And, to my growing horror, he confirms that my suspicions are correct.

But even now he's caught out in his trespass, Robert does not offer an apology. He is buoyant, even brazen, as he faces down the indignation and the fury that he might expect.

Perhaps to fend off the recrimination that he fears, he tells me that this "hurried coupling" was exactly what it took to clarify his life – and mine.

"I needed this," he says to me of his brief fling, "to understand how much you mean to me. Don't stay away. Come home. Darling, I'm ready now. Let's settle down. I want to buy a home for us. There has been enough delay. It's time to start our proper married life."

It seems that Robert does not notice or perhaps he does not care what this discovery of his unfaithfulness has done to me.

Yet I'm his wife and I'm in love, or so I tell myself, and, as he hopes will happen, I am charmed by this fresh promise that he makes. I long to move beyond the faltering start our married life has made.

I murmur softly, "I will come."

And since I am determined that the marriage of which I dreamed will flourish and survive, I push away reality. I do not want to see that the analysis that Robert makes ignores the feelings of his wife.

Nor that our life together is to be entirely on my husband's terms.

In time, I'll learn this man will only welcome my appearance on the stage he occupies when it enhances what he sees as his success. Or when he needs that reassuring comfort that my ever-loving arms will bring.

But for the rest, it is as if I don't exist.

Heathrow

At Heathrow, hopeful, eager still, despite it all, I walk through the arrivals lounge – where Robert waits. My eyes alight on him. I meet his gaze.

And then, as in some final movie scene from long ago, all motion seems to slow as we embrace. All lingering thoughts of faithlessness dissolve within the reassurance of my husband's arms and in the passion of his kiss.

But suddenly the luggage trolley, waiting ready by my husband's side, spins backwards to his left. Distracted, my eyes follow, till they rest upon a figure standing in his wake. Beyond my husband's shoulder, shy, uncertain and confounded by this scene, my husband's teenage son waits.

At once, despite the joy I feel to be again within my husband's arms, I see the cowardice that skulks behind the welcome that is shown to me.

And pity and repugnance rise within me as I gaze upon this callow lad.

Reluctant and unready for a battle that he cannot understand, he has been chosen as his father's shield.

"Of course," says Robert in response to all the questions that I do not voice, "now that we are to have a proper home, young Jamie will be living with us too."

Strangers, united in our apprehension of what lies ahead, Jamie and I stand frozen, knowing neither of us can control what is to happen next.

25

FROM DAY TO DAY

1985

Health and Home – Surrey

Weeks pass in wilful blindness and confusion as my body makes the protest that my mind and voice will not.

The pain returns. It's stalked me tirelessly throughout the fifteen years gone by. It overwhelms me now and there are other symptoms too. Blood leaves my body, fleeing desperately as if aware the vessel that contains it may not stay afloat for long.

Robert is solicitous and kind enough. At once, a specialist is found. Jamie is told that "we" – he and his father – are to care for me. Surgery, first recommended all those years ago, is once again proposed.

I think back to the agony and the indignity that all too often would disrupt my life as sudden pelvic pain would see me back in hospital again. These were the trappings of a womanhood that would not lead me to the joy of giving birth.

I'd tried so hard to shun what started as a whispered murmur of my likely childlessness. Yet as the years went by, that murmur grew until it shattered the complaisance that I liked to feign. And since that day in 1977, when Mr Fincham told me with such starkness that I never would conceive a child, my grief has haunted and directed me in everything I do.

And stubbornly, I had refused to be complicit in the ending of my dream. Thus, I had not agreed to surgery that would remove my womb.

It's different now. I'm anchored by my marriage. There's no more time in which I can look forward, still believing that some miracle of science or of faith will change my fate.

And finally, I face reality. I am weighed down by sorrow and despair. But I am passive now, uncaring of the practicalities to which my husband now attends alone.

And all that matters now is that I shut out thought.

The Dormitory

The necessary house is swiftly found. I will not call it home. It keeps a distance from me. It is solid, hung with tiles, hidden behind high beech hedges in an anonymous Surrey road. In this dormitory village there is little sign of life for here it seems the norm to insulate oneself from what goes on beyond one's own immediate world.

Behind the drawbridge of their cretonne curtains and their doors of oak, the household heads are masters of their own domains, just as, I understand at last, my husband too intends to be.

I know at once that what is left of me will be extinguished here.

Despite my failing health, I drag myself to London and to work and to activity. On the platforms of the railway station, commuters, though not strangers, do not speak, though now and then they almost nod. They stand, stiffly, brandishing their briefcases. Once they are aboard their train, their newspapers shield them from the ones they do not want to see.

My senior partner, Mr S, lives in this village too. I glimpse him now and then. He does not ask us round to dinner, nor for drinks. He makes it clear to me that we will not be welcome at the tennis club where he holds court. I sense his fury that I, his junior partner, have dared to trespass on his territory.

I realise how similar these two men are – my husband and the man who dominates my firm. Each of them chose me to adorn the world he thought was his and placed me there to play a part that he designed. Neither envisaged I might move beyond the boundaries that each had set for me.

Now, longingly, I look back at the decades that have passed. A vision flashes through my mind. A mélange of the rooms and houses that I've shared and all the multitude of people crowding through the corridors of life. Life in that distant land was unpredictable, a veritable kaleidoscope crammed with ever shifting shapes of many hues. Despite the many challenges they brought my way, each aspect then was glorious to me.

I was alive then. Is this also life?

My body gives its own response. The haemorrhaging and the pain increase. My husband urges me to heed the medical advice that's clear. Perhaps it's time, he tells me, to let go – and jettison my womb. I do as he commends. I will not say command. For all of my passivity, I'm conscious that my body is my own to care for and to guard. The choices that I've made in life are my responsibility.

Chapter 25

Yet others are concerned.

"You are my wife. You have your family now. I need you to be well – and I don't want to see you suffer in this way," says Robert kindly, but impatient that I dither still.

And I cannot escape the logic of my husband's words.

Despite my new resolve, my mind flies back to the choices I have made. It's true that, had I all those years ago accepted what the doctors said, I would have been spared pain. Yet I can't feel regret.

And maybe now that youth has fled, my choices are irrelevant.

The End of Hope

In days, I'm back at the Masonic Hospital. I bring to mind the times when in the past I've been a patient here. But those were times when I would have some test or else a small procedure that might keep alive the fantasy that I might yet conceive a child.

It's different now.

For once, I cannot think about the future or the past. I push emotion back. And in this present moment there is nothing more to feel.

The surgeon strikes. He smoothly strips me of my dreams, my usefulness, the motherhood for which I had believed that I was made.

And lying in my sterile bed, I ponder how my life has come to this.

This marriage had been meant to offer solace to us both. It was to represent a fresh beginning where in time we could forget the failures and the often self-inflicted hurt our adulthoods had seen.

Yet all the fluctuations in my husband's moods have stood between us and that goal. At times I am cocooned in Robert's love. At times it seems his only mission is to lift me high above the difficulties of life. And when I'm in his arms it is impossible to think that we could ever be apart. But then, sometimes in moments, it's as if I have become the irritant he'd like to sweep away. He makes it clear I am the complication that he'd sometimes rather be without.

I can't escape the fact that though within our marriage there are times that Robert will indulge and humour me, his world does not include a place for 'us'.

I try to tell him how this feels and how impossible it is to build a life for us upon the shifting sands of a commitment that he will not fully make. And though I've tried to overlook my husband's faithlessness, I can't ignore my growing certainty that there are many days when he regrets that I'm his wife.

Childlike, I count the days since we were wed. He loves me. He loves me not.

Yet, even in this hour of need, Robert's impatience cannot be disguised. He leans back in his chair. His shoe-clad feet are stretched across my bed. Arms that I long to hold me are clenched by his sides, his hands in the pockets of his overcoat. His lips smile, though his eyes do not.

"Stop this," he says, "for you're in luck. Today is a day when I do love you."

And in thus saying what he thinks is all I need to hear, he fends off all discussion of the things that break my heart. He turns away and marches briskly to the door.

London

The panelled walls that line the flat in which I convalesce are death to me. Our London home is several floors above the street. But there's no skyline to amaze me and distract. The only windows, to the rear, look out across a well. Though our apartment boasts new furnishings, as well as paintings that my husband loves, I cannot breathe the air I crave. There are no plants, no trees, no blades of grass. Yet I am told that here I must remain for weeks, until my strength returns.

But suddenly I have a visitor. It's Mr S. He's agitated – clearly irritated by the present circumstance.

He tells me that a client has arrived. Without appointment. From Hong Kong, it seems. Mr S would send him packing if he could but, since the client is connected to a man of influence, my senior partner knows he cannot risk offence. The client says his son, a child of nine, has been abused. There's talk about interrogation and a cruel stepfather. It's nothing Mr S has ever come across before. It bears no likeness to the deals and contracts that he knows.

"If only you…" his voice trails off. "Of course, that isn't why I'm here. I've only called to see just how you are. But since I'm here, I'm sure you'd like to know…"

And at this moment energy floods back. At times like this it always will.

"I'll come this afternoon. I'll take a taxi. It's OK."

Chapter 25

And thus, my convalescence is cut short as I decide that this young child needs all the help that I can give.

And though my husband chides me that I need to take more care, I sense that any absence that I choose to take from hearth and home comes as relief to him.

Reflection

From this time on, a darker veil of sorrow is to lie between me and the pleasures that so often seem to be within my reach. But though I cannot know it yet, this mortal wound of childlessness will open up a world of sensitivity to others' pain. For this fresh loss compounds the understanding which was Bethlem's legacy. And though I'm devastated now, in years to come, I'll see this for the miracle it is. For in the quest for healing and relief that suffering inspires, I am uncaged. I am released from all the narrow circumstance that is dictated by convention and by birth. Misfortune has positioned me within a wider world in which I am set free to walk with strangers all my life. As they have walked with me.

And it is through this liberation that, in times ahead, I'll come to know compassion, inclusivity and joy.

26

THE FALLOW FIELD

1985

Paris

Yet even in the midst of sadness, there are unexpected pleasures if I only let myself delight in them. And Robert does his best to cheer me and distract. He is a member of an international panel which meets to deal with global banking issues far beyond his day-to-day routine. He is uplifted by these gatherings which meet in Paris several times a year. Despite the darkness that envelops me, my mood shifts, slightly, as my husband makes it clear that he would like me with him when he travels in this way. And, so, when work permits, I am.

Thus, now and then, we visit this metropolis, the city of both light and love. And whilst my husband works, I'm free to wander as I please. I am at liberty to roam the boulevards and avenues. I can absorb the aura of the city's present and its past. And, if I choose to do so, I may sit for hours within a gallery and ponder all the beauty of a Monet or Le Brun. Within the pavement cafés, I can lunch alone with confidence I rarely feel elsewhere. I am at ease. I am reminded of the thinkers and the writers who would sit alone in cafés such as this. Their presence is companion to my solitude and to my grief. This city draws me to it as other cities have not done. Its ethos nurtures me. Its language and its books and its philosophers have helped to shape my life. Its culture stimulates my senses. Our rhythms harmonise. Paris embraces me and, when it needs to do, unerringly, it offers me support. It sees me for the woman that I am, with my own attributes and needs. It does not see me as a thing that's subjugated and absorbed within the married state I was so eager to adopt.

And suddenly, to my surprise, I realise that, for the first time since my wedding day, I am relieved and thankful that I am alone and free.

Chapter 26

La Madeleine

The small apartment we frequent is near La Madeleine. Its rooms are dark and intimate. As we repose within the shelter it provides, I sense the history of its former occupants, their influence benign. And, strangely, here I am not stifled as I was within our London home. Invigorated by the stimulation of my daytime wanderings, I can fend off the oppression that has sometimes marked my wifely role. Beyond the evening hour, we can relax as moments of togetherness remind us that we can at times be happy in each other's company. But even here our unity is fleeting and in the world beyond these rooms our closeness disappears.

One day I stroll with Robert in the street. And, as I often seem to do these days, I somehow irritate the man I love. His voice is raised in anger. I recoil. But there's no space within which I can move and, as I fall against a bollard, his exasperation grows. Instantly, hands reach out to catch me, though they are not his. The passers-by, who rush to help me, gently and in some amusement remonstrate with him for chiding me. Disconcerted – shamed perhaps – Robert retreats in silence.

Back in the apartment, a phone call interrupts the tension that is apt to stalk a married life when partners are too formed to change and blend into a seamless whole. Where there's no dovetailing of need in which each can provide the thing the other lacks. Where all that fits is circumstance. Where neither has the instinct nor the courage to accept that passion and affection may not offer them the consonance they crave. And neither has the will nor the ability to strive for harmony beyond that point.

When Robert takes the call, I find, to my surprise, it is for me. The caller, Mrs B, the mother of Sebastian, a feckless friend I've known for years, has somehow charmed my office staff to tell her where I am. She is desperate. She tells me that her son has had a fall. He languishes, unconscious, in a London hospital. She has been told he may not live. In strained and strident tones, she answers my unspoken query, for, though I'm shocked, this is not, surely, my concern. Sebastian and I were close once. But he is married now and so am I.

"In the name of my son, I appeal to you to come back home to London now. I know that if you come to him, Sebastian will live."

Though I recall it well, I'm taken back by her indomitable nerve.

But in this moment, I remember that once, in another life, I was myself. A self for whom a stranger's life would have been of concern. And

Robert seems to know it too. And as I ask him haltingly what I shall do, he shrugs and says that he would happily ignore the call. But grudgingly, he tells me that he understands this is not possible for me.

"Because you're you," he says, "you'll have to go."

He seems resigned. He says that he will drive me home.

Homeward Bound

Stunned by my husband's recognition and by this willing sacrifice, I gather up our things. Soon the dark blue Jaguar is Calais bound. The radio is all that breaks the silence of the shock we feel at such a sudden change of plan. The strains of Beethoven emphasise the sense of urgency that dominates our flight. The trees that line and guard the road stand straight backed and alert, as if in honour of our charity.

For in this rare moment of our marriage, we strive to achieve the same goal.

But harmony does not last long. Our car is halted. Gendarmes tell my husband we are driving far too fast. In my anxiety to reach Sebastian, I plead with them. Robert grimaces. I realise too late that only silence is required of me. He exhales loudly then, frustratedly, he says, "Life was so simple once."

In Dover now, my husband's eyes light up. He talks of all the things he plans to do now that he's home. I realise, with sadness, that his unselfish gesture was not, perhaps, entirely because of me. Sebastian's calamity has given Robert the excuse he needs. He wants, it seems, to get away from me.

I telephone Sebastian's wife. I marvel at the grace with which she welcomes the intrusion that is my return.

"I'm glad that you are here. Let's sit together at Sebastian's side."

Days later, as I sit beside Sebastian, he wakens from unconsciousness. And from the side room where she sleeps, I fetch his wife. Calmly she brings her husband's favourite soap and washes him. She speaks to him in gentle and familiar tones. In the face of this uxorial intimacy, I am humbled and superfluous.

And when I'm back with Robert in our Surrey home, I start to wonder if there is a place for me. Between what seem like critical events, I try to please. My focus is on Robert and the way I think he wants his wife to be. Sometimes I get it wrong. One night he hosts a bridge game at our home.

Chapter 26

I bring refreshments at the time my husband has proposed. Mistakenly, I do not wait for his command. The vocal fury I unleash in him reduces me. I slink away.

Yet though I am prepared to follow Robert's lead, just now and then come moments when I can't restrain myself from speaking out. It's rare for me to criticise or challenge his beliefs. Yet when we differ on a moral stance, I cannot subjugate my principles to his. It is too much for him to bear. He sought to place a rose within his home. He had not understood that deep beneath the petals there might be a thorn.

Riverview

In search of respite, I arrange to spend a weekend with a friend from student days. She lives in Yorkshire, but I stop en route in Hertfordshire, where we agree to meet. And while we're there, my friend suggests a change of plan for she would like some respite of her own. She asks if we can spend our time in Chiswick, in the small Edwardian cottage that I rented in my student days and bought when, finally, my legal studies were complete. Its dated charm has always nourished me and more than that, it's always been a haven for the friends and strangers I have taken in. In time, it will be sold, but now it still belongs to me. It isn't occupied.

"Of course. Let's go to Riverview," I say with matching eagerness.

When we arrive at dusk, what greets me at my former home is shock. For where there were bare windows, there are curtains now. Curtains which I had intended should be hung but which had lain neglected in their box. I leap to the conclusion that Robert, so attentive to our practical concerns, has once again been helpful here. It must be he who has decided that the curtains should be hung while I am gone.

"How kind he is," I say.

But then, in some alarm, I notice other things. Empty cardboard crates are piled beside the rubbish bin. What could they have contained? With mounting tension, I unlock the door to this beloved and familiar home where stained-glass windows flaunt the gentle beauty of a long-lost past. But even here, tranquillity has fled. For, as I step into the hall, I see that other boxes have been crammed into the tiny space. With apprehension, I tear off a lid and, in dismay, I see my precious books which were in Surrey when I left home yesterday. It's clear that Robert must have brought them here. I understand these books were always loathsome to my husband's jealous eyes. I used to hide them, furtively, beneath a cushion if he came home unexpectedly. But Surrey is our home now and I cannot understand why these same books are here in Riverview.

Reluctant to admit the thought that's forming in my mind, I telephone and ask my husband what has happened here.

"Ah, yes, *those* things," my husband says with studied nonchalance. "Jamie and I both think it best if you move back to Chiswick. We intend to bring the rest of your things tomorrow."

I am stunned. However, I am not too shocked to speak. Calamity has stripped away my diffidence.

"Come now, at once, and fetch me home."

In times of crisis my mother's tone, Edwardian and firm, usurps my gentleness. Now it is Robert who is shocked, and he capitulates at once.

"I will be there within the hour," he promises.

My faithful friend, appalled, declares she will not leave until she's seen my husband come and watched us drive away.

"I will not interfere," she says. "I'll just sit in my car. I will not go till all is well."

I gaze at her uncomprehending. *How can all be well?*

Within the hour the dark blue Jaguar returns. Its smoothness and its power swallow me.

27

REVELATIONS

1985–1986

In years to come, I'll long to say that this is where the story of my marriage ends. By now, it's clear that marriage does not mean the same to Robert as it does to me.

For all my optimistic stubbornness, I start to understand that we can't live together anymore. To ease the pressure, I suggest that, just for now, I'll spend some weeknights at my London home. My husband looks relieved. But this is not enough for him. His daughter visits me at Riverview – at his request. She comes to have the conversation he can't bring himself to start. He knows that in his daughter's presence, I won't argue or complain. In any case, I scarcely listen. I am numb. But then she tells me that her father weeps. He cannot bear, she says, to contemplate his "great mistake". That is enough to shake the lingering trace of hope. I cannot bear to think that this insouciant man who lifted me from all my insecurity has been reduced to this. And that, for all my efforts, I have somehow caused it to be so. It's sobering. And, as illusions shrink, I understand I cannot keep him where he does not want to be.

And with a sadness that I think will never dissipate, I sign the papers for a separation prior to divorce.

And suddenly the tension seems to ease, although the silent hopes we cherish are at odds. Whilst Robert sees an ending to a yoke he does not want to bear, I am ambivalent. For all the signs of pressure and discontent, I can't accept our marriage is to end.

Curiously, in the relief that we each feel at this unhappy truce, our passion and concern for one another are revived. As Robert's visits to my Chiswick home increase, I start to wonder if there is yet hope that we might reconcile. There can be no divorce until two years have passed. For now, we are still man and wife.

The Journey

In Business Class I sit, downcast, unheeding of the beauteous clouds that once would mesmerise me and enchant. Always, I have been drawn to these. Always, I've vowed that if I could reach out into that other world that's parallel to mine, I too would float on angels' wool and rest on thistledown.

But not today.

And, as I look at all that's dead or dying in my life, I weep.

Yet I am not alone. Beside me, sharing all the intimacy offered by a journey such as this, sits my companion for this business trip.

David is a patent lawyer. He is a lean and wiry man, at ease with life, yet rarely still. His constant motion, his unruly curls of black and his antipodean twang present a perfect contrast to the pompousness that permeates the legal world. His laugh evades all efforts to impose formality. His mien reflects the energy and zest that have the power to infect and to transform all those he meets.

And I am fortunate that it is he who sits beside me now.

The two of us are bound for Stuttgart where we are to join an international team to talk about the litigation that has overwhelmed the client we all share. And it will fall to me to make the presentation that will launch our talks. I'm doubtful that I am in any state to carry out what's asked of me. For, in this moment, I exude dejection and despair.

I look inside myself and think of all I vowed to cherish and to love. And sorrow buries me.

And David, who's a long-established mentor to this firm that is completely new to me, must wish that he'd appointed someone with a wiser, cooler head than me. Someone who had already learned to float serenely on life's surface, regardless of the obstacles that lie beneath.

But no.

For David is a man who does not recognise defeat. Someone who knows that challenges exist to draw out all the latent strength and talent that we have. And who believes that all will flourish if only they would understand they can.

And in the years to come, he'll use the money that he makes to build a firm where all are equal and where those who struggle learn they too can shine. And in my modest way, I'll help him launch the enterprise of which he dreams. And Robert, the enabler, is to help him too.

And David, in his turn, will make me see the strength and the ability in me that I so frequently discount. He will encourage me to fight for what he thinks is rightly mine. I cannot yet foresee this litigation is to bring my partnership success and wealth, but in the next few years the profits of my firm will double and then double once again. And David's energy will help to galvanise support. He is to orchestrate a plethora of praise that Mr S, my senior partner, can't ignore. With David's backing, I will move beyond my natural timidity. I will successfully insist that the agreement in the partnership must be redrawn. Thus, all I thought was unattainable in terms of independent status and prosperity, is to fall within my reach.

But, just for now, I fear my only future will be failure and defeat. And in this momentary lapse of vision, it is David who now takes my hand and reassures me that I can do all that's asked.

"We'll take them on together, Lesley. We will fly the flag for England. Let us help this client but let's also do it for ourselves."

And thus, we pledge allegiance to each other, and we will uphold this pledge in years to come. And each of us will count the other as a friend and fellow traveller upon the journey that, for a while at least, we are to share.

Endgame

Two years have passed since I returned to Riverview to live. I am still Robert's wife. These years have seen our life continue in its half-connected way. But now, in 1987, it is time for me to keep the promise that I made. I must submit the papers necessary for divorce. These papers are prepared and signed. But though the details are correct, we learn that there are technicalities that lead the judge to stipulate that we must wait a few more months before he'll grant us a divorce. Inside, a part of me is thankful that a final separation is postponed. But Robert's anger at this setback is a shock to me. Although he has so often spoken of divorce, my husband's actions have at many times belied his words. When he is with me, he behaves the way he's always done. And though we have two separate homes, we are together just as often as we ever were.

I've tried to make myself believe that though my husband seeks his freedom from the married state, his love for me remains unchanged. Now, in the face of Robert's sullen fury, I begin to see that perhaps I was wrong. I contemplate with sadness that, in Robert's future, there may be no place for me.

With synchronicity his bank now moves location. With it, Robert moves to Bath. I visit, but our time is shorter now. As ever, Robert vacillates. He tells me that his daughter is to wed. He asks me to be with him on Catherine's wedding day. But then abruptly, cruelly, the invitation is withdrawn.

Now Robert, in his turn, succumbs to illness and an operation is required. He finds himself alone. He begs me for support. From far away I listen, and I try to allay the concerns my husband has. The small disruptions to his life are mine to hear of and resolve. And so, my arms extend to comfort him. I pack a case to travel so that I can nurse my husband as he asks. But then he rings and tells me not to come.

"It's complicated," Robert sighs.

Yet he insists he will continue as a mentor to me in my business role. He continues to travel with me on the business trips that I must make. He decides to travel widely, for his pleasure too. Mostly he's alone but, now and then, he takes me with him.

The ties that bind us are now frayed but they are not cut yet.

One day when I am home in Riverview, a policeman phones. He tells me that there's been a break-in at my husband's home in Bath. He says that Robert is away. They need to find him and somehow, it seems, they've found my name.

"Are you the wife?" the policeman asks. "Where can we find your husband? It's important that we speak to him at once."

Though I can't tell them where my husband is, I know that Robert has left documents and notebooks in our bedroom here at Riverview. Though I am hesitant to look into my husband's private things, I yield to what the policeman tells me is the urgency of his request. I hope to find a name and number that will help. But, as I leaf through well-thumbed pages, I find only names that are unknown to me. They are women's names. I shudder but I manage not to gasp. Quietly I give the police his daughter's name.

And, finally, I understand that our relationship is dead. It isn't marriage that my husband does not want. It's me.

It is inevitable and there is just one more step for me to take. I must make one last application for the court's decree – an edict that will end the hopes I cherished on that late November wedding day.

Weeks on, in Bedford Row, I stand before the oval pillar box. I hesitate and linger till at last I post the letter that will end our married life.

Chapter 27

My mind flies back to 1974 and Exhibition Road. It was a post box then that swallowed up my dreams. And strangely now this memory reminds me that beyond defeat and sadness, other joyful days may come.

My office now is situated here in Bedford Row. I do not know it yet, but it is here my working life will end. And I will pass this scarlet milestone each and every day for thirty years.

And though it speaks to me of deep-remembered pain, it offers me the hope of resurrection too.

28

WILDERNESS

1987–1989

A Harsher Landscape

Thus, life becomes for me another wilderness – though not one now where I will struggle for my health or for my daily bread. I have an income that would feed a family or two. I have the shelter that is Riverview. I have an occupation where, each day, I have new challenges to face. Where even now the energy I have can find a use. Where curiosity and my desire to serve can be assuaged.

Despite all this, the landscape's harsh. The desolation that surrounds me is emotional. I cannot see beyond the wasteland that now separates me from the hope that I once knew. From time to time, I feel that I am welcomed for the role I play, and yet it seems that there is nowhere I have been accepted for myself.

And I feel shame that despite all the opportunities, ideals and gifts I have, there's disillusion in my personal life. I can't escape the fact that I have failed to understand the challenges that stem from different backgrounds or conflicting aims or latent prejudice. I realise that even love that's shared is sometimes not enough to form a lasting unity.

Yet life continues, as I understand it must, and I am fortunate. The legal cases that I must now pursue absorb me and distract. They are both complex and intractable. But I will not accept that fact. I've learned to persevere and not to yield. It is curious that this same quality on which I've built professional success has sometimes seemed to be a weakness in my private life. For often it is when I do not walk away that I expose myself to pain.

Yet though I grow in confidence at work, I am subdued. My clothes reflect the changing seasons of my life. A blouse of French blue silk beneath a chocolate paisley costume in the finest wool becomes my signature. The black and scarlet outfit with the studded leather cuffs is relegated by me now, for that was Robert's gift. The clothes I wore with boldness in my married hour give way to subtle tones as, once again, my diffidence and my uncertainty prevail.

Perhaps one day I'll learn that self-belief is more important than the validation of another human being. And that those of us who stand alone in life also have worth.

Mountains of Discovery – Italy

I fill my private time as best I can. I take a trip to Italy. The mountains and the lakes are healing. But I am not alone, so I don't always choose the route or pace at which we walk. I am content that someone else should take the lead.

Neville is dark and tall and strong. A northerner, he walks for miles each week. And it is when he leaves behind the wreckage of his private life and the mundanity that is his work routine that Neville comes into his own. And now he has a group of straggling followers to lead, he comes alive again. He senses that we will not challenge what he sees as dominance. And I for one don't question that he knows the way and understands what's best for me. Until I find that the ascent he chooses is too steep for me and so I slither backwards till I reach the valley once again.

And later, as I lie in bed with aching limbs and battered knees, I ruefully regret the willingness with which I offer up control to any stranger who suggests that he may have a better plan than I.

And dimly it occurs to me that all the Nevilles that have flitted through my life could never understand nor shape the future that would perfectly accommodate the person that I am. And though I am so grateful to the ones who've offered me their vision and support, I cannot always place my future in their hands. And I remind myself of this: my life is mine. It's my responsibility and I must build my own prosperity.

Beyond the Divide – Berlin

The wider world around me is also witness to a change, one more dramatic and far-reaching than the change imposed on me. In 1989, I'm at a legal conference in Germany when news comes that the Berlin Wall has fallen, bringing hope for unity. The delegates are stunned. I know that Germany has longed for this for almost thirty years. In 1961, I wore a silver lapel pin of solidarity shaped like the Brandenburg Gate. That Gate is open now. It's hard to understand that this has really come to pass. The European landscape is transformed.

My mind flies back to Easter 1965. A student then, I'd flown to Germany to join my childhood friend. And Hella had a plan. The airspace to Berlin was newly opened. And, just because we could, we took a flight.

Four times a year the West Berliners were allowed to visit family in the east. Though neither of us had such ties, we saw no reason why we should not cross as well. The soldiers at the border separated us. At their insistence I, a foreigner, was made to walk alone beneath the checkpoint where so many died. I saw the guns of soldiers trained on me. I saw the sternness in their eyes. I felt a tiny trace of fear.

But minutes later, above ground again, I found myself a witness to the elation and emotion of those strangers who, beyond belief, were reunited with the ones they loved. I watched as gnarled and trembling hands reached out to touch the babies who betokened life and hope. I saw the disbelief and joy that, even after all the brutal changes life presents, we can survive if we have patience, fortitude and hope.

We rarely are prepared for change imposed on us, especially if it's visible and swift. Sometimes it's even hard to welcome change that's positive when it moves faster than we can accommodate. And yet, in time, adjustment comes.

In 1989, the legal conference closes in a Europe that has been recast. Yet I am glad that change is not ubiquitous. I think of Hella and the friendship that endures despite the very separate lives that we pursue. It's several years since we last met. In adulthood, my friend has travelled widely and in 1989, her husband's work has taken her to live in Pakistan.

And suddenly I feel a tremor of excitement that is rare for me these days, as it occurs to me that I am free to join her there. I marvel at the solid ties formed in the adolescence that we shared. With thankfulness, I understand such ties will help me shift beyond the bleakness of my married years. And as she has done through the decades that have passed, this dearest friend will welcome me.

29

A PAST AND FUTURE FAITHFULNESS

1989–1990

And now my life is crowded with the plan I have. As I expected, Hella graciously extends a welcome to her self-appointed guest. I reread all the letters she has sent me in the past few years. They have new meaning now I'm drawn into the world she occupies. Her letters speak of muezzins and minarets. Yet, as she feeds my dreams, my friend does not neglect the practical advice I need. She speaks of teeming crowds and of the isolation of a woman who has not yet learned to bow to the seclusion that this other world prefers. She tells me that my solo journey may be fraught with risk and sets out all the safeguards I must put in place and all the rules that I must follow if I am to travel safely from Karachi to Lahore.

Thus, Hella takes command the way she's always done. Despite the disillusion that sometimes haunts my mind, I am content to place my trust in her. She is unwavering, this constant and forbearing friend.

In 1989 she is the only one whose present remains faithful to the ties which were our past.

Holland 1989

Just weeks before my Asian trip, I fly to Holland for New Year. I am to join a party of the unattached. The ones who lack those precious bonds that grapple us together when we mourn or celebrate. Though Christmas is a time for joy and family fun, I always try to hide when New Year comes. It seems to ask such bravery. I often lack the courage to look forward and I vow I won't look back. I want to disappear and hide myself. I cannot bear to face a string of questions asking how I am and what my plans may be. Especially when I know my answers will dismay. I long to be unpressured and anonymous. For in the company of strangers who don't know or care about my woes, I can relax and be myself. And so, I choose to mingle with the social discards and the fugitives or with the restless ones, like me, who cannot be at ease within a world where expectations cannot be fulfilled.

But now, in late December 1989, I feel a lightening of my mood. Despite my cowardice and my innate timidity, my mind cannot dismiss a touch of eagerness when thinking of the escapade that lies ahead. In preparation, I try on the newly purchased clothes I've bought for Pakistan. I decide that I will wear them as I tour the sights of Amsterdam. The trousers that are black and gaberdine are softly pleated to conceal my abdomen. They're partnered by a heavy woollen tunic on which silver spangled edgings are affixed. They are intended for the visits I expect to pay to souks, and even mosques, perhaps. In my imaginings, I picture Hella and myself, in modest dress, our hair and faces swathed in knotted scarves of silk.

Thus, even here, in Holland's dark museums, I am transported to another corner of the world. And in this frame of mind the Rembrandt paintings seem to merge into a sea of blackened tar, and I pay scant attention to my fellow guests.

Until I reach the Anne Frank House.

For here, I can't escape the poignancy, the waste, the sense of urgency that drives us when we know but won't admit that we are doomed.

But as I contemplate, I feel a presence at my side. And then I hear a voice. It's clear but yet it's hesitant. There is a gentleness. It catches me and brings me back into the present hour. This is the voice of one who watches and observes.

"Excuse me. May I just...?" The voice trails off as if the speaker is unsure that he should speak. "The fastening on your tunic is undone. Here, on your neck. It's catching in your hair. If you would let me, I will do it up for you."

I'm startled by this interruption and the intimacy of this man's request. And to my own surprise – and perhaps his – I nod and murmur, "Yes. If you would."

And, as I stop and step aside, I don't question or appraise this presence that is now attached to me. My back is turned to him as he attends to what has caught his eye. Then on my neck I feel the fleeting brush of flesh on flesh. It wakens me. And, as he fumbles with the fastening, I am aware, if very dimly, that this is a moment that I won't forget. The moment when this man who is for now unknown, unnamed, obscure, has transformed all that is to come for both of us.

Chapter 29

And even as, with mumbled thanks, I move aside, I recognise my life has shifted in that single moment when he touched my neck.

If only I could see ahead into my sixth and seventh and even eighth decades, then I might understand that, from now on, my life will pace itself more evenly. And yet I cannot know what this encounter is to mean throughout the years to come. Despite what seems like forwardness, I do not feel this man intrudes. There is no drama here. This stranger's simple gesture shows me that an easy everyday concern is born of naturalness that all too often has been absent from my life. His presence offers me a momentary glimpse of something that in adulthood I have never known till now. It is a life more ordinary, one without the tempests and the turmoil of the years gone by. And in this instant, new life is conceived, where richness blends with quietness of soul. A life where I can pause to see the beauty and compassion of the raindrops that still linger on replenished earth, now that the storm has passed.

30

ORDINARY TIME

1990

And thus, this year begins with positivity. No introspection shall intrude upon the unexpected impact that this quiet man has had. For here to share with me the dawning of this new decade is Alistair, the stranger who I met within the Anne Frank House.

He is different from the powerful men who've beckoned me in years gone by. Yet, though I cannot foresee all that is to come, he is the one who from the start determines he will stay with me and see me through. He is a gentle man. An academic, he is most at home in tweed and cords. And yet he has a sense of style that elevates his presence and the things with which he chooses to surround himself. A thoughtful man, who never says a word he does not mean, his depths will take me by surprise.

He is a man of almost fifty years who is settled in a village life where he's accepted for himself. He feels at home within the folk clubs and the pubs that form the heart of his community.

And yet I am to learn that he has weathered storms that equal the intensity of those that have surrounded me.

In time, I am to understand the reasons for the sorrow that still lurks within those large and lustrous eyes of grey. And all my life I'll want to soothe and kiss away the rigid furrow in his brow that speaks of time-worn sadness and distress. This cleft belies what passes for contentment in the life that he has carefully reshaped. This grief is his alone to bear. Though I may feel compassion, I have not lived the sorrows of that past. And yet the earlier despair that he and I have separately known will bring us closer in the years to come as peace is found within the soothing silence of acceptance and companionship.

In any case, the joy he brings is in the ordinary things of life. The pleasures that have almost passed us by, so overwhelming was the drama of our separate lives. But Alistair is some steps further from the trauma of his past than I. Thus, he can take my hand and help me to discover once again the pleasures of a settled life.

Chapter 30

It is unsettling that just days after we have met, I must fly eastwards on the visit that I have arranged to Pakistan. My diary has been cleared. And this disruption gives us space in which to breathe and to reflect. I am touched that Alistair sends letters and that, now and then, his phone calls reach me too. In turn, I write to share with him my rare experience.

When I return, I celebrate with Alistair the things that have been absent from my life for many years. I visit him at his small cottage in the English village where he's made his home. Shyly, I sit beside him in the hostelries where he has found some shelter from the sorrows he has known. At other times, when visiting his mother, I am transported to a gentler world where all the cares of life are swept away as tea is taken and as pleasantries are shared.

And in the freshness of the country air, I walk with Alistair and, like some child reborn, I kick my feet through leaves that carpet woodland paths. One day we walk along a country lane and chance upon a humble donkey being led in silence by a farmer who inclines his head in greeting as we pass. I am struck by what I see. For though this donkey is by nature stubborn and perverse, it is now docile and at ease within the confines of the path that it has come to know.

And, musing on this scene, I contemplate the wonder of a life where all that changes are the seasons and the ordered times of life and death.

In London, Alistair is eager to explore the city and the riverbanks. At weekends, he arrives on Friday afternoon at Riverview and waits for my return from work. And when I turn my key and pass beyond the door that opens on the home I love, I find him waiting patiently. And we embrace.

We dine at home on food from Thailand or from India. Yet as we talk and share the confidences hidden deep within ourselves, these delicacies lie, almost untouched, congealing in the multitude of aluminium trays that each week Alistair will walk so faithfully to fetch. Later in the evenings there's no need for words as we replay the songs that formed the soundtrack of our youth. And as it brings us into harmony, this music of our past revives our energy as, gradually, it speaks to us of hope.

In February, on his birthday, though it's only weeks since we first met, I hurry home with eagerness to greet Alistair with all the preparations I have made. And when he sees the simple cake and candle that I have arranged for him, he cannot quite hold back his tears. And I am stunned to realise this gentle man cannot recall a time when he felt welcomed in the way he is today.

And for my part, I sense the sorrows of the past are fading now. Perhaps in this decade they can be laid to rest within my soul.

Yet idylls of the kind that I describe are for the dreamer or the very young. Such perfection is unlikely to endure. Between us Alistair and I have lived almost a hundred years. If we display a superficial semblance of the stoic evenness that comes with middle life, inside us lurk the pain and brokenness that marred our early adulthood. However valiantly we fight to change our past misfortune into wisdom and experience, it cannot quite be done.

At least, not yet.

And sometimes, as we notice tiny cracks within the façade each of us has built, we hesitate, remembering the betrayals of the past.

For who of us, although distracted by some superficial charm, can forget pain that comes with unexpected callousness? And who of us, however dazzled and beguiled, can banish every memory of faithlessness and loss?

Thus, in the months to come, our past realities intrude into these halcyon days as we discern the foibles and the failings each of us has gathered in the years gone by. And though they are just modest blemishes, they sometimes give us pause.

At moments such as these, I falter, though I do not step away. For all the wounds that sensitivity can bring, it offers us the gift of understanding too. And those conscious of the flaws they carry deep within themselves are slow to judge the frailties of other less than perfect beings.

For his part, Alistair reveals his steadfastness. Whatever he observes in me, this man accepts me as I am. And if I rush headlong into a life beyond the domesticity we share, he is content to follow or to wait. Just now and then, if he can see that danger lurks, he will reach out to pull me back. But for the most part, he will let me be myself. He's made his choice and here, beside me, he will stay.

And in the confidence of one another's care, we do not rush to plan ahead. We are content to linger and to take our time.

And gradually I learn that if we love each other as we hope that we are loved, our lives will be transformed. For in the love we give to others, we ourselves are healed.

31

CHOICES

1992–1994

Transition

Now, in this century's last decade, illusion's mists begin to part as finally I understand that all the choices that I have are mine to make. No longer will I let myself be wholly swayed by others' views, by passion or by circumstance. Though these will have important roles to play, they won't usurp the power I have to influence.

And to the fortitude I've slowly built is added something that I've never known till now. And though it's tiny and not fully formed, the seed that's growing in me cannot be mistaken. In 1992, at almost fifty years of age, I sense a kind of confidence.

I'm thankful that my sight is clearer now, for I can see the legal partnership that means so much to me needs new direction if it is to last beyond a year or two. For Mr S has no ambition other than to languish in a place of comfort through his semi-working days until the partnership can buy him out. But partnership reserves are few and it is plain to see that to survive we must abandon independence and ally ourselves with others in a larger entity.

To my astonishment, I am the one who calls for forward thinking and for strategy. Yet, with the power and authority that none has challenged in the years gone by, it's Mr S who will determine with what other firm our future lies. It's Mr S who brings us details of the different firms with which our partnership might find a home. But it is clear that some of us are vulnerable. A partnership that's looking to acquire a smaller firm will seek out individuals whose contacts or whose proven efforts promise a prosperity beyond what it has managed to achieve alone. The German clients who I serve will surely guarantee that I will be accepted by a larger firm. But gradually, I realise that others won't survive. I understand there's little to be said. But I'm subdued by what I see. And if the meagre influence I have may be still more reduced within a more established partnership, this is the price that I must pay if I am to continue with the work that nurtures me. I tell myself that I will be content to focus on my clients, thankful that in years to come I'll have a base from which I can support and serve.

Yet, though I'd like to think the partnership in which I work is founded on professionalism, ethics and ideals, I can't escape the truth that, when a crisis comes, self-interest and expediency matter too.

A Backward Step

Although the shift to which our partnership commits itself is radical, the outward signs of change are small. The business in which we are to be absorbed is situated only yards from where our firm has practised for the past five years.

And thus, in 1993, my partners and our tiny staff move with me to the handsome Georgian house that fronts on Bedford Row. My mind flies back to Dorset Square and to that other Georgian townhouse where many years ago I chanced upon the legal world. Reflections on my past entwine with images of those solicitors who flourished in this building in the centuries gone by. Solicitors have practised their profession here since 1784. The names of some of them are etched in brass beside the black front door above the three worn steps which lead up from the street.

Before the house, a false acacia stands. Its feathered fronds of primavera green bring softness to the grandeur of this elegant address. Its lower branches point at curious angles towards the earth as if the weight of all that they have witnessed is too much for them to bear. This tree has watched for centuries as clients, lawyers and their staff have passed beyond the door that seems so solid and unwelcoming. And I reflect that in the rooms behind this dark, forbidding door, a multitude of arguments have taken place and been resolved, and countless lives have been affected, some perhaps transformed.

I understand my presence here grants no enduring right. I am to be a transient lodger in these rooms, with temporary access to the knowledge and the wisdom stored within. Perhaps one day I too can add my own experience. From now on it will fall to me to offer comfort and encouragement to those who visit here. And when I can, I'll offer resolution too. Now and beyond the present century, this house will be the backdrop to the dramas that are other people's lives.

Chapter 31

But in the present hour, I cross the threshold with a junior colleague at my side. Excitement mingles with the trepidation that I feel. Inside, I see that portraits of my predecessors line the walls. Above the entrance hall, a picture of a hunting scene commands my gaze. It's vast. By contrast, the receptionists are housed ignobly at a spartan desk pushed far into the corners of the room.

I see at once what is important here and what is not.

The senior receptionist, slight, fair-haired and anonymously pale, jumps to her feet.

"Good morning, Mrs Cox. Please come this way."

She ushers me towards the staircase, its balustrade and sweep magnificent. I beckon to my colleague, but before we reach the second stair, the fair-haired lady leaps in agitation to her feet. Hands raised and flailing, she demands that, though she will allow me to proceed, my young companion must retrace her steps.

She glowers at my colleague. "Oh no. I'm sorry, but not you." It is clear she has been briefed on what must happen here and who should pass. "This is the partners' staircase. Members of the staff must use the other stairs."

The rights and duties of a partner in this firm seem little different from those that have pertained throughout the past two hundred years. Change will come slow to Bedford Row.

I learn that every morning, as has happened through the decades that have passed, three partners are required to supervise the opening of the post, and every Friday I am to be one of these. We sit at a mahogany table in the downstairs library. Beside it, empty wicker baskets will be filled with all the post that each department will receive this day. The room is darkened by the bookcases that line the walls. The door is left ajar, propped open by an antique hole punch, its black contour embellished with a fading gold. The full-length windows are obscured by opaque, semi-frosted film. The shabby curtains echo the disdain of those who are established and secure.

But I am here to work and though I'm fascinated by this glimpse into the past, it's not the setting of my workplace that will dominate my mind. Each weekday through the years to come, unless I'm travelling to some far-flung court, I am to pass, unseeing, through these rooms, my only focus being the dilemmas of my clients. Elegant and full of history as they are, surroundings count for little in my clients' worlds.

Strange New World

I too am, for the most part, unaffected by the shabby grandeur of the building that is to be my home or by the rigid rules prescribed by those who've followed them since they began their working lives in Bedford Row. I am surprised to find that many of the partners in this firm have only ever practised here. No other way of adult life is known to them. In time I'll learn that I must tread with sensitivity if I'm to gain support for any innovations or new working pattern I might hope to see. It is clear these partners will not lightly yield to any threat to their established way of life.

For now, I simply shrug and build myself a sanctuary where I can work untroubled by new partners or by unfamiliar ways. The antique desk with rounded corners that I bought in Exeter to celebrate my partnership is wheeled across the road and carried up the stairs. Upon my office wall I hang a print of nineteenth-century Chiswick riverside. Its opaque tones of white and grey evoke the magic of the early morning mists that shrouded fishing boats at rest. My mind recalls the silent world of which I also was a part, as twenty years ago I walked the river path to catch the bus to college where I studied law. This image of tranquillity is solace to the dramas that unfold within my clients' lives and mine.

And on the mantlepiece I place a tiny cardboard box of palest blue, within which is contained a silken bag of pebbles that my aunt collected for me from the banks of Knighton's River Teme. Inside the box lid is a rhyme that she once penned to soothe me as I faced the turmoil of a life beyond the peaceful haven of my childhood days. The stones are rounded, cool and comforting to touch. This loving aunt has always understood that nature and its deep-remembered joys would be my consolation through the storms of life to come.

And settled in, I find all else irrelevant for now. In any case, I am distracted as the telephone intrudes. A would-be client gives a monologue in deep Germanic tones. In his distress he lacks coherence but his story's mine to comprehend and gradually I learn that, through a challenge to his daughter's right of custody, this man's beloved grandson has been made a ward of court. And thus begins a saga that will last for years, as parents vie to keep the care of this young boy. The old man finds it hard to understand the role the English courts must play in German lives because the child's family has dwelled here for just months of his young life. No member of the child's past or future family plans to live in England once this case has been resolved. His mother wishes to return to Germany and to her family home. His father claims the mother's parents are unfit to have an influence on his child. Thus, though he also plans to move back home to Germany, he asks the English court to halt the mother's plan. His desperate ploy will bring the father time. It also brings disharmony, uncertainty and pain. The case will take two years to resolve. And in the meantime, rifts that could with understanding have perhaps been healed will widen into chasms that are never to be bridged.

I am conscious that although for me a case like this is just another day or month or year of work, for every child and parent caught up in a struggle of this kind, the outcome will forever change the future that they once believed was theirs to fashion and to build.

It falls to me to understand and to illuminate each client's hopes and fears. But I commit myself to more than this. In every case, regardless of the adults' rights and wrongs, I'll strive to shield the innocents concerned. I realise, with sadness, that so often children are the helpless casualties of conflicts caused by those who claim to love them best. And whilst I cannot change the past behaviours that have brought such parents to dispute, I have a role to play. My quest will be for harmony, for reconciliation and for peace.

4 January 1994

At home in Netheravon Road, I wake. My eyes alight upon the silver stars that glitter on the ceiling of what just weeks ago was someone's nursery. Today the shining stars reflect my mood.

This house is new to Alistair and me. It does not bear our personality as yet. Our furniture is only partly here. Yet it is in this house that there will be a gathering to celebrate the wedding that takes place at noon.

I rise and take a bath and quickly wash my hair. The skirt and jacket I decide to wear are ones that are familiar and well loved. Above the gentle, unassuming beige are folds of palest cream. This silken collar forms a ruche that swathes and frames my face. It brings an echo of celestial piety that contrasts with the tumble of my dark brown curls.

Today I'm organised. At seven o'clock the cleaners come. They do their work and go. The flower man arrives. He brings in three large terracotta vases, each one filled with simple flowers of white.

"Here?" he queries, looking with disdain at the utility sideboard squashed beside the green-tiled hearth. "Yes, there," I say, with all the certainty I feel today.

The caterers are here as well. I will not cook today. So, James and Emma will prepare the salmon and the courgette salad that I want our guests to eat. The guests are few and most of them are elderly. I do not want them to be taxed by food that is too rich for them.

And some hours later, we return from church. Alistair and I walk hand in hand along the road where sycamores are bare but where in weeks to come hope is to be reborn as buds appear and springtime comes.

My parents come inside. They both remove their shoes and put their slippers on. I want to tell them there's no need. But now and forever I'm their child. I do not tell them what to do.

My husband's mother stands beside the cousin she has brought with her to keep her company and ease the nerves she feels. Her hat and costume are of royal blue. I cannot read her thoughts, but I am gladdened by her gracious smile.

And camera in hand, her modest presence boldened by her faux fur hat, my Aunty Florrie hovers anxiously.

My sister and her family sprawl on the sofa, hiding its shabbiness. My younger niece darts to the kitchen – in and out she flits and flirts. At twelve, she's rather drawn to James and is determined he should notice her and all the charm she's learning that she has.

And then comes Mrs Ray, my neighbour from the house at Riverview where I had lived since 1972. Our parting had been sad but stoical. Life shifts and we move on.

"Twenty years," she'd sighed as I returned the crockery and garden tools I'd borrowed in the years gone by. "And never one cross word."

Mrs Ray refused to join us at the church. She says she's had enough of church. I'm glad she's with us now. I understand.

Her husband died quite recently. He was the keeper of our street, checking constantly that things were as he deemed that they should be, bemoaning those who made a noise at night and watering my plants when I was not at home. Through all the turmoil of my personal life, I felt so safe with Mr Ray next door. In his last weeks, I visited him each day. I often picked for him a single rose of palest apricot and brought it to him in a crystal vase.

"Ooh! Big as dinner plates," he'd say, his rheumy eyes protruding

Chapter 31

from his shrunken yellow face. As if he'd never seen a rose before. Or else as if he feared each rose might be the last bloom he would see.

I glance towards the sofa where my younger niece writhes, full of energy. Her elder sister is composed and slightly tense. It's almost time for me to grace my wedding day by passing on the joy and the good fortune that my bouquet represents. And so, I take my flowers from the table where they rest, and I caress the ivory roses and the lisianthus that I carried to the church. With care, I separate the stems as I untwine the tangle of the clustered blooms and fronded ferns. And, as I plan that it will do, the bouquet parts as it is tossed across the room. And thus, with outstretched hands, my nieces each receive the blessing that this token of my married love imparts.

At last, we sit to eat. Champagne is poured for everyone apart from Mummy, who I know won't drink.

"Not this one, James," I say.

But Mummy is indignant.

"You have missed me out," she says, her lips drawn in.

A quarter of an inch of Bollinger is poured into her glass as she demands.

Our glasses raised, I look at Alistair. He looks at me. I wonder at the peace I feel. On this rare day, I seem to have no nerves at all. And Alistair is calm itself. It is as if we understand that God approves the plan we have.

I smile and sigh a little. I am married now.

32

BITTERSWEET

1994–1997

New Beginnings

And now begins a married life that's shared – something that I've never known before. A life that in my youth I wrongly thought would come my way with ease. It brings the simple pleasure domesticity affords. It brings companionship, a precious gift I never had the chance to understand. It shows how marvellous an ordinary life can be.

I will not tire of it. I'll never find it boring or frustrating when my husband watches cricket for what seems like days on end but always finds his way into the kitchen when it's time to lunch. I'll cherish all the hours we'll sit in silence on our sofas reading newspapers and books. And every weekend, I will marvel when it is my husband's turn to bring the mugs of coffee to our bed.

The tiny ripples that will surface on the face of married harmony are transient. They don't disturb the balance that this marriage brings to all the dramas of my working life. My husband watches silently as working hours expand to fit the needs of someone else's tragedy. He'll sometimes find it hard to hide his irritation when our phone is used for messages that I accord priority above our comforting routine. He frets and grumbles when I am late home, exaggerating all the risks that he supposes face a woman on her own at night. Just now and then he'll tell me that I love my clients more than him. But then the mask of fractiousness will slip.

"Now tell me," Alistair will ask me with concern. "Have they found kidnapped Tristan yet?" Or "How is little Mario today?"

For all the irritations, he accepts me as I am.

And I accept him too.

Chapter 32

Knighton

In 1996, we travel back to Knighton for a visit to my Aunty Florrie and the sleepy border town that was my childhood home. In Knighton it is just another ordinary day; yet in its changelessness, it is exactly as I hope that it will always be. Beyond the grey stone wall where sheep once grazed, the willow trees still grace the riverbank. And watching like a sentinel upon the mound that rises high above the yellow green stands Knighton's church. I sit upon the well-worn steps where once I played with pebbles or with ration books. The sun streams down upon another perfect Knighton afternoon as memories reunite me with my childhood joy.

But yet, for all the recollection of that sweet familiar past, there is a difference today for here beside me now sits Alistair. His hair is tousled but his gaze is steady and there is no tension in his stance. My arms enfold him as I smile for Aunty Florrie's camera. My brown curls tumble carelessly. They match the casual shirt I wear. I have no thought today of how I look or what the camera will reflect. But in the photograph that Aunty takes, the happiness that I exude will lighten life throughout the years that lie ahead.

To this same cottage many years ago my Grandad Taylor brought his shy Edwardian bride. And in the background of the picture can be seen the window of the room where I was born.

And now at last, my husband is a part of this. All that I loved, and love, are melded here today. And in this instant, captured by my aunt's unerring glance, is glimpsed a life that is forever free of all the sorrows of the past and all the cares that are to come.

If only I had known how close those cares might be, would I have faltered in my happiness?

The First Cloud

A few months on, the mood has changed. Around me everything is gathering speed and moving with relentlessness towards a destination I try not to see.

At Christmas time, the first cloud scuds across the azure sky. For, visiting my parents at their Hemel Hempstead home, Aunty Florrie suffers what will be the first of several strokes. In consequence, her movement is impaired, and she is stranded scores of miles and more from home.

And my role changes now. No longer am I simply Aunty's loved and loving niece. I have become her legal guardian too. Despite her closeness to my parents, common sense dictates that someone younger now must be her voice.

As I now ponder ruefully how I can help my aunt, I call to mind that once, in poetry, she wrote that Knighton, "sheltered by hills too gentle for renown" was "where I was born and where I hope to die".

Now more than ever it is Knighton where she longs to be. Her words will haunt my conscience for a lifetime through.

For I'm aware of all the difficulties that must be overcome if she is now to go back to her Knighton home. She is too frail to live alone. In Knighton there are few resources that are able to provide the care she needs. For all that Aunty Florrie's life has focussed on its school, its church, its poor, the town she loves is not equipped to help her in her hour of need.

But Aunty does not know this as she gazes at me from her bed.

"I leave it up to you. I give you my implicit trust," she says in tones that tell me that her future's mine to order and resolve. She turns away to contemplate less worldly things.

I won't give up. However difficult my struggle with the doctors and authorities may be, I am determined that I'll find a way that Aunty can return in safety to her home. I think that I'm the only voice my aunt has now. But I am wrong, for there's another voice that matches mine in its determination and its strength of will. For Mummy, practical and unemotional, is of the view her sister's needs will be much better met if she remains in Hemel Hempstead in my parents' home. She disapproves of my attempt to satisfy my aunt's desire to return home. At eighty-nine, my mother still believes that she can take care of the younger sibling who she loves.

And, as in childhood, I now feel again the fierce ferocity that is the conflict of our wills. And, as in childhood, Mummy's will prevails. For Aunty Florrie gives a final word I know I must respect.

"What is important," she instructs, "is that your mother's not upset."

A Deeper Shadow – August 1997

But suddenly this struggle is irrelevant as now we learn that it is Mummy and not Aunty Florrie who is close to death. How could we not have

Chapter 32

noticed this? Her shrunken body with its lately jaundiced skin is host to cancer now. It is untreatable. I wonder how much pain she must have borne without complaint. It is too late to help her, and she has just weeks to live.

It is unthinkable that anything can vanquish her determination and her eagerness for life. Her power has always dominated and eclipsed. She's always strived to forge a path for me. Her tireless energy propelled me where she thought that I should go. And even when she realised the will masked by my gentle mien could match her own, she would not let this stifle all the certainty that she possessed. Yet as I moved beyond the world she understood, we found ourselves adrift and stranded on the separate shores of lands the other could not enter or regain. Although we always travelled with each other in our sights, there was a distance that we could not cross. We never talked, except of trivialities.

It's different now.

Firmly, Mummy gives her last commands as she insists that if she is to die, she'll die in her own bed. She tells us with precision how she wants us at her side as she departs. And she is adamant that she won't leave us on a day the sun she loves shines bright upon the earth.

But following these insistences there is serenity. The worries of the last few months and years and decades are behind her now. She lets them go. And finally, her words are personal. She speaks of things that she has never brought herself to say before. The words I hear her utter to my father break my heart. To me, her sometimes troubling child, she makes one first and last request. She's always feared for me. She worries when I offer help or shelter to someone I barely know. And in her final days she makes this clear.

"Darling. No more waifs and strays. Please."

I know at once that this request is given out of love and from concern. I know at once I cannot honour it.

Chiswick

Beyond my mother's bedside, life continues as it must and as she urges that it should. Thus, on a sunny Sunday afternoon while Mummy languishes and waits for death, I go with Alistair to see a house that is for sale. It is in Elmwood Road, a Chiswick Street with houses built around the year of Mummy's birth.

Our search has been desultory. We are not really certain we should move. But as the owner opens up the dark green door, we are beguiled. Before us lies a vista of successive rooms. Each one is dressed in shabby chic though this style has no name as yet. Antiques and paintings complement the elegance this house displays.

My gaze is drawn beyond the well-proportioned rooms, and it alights upon the terrace which is crammed with tables topped with pots of daisies and geraniums and pinks. Beyond these, I espy a smoke bush with its fluttering purple leaves. They form a graceful backdrop to a perfect rose of purest white.

And, as at Riverview so many years ago, enchantment claims me, and I know at once this place will be my home. And as my husband turns and looks at me, I see he knows it too.

3 November 1997

In Bedford Row, I try to focus on my work. But time is shorter now, so one day on an impulse I postpone my conference and make my way with speed to Mummy's side.

I am too late.

A nurse stands at the open door and greets me as I hasten up the garden path. Her outstretched arm together with the pity in her eyes inform me that her task is over now. Indoors my father and my aunt sit downcast and subdued. I cannot speak and nor do they. Our voices have been swallowed up by incredulity and pain.

Only the nurse has words.

"Lesley, I told her you were at the garden gate. I think that she was reassured. It made it easier for her to leave."

I tell myself I will not let her go. I am not ready yet. I hold her. She is still warm.

At last, I creep away and join my father and my aunt.

I'm shocked by what I see. My father is reduced and somehow shrunken now. He seems to be much smaller than the father who, though eighty-four, was weeks ago a handsome man. What only yesterday was healthy sun-kissed skin, is dull and sallow now. Clothes that were freshly pressed and amply filled, now seem to gape and sag.

His eyes are heavy as with unshed tears.

The nurse returns and hands to him my mother's wedding ring. He

Chapter 32

trembles as he looks at me. Wordlessly he passes me that simple band of gold worn thin in service of her family.

And then he indicates my mother's bag. It's small and unobtrusive but she always kept it by her side. He gestures to me, and I understand this, too, is now in my charge.

It seems impertinent to open it. But as the evening deepens, finally I look inside. The contents are at first predictable. A lace-edged handkerchief of white enfolds an unused comb. But further down, my fingers touch upon a photograph. I look with incredulity. There, radiant, full of life and eagerness, a woman smiles, and I behold my younger self. I'm dressed in academic robes. My mother took this photograph upon my graduation day. And I am moved to realise that love and pride have kept it close to her for thirty years.

33

A WIDER WORLD

1997–1999

Aftermath

Within a few hours of my mother's death, the Knighton undertaker comes to take her body home. And on Remembrance Day, her burial takes place. It is a glorious late autumn day. The great red oaks look down upon her grave. I marvel at their splendour and their fortitude. Through every season Kinsley Wood endures, an ever-watchful witness to our lives.

My aunt sits in her wheelchair, silent and downcast. My father trembles as he points towards the open grave.

"Me next," he mutters as I scan his face, uncertain if this is a statement or a plea. Surely, I think, this cannot be a wry attempt at jest. Whatever his words may mean or seek to say, I understand that what he says is likely to be true.

In months ahead, there is a further blow as Aunty Florrie also dies. My father lingers on for just one year.

My world is shrunken with these deaths. For, though I've told myself that I have lived an independent adult life, I realise that this has been, in part, delusory. The truth is that for more than fifty years, my world has been marked out and framed by the solidity of family. Now suddenly, in months, the pillars of my childhood are dislodged. They crumble and they vanish from my sight.

But I take comfort in my husband's steadfastness. His presence anchors me.

Despite my grief, my world continues to expand as all the gifts that I received throughout my past are mine to use and share. And now, perhaps because there is a wider gap to fill, I focus yet more energy on others who, though strangers, cross my path in need of friendship and support.

Chapter 33

Climbing the Mountain

In parallel to my instinctive wish to nurture and to serve is my belief that I must always rise and do the best I can with what I am and what I have. In childhood, I was often told that I would shine in life. Yet I have shown it is so easy to fall back and not achieve the things that others think I should. The things that challenge me are sometimes trivial. They are so often things that other people do with ease, like going to a cinema or simply standing up and letting people notice me. Yet I am resolute. Despite my ever-present anxiousness, I must face up to every challenge that may come my way. The grim assessment of the Bethlem doctors lingers in my mind. I will not justify their negativity. I will make something of the life that I've been given. I will not let their caution hold me back. I won't be cast aside by them. Or anyone.

In 1999, I'm asked by Mr S if I will be the English speaker at a German legal conference on Family Law, a gathering of academics and professionals. I am aghast. Inside I tell myself at once this is beyond my courage and my capability. Yet, strangely, I can see that Mr S is almost hoping that I will say no. Although he likes to revel in the benefits that my professional success has brought, he is unsure of me. Perhaps he's anxious that I'll move beyond a script that he himself approves. Perhaps he also doubts my competence. He is the chairman of the Anglo-German legal group. It's his responsibility to find someone to speak. I am a natural choice. He once was brave and generous enough to offer me a tiny share within the business that he had created for himself. Perhaps it suited him to harness the enthusiasm that he saw in me. Yet in my presence, he is uncomfortable. He needs the women in his life to soothe him and to make him feel at ease. I will not flatter him. I cannot do the things that he's accustomed to expect. And now, as always, I can see he is reluctant to invite a new initiate into his private world. Especially a woman. Especially me.

Sensing his ambivalence, I answer with a rising flood of energy and pique. "Of course," I say. "I'd love to speak."

I will not be diminished by his doubts. And now the mountain's mine to climb.

In weeks, I stand behind a lectern on a rostrum in a crowded room in Bremen's best hotel. I'm eaten up with fear and yet I somehow smile and hesitantly test the microphone.

"Good morning. Can you hear me?" I inquire.

"Nein."
"No."
"Speak up."

The brutal answers devastate. Then, as at last I start to read the script I have prepared, I hear a crash. A late arrival trips and almost falls as he makes haste to join the audience.

"I am so… sorry," says the lawyer with the flaxen hair and deep Germanic tones.

"It's quite alright." Instinctively my answer seeks to soothe. I pause and then, from nowhere, comes a thought I can't suppress. "It would be so much worse if you were trying to get out."

I hear a murmur of amusement. It isn't quite a titter, yet it's tangible and tolerant, and as the ripple spreads, it reassures me that this audience is willing to accept me for the person that I am. And as I'm lifted on the crest of their encouragement, the hour passes in a mutual camaraderie as my imagination planned that it would do.

At lunchtime, as the delegates disperse, I see that, hovering and watching with his slightly twisted smile, Mr S prepares to speak to me. And for an instant I imagine that he may tell me that I have done well. Perhaps, I dare to think, he will invite me to have lunch with him. But this self-centred, agitated man now fidgets and contorts and can't disguise his feelings of relief.

"At least," he sniffs, "you were not a complete disgrace to me."

Impatient to be rid of me and all the complications that I represent, he turns his back and disappears within his coterie.

Standing alone within the now deserted hall, I'm left to contemplate that as we rise and take life's challenges, we have to be prepared to walk our paths alone. For as we dare to differentiate ourselves, we sometimes sacrifice the comfort of the crowd.

A Quest for Justice

Meanwhile in Bedford Row, another tiny miracle occurs. The leading partner of this firm that is so steeped in hierarchy and class proposes we should also serve the ones who cannot afford legal fees. Thus far, each lawyer has been free to take on legal aid work as and when they choose. It isn't lucrative and it's not often favoured when each partner must have profit as a primary goal. But cases have been squeezed into a busy schedule

Chapter 33

as a personal choice. It will be different now. The Government decrees that those who give a service paid for by the state must prove themselves entitled to a franchise granted on the basis of efficiency and competence. It will take many hours of unpaid work to put in place the systems that will justify a contract of this kind. And there will follow many years of working for a meagre recompense. But if we can succeed, new worlds will open up and barriers to justice will be broken down. It is a worthy aim. It's heartening to realise that common ground may lurk behind the very different facades that individual partners may present. Perhaps, I think, I have misjudged the characters of those with whom I am in partnership. But I soon realise that very few agree this is a goal we should pursue.

It is proposed that I should be the franchise representative. The partners gathered round the table in the meeting room are for a moment stunned. But soon enough they have their say.

"This isn't quite the kind of client this firm serves."

"But Lesley, you are one of those who brings in all those hefty private fees we need."

"You'll have to work much harder for your keep."

"I think you must have lost your mind."

But somehow all objections of this kind are swept aside if not entirely overcome. And within weeks we pass the necessary audit, and I am free to work for all who seek my help. It's been a test for me to undergo the necessary scrutiny whilst facing down the general disapproval and dissent. But in exchange for all the extra work that I must do to keep my equal place within the partnership, I have unlocked a world in which I am at once at ease. It is a world of strangers stemming from all sectors of society and from every corner of the earth. And all these clients have in common is the present trauma in their lives, their anguish and distress. Their solitary paths are mine to tread with them. My past experience and strength are theirs to use. What is to bind us now and always is our shared humanity.

In years to come I'll persevere to reunite those stranded by the ravages of separation and divorce. I'll share the blows of the injustices made manifest when power is unequal and truth is sacrificed upon the altar of expedience. I'll soothe the parent of a kidnapped child. And, if it takes me years, I'll fight for justice for the dispossessed. And now and then my mind will fly back three decades to Bethlem and the moments of compassion that I witnessed there. And I will watch once more as foul-mouthed Josie kneels at Diane's feet and shares her sorrow as she weeps. And with humility, I will recall the strangers in whose presence seeds of charity were sown as I absorbed the precious gift of selfless love.

34

MILESTONES

2000–2013

Birth of a Century

The new millennium is here. It seeks to separate us from our past. We are exhorted to be bold and to imagine wondrous new achievements and experiences. We must shake off the gathered cobwebs of the century that gave us birth and embrace what is now unknown. We are swept up within the vision of a future in which we transcend the shackles of the past. Yet time is merciless and even in this hour of joy, it does not falter as it surges onwards, counting down the minutes, hours and years until, in this millennium, we reach the moment of our death.

But Alistair and I don't bring such thoughts to mind. We raise our glasses of champagne and tell ourselves the future is our own to mould. Next day, a perfect morning dawns. The sun streams through the window of the bedroom that we share. In bed we linger with our coffee and our papers in the casual comfort of another ordinary married day. Then as my husband browses through the pages that have extra volume at this festive time, he chances on a list of all the pop songs that have topped the charts throughout the past decades. And side by side we recollect our separate pasts until in harmony we sing our solid memories. And, as we do so, we create what in the years to come will be a joyful memory of the present day.

The Anchor Found

And now in Alistair I've found the anchor that has all the solid certainty to harness me throughout the storms of life. The anchor cleaves to me as we explore the universe that draws us ever outwards to infinity. Yet here, on more familiar ground, the anchor is indulgent in its faithfulness. It gives me space and latitude so I can stretch, my energy unstifled, as I reach to others who still flounder in life's shallow lands. The anchor understands my restless need to succour and to serve. It watches with forbearing as just now and then I float away. And in its steadfastness, it waits for me.

Beyond the Sanctuary

But life for me extends beyond this precious sanctuary, and all the energy that peaceful life conserves flows over into my professional role. My clients' traumas are my personal concern, their distress mine to heal.

In court, I sit beside the father who is not allowed to see the children that he loves – and who love him. Their mother claims it's so much better for them all if he and they are kept apart. She details tiny imperfections that she somehow manages to transform into stumbling blocks. And even though the anguished eldest child writes to the judge and pleads to see the father he adores, the letter is dismissed as sheer recalcitrance. The judge holds this a greater sin than parting children from someone they clearly love. Beguiled by her, this judge will not accept the mother can be cold and cruel as her child describes.

"Who is it who puts words like this into a child's mouth? I won't accept this lovely lady does not speak from goodness and from truth."

Perhaps this young boy has been taught that actions will speak louder than the words he penned. He runs away. He runs away again and shelters in his uncle's home. And while we wait unknowingly in court, the judge sends police and tipstaffs to break down the doors behind which this brave, frightened boy has put up barricades. And when the news of this young boy's removal from his place of refuge is announced in court, this gentle father is impassive, even though inside his anger burns. And I am witness to a justice that, against all moral sense, requires that the protection of a child shall, on occasion, justify arrest, displacement and abuse.

The Woman and the Child

And so begins this new millennium. Somehow, I am at one with all that matters now. I have learned that other people's travails can be lessened if they are shared. And Alistair stands by to give me respite and to catch me if I falter or I fall. And when I leave the shelter of my ordinary life, I am a witness to the things that need to be uncovered and disclosed. And in the years to come, the sustenance this marriage brings emboldens me to use the voice that will speak out for justice and for truth.

Chapter 34

Yet deep inside the woman that I have become, the vestiges of childlike anxiousness remain. Like every human being I am a mélange of fragility and strength. And if at times I seem to stride with certainty along life's toughest paths, at others I may be undone by panic at some triviality.

In my professional role I must conceal the weaknesses I have. With Alistair there is no need for me to hide.

One day as we traverse the jungles of Malaysia, we reach a resting place where bamboo houses sit on stilts beside a lake. Inside, the décor mixes comfort with an ethnic authenticity and charm. It seems to offer everything a western tourist might demand. But as I venture to the bathroom, I recoil. For there, inhabiting our washbasin are two enormous creatures of a species that I cannot quite identify. And as they rear and display giant legs and wings, I scream and flee. Hysteria does not befit a woman of my years. Yet as I throw myself beside my husband on our bed, he gently puts his arms around me as he slowly speaks. And as he cradles me, he does not chide or ridicule. He simply asks me to think back to childhood and to Kinsley Wood.

"Do you remember little Sammy Squirrel? Little Susie Squirrel too? You say your grandad told you that they were your friends. Well, it's no different now. These are not squirrels. But they are your friends. Billy and Betty Beetle, let us say."

The child within relaxes in response to Alistair's acceptance, sensitivity and love.

Three Score Years and Ten

Thirteen years have passed since the millennium. But now there is another milestone, this time of a far more personal kind. In January, I will reach the age of seventy years.

South Africa is where we choose to spend these days of celebration and of thankfulness. The villa where we linger stands between the barren mountain and the sea. The brightly coloured bathing huts illuminate the scene as False Bay stretches out into the vastness of the ocean reaching far beyond our view.

We are the only guests, and we are cared for by Good News, the owner's general factotum, who is as efficacious and as cheerful as his name implies. A housekeeper comes in each day to cook. Cocooned within this sheltered household, we unwind.

"I've never seen you so relaxed," says Alistair.

But one day, as our driver waits to ferry us along the Cape, my husband can't be found. And though in minutes Good News shepherds him towards our car, I am disquieted.

Good News seeks to reassure. "So many strange rooms. A visitor is easily confused."

The word strikes like a hammer on a corner of my mind that is reluctant to admit our peaceful life will one day be disturbed.

Confused? Not Alistair! I push the treacherous thought away.

The Mask

As I return to Bedford Row, I focus on the problems other people introduce into my life. My clients hail from Denmark or Dubai or from Australia or France. As fewer people can afford the cost of rising legal fees, I learn to deal with those who have to represent themselves. I write and speak about the challenge that this brings. For those who have no choice in this, I express understanding and concern. But lawyers find that they are often challenged by the litigants who choose to throw off the restraint that legal customs bring. Especially by those who seek to exercise manipulation and control. And sometimes, with the stripping back of objectivity and courtesy, we lawyers have to face the rawness of accumulated anger and distress. For here, unfiltered by professional skill, we see and feel the anguish of the very conflict that has brought our client's marriage to an end.

One day a colleague puts his head around my office door.

"I see you're in the news," he says. "At least the legal press."

His head cocked slightly sideways, his expression quizzical, he thrusts a copy of *The Law Society Gazette* before my face. It's open at a page that shows a list of those who have been recommended by their peers for special designation in their chosen field. And there to my amazement is my name: "Lesley Pendlebury Cox. Super Lawyer, Family Law".

It's hard to comprehend that I, once clothed in so much negativity, should be selected for this accolade. It is a wondrous affirmation of the way in which I choose to exercise the skill and the experience I have. And yet, despite my satisfaction and surprise, I sense a sorrow that I can't suppress.

For what if people knew the secrets of my past? Would my name still

Chapter 34

be recommended in this way? And what of those with whom, in Bethlem, I once shared repression and despair? Did they regain or find identity? Or are they, even now – if they are still alive – excluded and outcast? And if they have survived, have they the courage that I lack, to live without the mask? If they stood in my place, would they reveal their troubled past? What might they say if I were to unmask the sometimes flawed and fragile human being that is me?

35

A SENSE OF AN ENDING

2013

In Heaven's Reach

In early June, I sit with Alistair within the carriage of a green and yellow Alpine train. The Wengernalpbahn wends its way through meadows strewn with early summer flowers. It climbs the slopes that steepen gently, then it plunges into darkness as it traverses a copse of forest pine. In moments, light returns, as to our right the valley falls away and we are carried ever upwards till we reach the snow-capped mountains of the Oberland.

It's almost two decades since we encountered these majestic peaks and valleys that restore us each and every year. The air is cooler here and every breath invigorates. Each May and early June, we tread the mountain paths, in search of harmony and peace. Surrounded by the silence of companionship, we marvel at the changeless beauty that draws us back each year. For here, we feel at one with this great universe. And, now and then, we halt in awe as, suddenly, the clouds divide, and earth and sky are somehow melded in celestial light. And if we only stretch our hands towards the firmament, then surely Heaven itself will be within our reach.

And in the third decade of married life, we are in Switzerland once more. It is the first day of our visit to this beauteous land which brings us energy and joy. A land where we have never felt a moment of disquiet or anxiety. A land where we are sure that endless peace is ours to find.

But we delude ourselves.

For suddenly, as we walk side by side, my husband slumps against my left-hand side. I feel the pressure of a weight that in this instant he cannot support. Alarmed, I clutch at him, but I can't hold him, and he slips beyond my grasp and falls.

It's only minutes – less perhaps – until he speaks. Yet all at once our world has changed. This moment is to live forever in my mind. It is a moment that divides the present from the past.

Chapter 35

Unterseen

The doctors here at Unterseen assure us that their tests do not disclose an underlying reason for my husband's fall. They tell me that the complications of his long-term diabetes aren't to blame and that they diagnose no stroke or cardiac alert. They say that Alistair is medically as fit as, at his age and in his circumstances, he could hope to be. I'm puzzled but relieved. Yet Alistair complains of pain. His hip is fractured and must be reset.

"That is no problem," says the doctor who conveys this news. "We'll see to that."

I feel no qualm. My husband's sanguine too. His diabetes and his other illnesses have made us intimates with those who practise medicine. We trust in others' expertise and their assurances.

The following day, I wait while surgery takes place and suddenly, I feel a flicker of anxiety I cannot quite repress. The title of the book that I pretend to read disturbs me: *A Sense of an Ending*. And all at once I am aware that, in the farthest corner of my ordinary world, a tiny shadow creeps across the sun.

In hours, Alistair returns from surgery, and I am told that all is well. Yet somehow, I'm not reassured.

Wengen

That night, alone in our hotel, I gaze out at the silent splendour of the mountain peaks. I feel detached. I am enfolded in a separate, solitary world that seems to span the gap between the heavens and the earth. I'm shut off from the world where yesterday we felt so much at ease. A broken hip is surely not a threat to life. And yet, instinctively, I know that Alistair is now in danger of a kind that no one can forestall. I cannot share the trauma that engulfs him now. And yet there's nowhere else that I belong.

At 2 am, I am wakened by the telephone. I recognise my husband's voice, but I can't understand the words he tries to say. I only know that there is fear in every utterance he makes. And then there is another voice, much clearer but still filled with urgency.

"Mrs Pendlebury, you must come at once."

But I am trapped within this sleepy village nestling halfway up the mountain side. Only a train can carry me down to the valley far below and from there to the hospital. I have no choice. I have to wait for dawn.

Aftermath

When, hours later, I arrive in Unterseen, what greets me is a sight that I will never banish from my mind. My husband is awake but, in his agitation, he is not the man to whom just yesterday I bid a calm farewell. He is delirious. He raves that he is in a prison camp. That German princes come to visit him. That there's a Buddhist wedding for which he needs to source both food and wine.

But as he writhes, his face contorted, both hands clutching at my arm, the nurses sigh in thankfulness and relief.

"We'll make a bed for you. You have to stay with him. He is much calmer now that you are here."

The next two days don't see a change. So, timidly, I venture to the office of the nurse in charge. I need to understand what lies in store for us.

"Please can you tell me how much longer the effects of surgery will last – this temporary delirium that now torments my husband so?"

"But I am sorry, Mrs Pendlebury. I think you do not understand. The truth is it may never go away."

I'm stunned. I can't absorb the meaning of these words. What have they done to cause this transformation in the man I love? How is it that a broken bone has now become a broken mind? Why can't my husband be restored to me?

That afternoon I make my way back to the village to fetch the things my husband needs. Along its single street are scattered visitors returning from their daily hikes. Their chatter and their laughter seem inhuman to me now. How can they be so free of care? Do they not know the things I know?

36

COUNTERPANE

2013–2016

A Kind of Living

Our world has changed forever, yet in spite of Alistair's calamity, a kind of life goes on. For after all the horror of the fall and the delirium, I get my husband back. His ravings cease, at least for now. He learns to walk with crutches, and in days, we are at home in London once again.

Slowly I adjust and grow to understand our peaceful past will not return. Life from now on will be a patchwork counterpane – a makeshift coverlet that draws together all the different duties that now crowd the space in which I must contain a life.

And hide the pain.

My husband's need of loving care is now more evident. Painstakingly, he walks and tries to do the things that he has always done. But diabetic incidents increase and gradually I detect the signs of vascular disease.

The doctors say that our beloved mountains might be fatal for my husband now. It's hard to think that we may not return to Switzerland. I search for holidays that, at a lower altitude, won't tax my husband's health. Mallorca offers places where it's easier for Alistair to saunter safely and enjoy a different tranquillity. A small hotel we grow to love affords a perfect vista, and we sit for hours and watch the ever-changing, changeless sea.

But in between all this, there is still other work for me to do. Professional challenges increase. My clients may be few in number, but their situations demand empathy and fortitude. Just now and then, a colleague will suggest that surely I should give up work and stay at home to be my husband's nurse. I cannot contemplate what they propose. There is so much that's still for me to do. And if I am to find the strength and stoicism that my husband's situation asks of me, I need to balance this with action that is positive. Despite its pressures, my profession brings me opportunities to help my clients move away from trauma and towards a calmer, more rewarding life. Throughout the years, increasingly, I've struggled to accept a purely passive role in life. I need to change the things that must be changed. Yet facing Alistair's decline, I realise that one day there may be a challenge that it may not be within my power to overcome. And if I am to face this challenge with acceptance and with grace, I need to cling to the familiar consolation of that part of life that is unchanged. I need to reassure myself that I'm still me.

The Sad-Eyed Man

A client is imprisoned, briefly, on the basis of the allegations of his wife. She claims he's violent.

And when he is released, his only contact with his children must be supervised. But one night, poring over records that the contact centre keeps, I stumble on some words that I cannot allow to disappear.

"Mummy hit you, didn't she? Will Mummy hit me too?"

The scribbled record tells me of the soothing words with which this sad-eyed man replies, "It is OK. Your Mummy is a lovely girl."

And through the weeks and months, I am to realise that in this client's marriage, love and loyalty have been betrayed.

And though it is to take me years, I know that I must right the wrong that has been done.

Thus, from now on, the spirit of the sad-eyed man will have a silent presence in our home. It seems quite natural. For gradually, I'll grow to understand that this man and my husband, though they'll never meet, both share the fundamental value of respect – for the commitment marriage asks and for humanity.

Towards the End

And even though his frailty and fear are greater now, my husband never asks that I should banish every other focus of my dedication and concern. He does not ask that I should give up any of the work that means so much to me. He trusts in me. He knows that when he needs me, I will come to him.

I teach him how to use a mobile phone and press a button that will bring me rushing to his side. And on the many days he spends at hospitals,

Chapter 36

I'll be with him. He'll never have to face a medical appointment on his own. Or any other trauma in his life.

But one day, three years on from Unterseen, my husband has another serious fall. He breaks his second hip. Bleakly, I sit beside him in the hospital now that the operation has been done. He is not rational. He's restless, writhing, desperately trying to regain the comfort and the confidence that he once knew. It is in vain.

And when I cannot get a nurse to give him what he thinks he needs, my husband swings a fist into my face. No one notices, or if they do, it is irrelevant to them. I'm scared for him. I'm scared for me. I do not tell the doctors of this incident. I try to shut my eyes to Alistair's belligerence. It is another sign I do not want to see. But, even so, the doctors are aware of a deterioration in my husband's equanimity and mood. I tell them I am sure that any agitation and confusion will subside, the way they did in Switzerland. I see that they are not convinced. They do not seem to understand that what my husband needs is reassurance that the life he loved can be restored. The strength of Alistair's aggression underlines the terror that he feels.

Meanwhile, the nurses put him in a bed with bars. And only after this is done do they announce that I must give permission for these bars. I question them.

"Must you restrict him in this way?"

"The bars are for your husband's safety. We don't want another fall," they say.

But I am shocked. For even though this is for Alistair's wellbeing, the bed with high restraining bars that rise on every side entraps the man I love and fetters all the freedom he once knew. I am distressed. I am appalled. It seems to me this frail, white-haired man, once full of eagerness for life, is now incarcerated in a cage. It is unbearable. They don't appear to see my husband for the human being that he is. I remonstrate with them. I tell them that I won't agree.

"You must. We cannot let him go back home unless you do. A bed like this must be installed within your home."

I have no choice. I sign the book they thrust at me. But I resolve that even though there is to be a bed like this at home, I'll set my husband free the moment we are on our own.

I do not see that I no longer have the power to influence or to change. I do not realise how much my husband's torment is to overshadow both our lives. I am not ready for the horror of the loneliness that is to dominate the nights when Alistair will call to me unceasingly for succour and relief. I can't foresee that rest is to evade us through the weeks and months to come.

And when at last I understand the wilderness that I have reached, prayer is my only consolation and my only strength.

I cannot know how deep and how significant will be the impact of the supplication that I make.

Strangers on the Loneliest Road

Yet from now on, I will not be entirely alone. There will be strangers on the doorstep of the home where we have cherished privacy and peace. I cling to those familiar things that mask from me the truth that our lives are forever changed. The olive tree we planted years ago to screen us from the passers-by still shades the herbs beneath. The scent of lavender pervades the air. But other things are different now and one day, there beside the Elaeagnus hedge stand Alistair's first carers: Faizah, large, smiling, swathed in black, and her assistant, a young man with a half-shaved head and diamonds in his ears.

Other carers follow, till at last comes May. She kneels beside my husband so that he is not alarmed. She is to be his last true friend. She does not see him solely as a patient she must tend. She sees him for the man he is, with weaknesses and strengths as well. As Alistair responds to her concern, I notice that he also cares for her. And when, just now and then, there is some problem that he can resolve for her, I see my husband smile with satisfaction and relief that even now, despite it all, he has some usefulness.

"May was upset today. She could not find a place to park. She got a ticket. But I calmed her down."

Sometimes May brings her children with her, after school. They question Alistair about the students he once taught. He talks to them about the lessons they enjoy.

Briefly he lives again.

And in those moments, I too am alive.

Soon, too soon, other visitors arrive. Medical men and women with cases and instruments. They rescue us so many times: groups of exhausted angels wearing big black boots. They always try to bring me back to sanity, distracting me with kindly compliments about our home. Beyond my gaze, they work so quickly to ensure that Alistair will stay alive.

Although he tells me death is now his wish.

The Cage

Alistair must now live out his life within the confines of four walls. A bedroom is arranged for him in what was once our drawing room. The walls are aubergine and gold, the curtains finest silk. It is a room of books and paintings too. Here, in another life, Alistair would sit for hours to watch the cricket and to cast aside his worldly cares.

Memory and beauty pale before the cruel domination of the bed with bars that has become his cage.

Now, surely, I must set him free. But after I have lowered those restraining bars, my husband looks at me so sadly and with watering eyes.

"Please put them back again," he begs me anxiously. "Without them I am scared that I will fall."

One night, to calm us both, I also climb into the cage. Gently I lay myself beside the man I love. My arms enfold him, and I feel him gradually calm. Slowly his muscles are unclenched. And then he speaks to me or to the one he thinks I am. Softly spoken, private words.

"I have a secret," he says. "I need to tell you what it is."

I wait, and in a second, from my husband's lips, is thrown a dart. I understand he does not mean to hurt.

"I'm married," Alistair confides. He clutches me and pulls me closer to himself. "My wife is Lesley."

There are no further words.

No thought can tell me what this utterance reveals. I dare not give a meaning to those words that have escaped my husband's tortured mind. A thousand infidelities might lurk within his brain, once brilliant.

But who could say if any one of these was real?

37

END OF LIFE

2017

Time is the master of the universe. Time extends forever onwards to eternity. Time has the power to halt us at a barricade beyond which we won't pass. And when time wills, it crushes us.

February 2017

Thus, on a February night that's cold and dark and bleak, time forces me to pause and look at what I cannot bear to see.

Tonight, there is no respite from my husband's restlessness. He twists and turns. His speech is jumbled now. The rhythm of his breathing is disturbed. Then silence comes.

My finger dials the digits I have dialled so many times before and soon the ambulance is here. We speed towards the hospital. I'm numb as, once again, our future is in others' hands.

I wait outside the room where imaging informs the doctors that my husband has not had a stroke. I breathe again, but only for an instant, for there's more to come.

"It is a haemorrhage," they calmly say.

I grip the stretcher as they wheel him to a ward. I will not leave my husband's side.

8th Floor East

On 8th Floor East, I realise that Alistair and I have reached the ward that is reserved for the acutely ill. Alistair is silent, almost motionless. He's drifting further outwards to somewhere that I can't go.

Mine is the only voice that he has now. Shyly, but insistently, I cast my eyes towards the doctors standing by my husband's bed.

"What will you do now?" I ask.

Chapter 37

Their backs are turned to me. At first, they do not seem to hear my voice.

"What will you do – to help?" I ask again, more urgently.

I put my trust in them. The medical men and paramedics have always brought relief, however short-lived this might be. I do not doubt that Alistair will be revived once more. But there's a pause. I'm apprehensive now. I cannot breathe. My throat constricts.

And then the senior doctor turns and smiles an urbane smile.

"Ah yes, my dear. There still are things that we can do to make it easier. We'll help. Of course, we will. We'll send the end-of-life team in."

The group of doctors do not seem to understand the impact of these words. They do not linger by my husband's bed. They do not reach to touch my quivering flesh or hold the hand that shakes with shock. They move away – a little bubble floating smoothly on the pool of ebbing life within this teeming hospital.

I'm overcome. I want to flee and yet I cannot leave my husband here. I'm full of fear as anger fights with duty and with love.

End of life. Not death – they didn't say that word. But end of life. I had no time to think of this till now. Only as I sit beside my husband's bed, passive and helpless, do I begin to realise what faces him – and me. And though I long for Alistair to be released from suffering and pain, I cannot contemplate the void that is to come.

End of life: these words evoke the vision of a perilous transition. For Alistair, I think that this might mean a path to the oblivion he seeks. For me, I know that it will herald a descent to chaos and despair. That's what dying is for those of us who have to stay behind.

Engulfed by isolation, I flee the lonely space beside my husband's bed. This is a spotlight I must shun. I will not stay.

I have to get away. I'm sweating now. Beyond the ward doors, there is life. I know there is. There must be life. I almost run till, standing by the lifts, I halt. I watch, in my confusion, as dark and hazy shadows zigzag into view and out again. Dimly, I realise that these are other people who don't seem to know or understand the torture in which Alistair and I are now submerged.

I telephone the faithful friend I speak to every day. But she's in Eastbourne, eighty miles away. I swallow and I mutter but my words don't come. End of life: words that in the months to come will stubbornly refuse to pass my lips. I can't go on. My hands are shaking and the phone falls through my fingers to the floor.

I turn. Despite my longing to escape, I cannot flee. For Alistair is still inside this awful place that I once thought so healing, friendly and benign.

I realise there is no exit from the hell in which I find myself. All that matters is contained within this present time and place. This hospital is now the only world we have. Here, God alone will dictate who may live and who must die.

And all who enter here are candidates for death.

Decorum and restraint have vanished and I'm sobbing now. Tears blur my sight as I press frantically upon the buzzer that will bring me through the doors and back to Alistair. I can no longer see or hear. Instinct alone will bring me to the bedside where I need to be. It must.

Yet I am wrong. For instinct does not guide me to my husband's bed. Sightless, I crash and hurtle sideways till I feel another human form which jolts against my bones.

Despite it all, politeness rises in my throat.

"Excuse me. I'm so sorry but…"

Then, as I raise my tear-stained face, I see a tiny miracle of sorts. In my confusion and despair, I almost do not recognise the transformation of the chaos that this figure brings. I can't believe the marvel that I see. For here is not some nameless form. Strangers there are within this hospital – a cast of hundreds, perhaps thousands: workers, visitors, the ailing and the nearly dead. Yet now, in disbelief, I look and see that here, beyond all comprehension, is my neighbour, Sasha – she of the kindly eyes, the ever-present warmth, the ragged jet-black hair.

A past and future comforter from that now distant and familiar land that was our home.

She takes my arm. My heart is pounding but it quietens.

"I need to go to Alistair. I need to be his wife until the end."

With sad assurance and compassion, Sasha nods and smiles. She comforts me. She tells me that in this, my loneliest hour, she'll walk with me.

"I'll come and watch with you awhile," she says.

And through the heavy veil of agony, I somehow see and realise that I am not alone.

Although I do not know it yet, I will tell someday that an angel brought this neighbour here. And that this miracle, so little and yet so immense, was just the first of those that were to come.

Chapter 37

And though I cannot know in this dark hour what light there is ahead, the truth is this:
In my end is my beginning.

38

AFTER THE END

2017

On the doorstep of our home, I stand alone. The sky is lowering and bleak. The scent of lavender has gone. And Alistair will not come back to me.

I won't recall his dying hours. One thousand times, with every tortured shudder of his breath, I felt my husband die. It is enough to say that I was with him to the end. And mortal angels who befriended me in this remorseless time surrounded me until he was at last at peace.

My body does not feel the same as it did yesterday. I can't be still, yet I don't seem to know the way to move my limbs. My breathing's shallow and each part of me is racked with rawness that I've never known before. Each noise is thunderous and each light blinds.

I am a stranger in a world that now seems hostile and closed off to me. I've lost all understanding of the way to navigate the life I've known for seventy years and more.

And yet in spite of this, I am compelled to live.

Somehow, I have to learn once more to do the ordinary things that in the past I have accomplished without thought. It's hard for me to step outside and walk along the street where I have lived for almost twenty years.

A neighbour, Charles, is passing, and he stops and asks me how my husband is. I try to speak but words won't come. I raise my hand and gesture, pointing to the window of the room where Alistair has lived for these past months. I shake my head. It's all that I can do. I cannot bring myself to speak the words that will announce that Alistair has died.

The Saturday Bus

It's Saturday and on this second day of widowhood, I force myself to leave our home. This is the day I always catch the bus to shop. At least, it used to be.

Chapter 38

Somehow, I reach the stop. I sit down on the slippery ledge where I have perched so many times before. I barely notice those who pass until my eye alights upon a figure that I recognise. Although I see him often when I go to shop, I do not know his name. And if I think of him at all he's just that curious man who travels on the bus I take each Saturday. It is his habit, as he walks, to pick up debris from the pavement and the gutter too. He does this every week. It is a task he relishes, it seems. His teeth tut. He mutters and he grimaces.

He turns the corner, and he strides towards where I am waiting for the E3 bus. He wears his blue checked cowboy shirt. His baseball cap is firmly pulled across his brow. A dangling shopping bag completes his weekend look.

His figure, tall and thrusting, stoops to scoop up cigarette ends from beside the bulging litter bin. My heart sinks for I hate to watch the irritation he displays. My eyes are lowered, for disturbance is especially unwelcome now. Why does he have to get *this* bus today?

Relief floods through me as the bus arrives. Despite my lethargy, I move a little swifter now. I will not let him trespass on my grief.

Somehow, I shop – although the pound I struggle to insert into the trolley slot won't fit. I try another coin, but the result is just the same. A stranger takes the coin and without effort frees my shopping cart. It's inexplicable. I do not realise that this new clumsiness is just another sign of loss and emptiness. My counsellor has warned me that perhaps I will not sleep at night. She reassures me that it's good to weep and let out all the anger that I feel. She does not tell me that the very rhythm of my being is to be disturbed. Or that the simplest tasks will be beyond me in the months to come.

Today, my shopping done, my basket filled with food I will not eat, I sit and wait once more for the returning bus. And once again I am disturbed. To my alarm I see that tall, familiar figure bearing down on me. The man on the bus is back.

He's angry now. And from his mouth, invective scatters, savaging my reverie. He spews out his disgust at Brexit and the gross insanity of those who voted to send home the Poles, who, he laments, are so much cleaner and much more hygienic than we Brits.

It is too much for me to bear. And suddenly I hear a plaintive voice and realise, to my astonishment, that it is mine.

"My husband died two days ago."

I see that he is shocked by this announcement of my pain – and so am I. He stops and for a moment all is quiet. I hold my breath. What have I done?

I cannot quite believe the impact of my words. For suddenly I see his arm is reaching out to me and, though he does not touch me, he enfolds me somehow as he shepherds me onto the E3 bus.

He sits beside me and at last he speaks to me in measured tones. He is detached. He does not speak of me nor of my husband's death. Instead, he speaks about a writer he has interviewed this week. He talks about the loneliness of age. His erudition calms as it distracts and, for an instant, I'm myself once more.

Our journey ends. It is as if our outbursts have not been. I walk away down Elmwood Road.

Dipa

Saturday has almost passed. But this tumultuous day is not yet done.

Back home again, I rest upon the sofa that is clothed in amethyst. I realise that I am seated where, throughout the years before his illness, Alistair would always choose to sit. Newspapers that engrossed him once lie folded and unread beside my feet.

My phone rings. It is May, the faithful comforter and carer who my husband loved. But she is brisk today and tells me that it is her daughter who has asked to speak to me. The voice I hear is clear. Its tone is pure.

"Mrs Pendlebury, this is Dipa here," the young girl says. "You must not be upset. Mr Pendlebury is in Heaven now. He's being so well cared for there. It is alright."

There is a pause and then she speaks with emphasis.

"And please don't worry. We are here – for you."

I'm stunned. I hardly know the girl who speaks. She's just a child. Her mother brought her to our home when I worked late and Alistair could not be left alone.

Dipa has a cruel muscular disease. At fifteen she is wheelchair bound. Yet in her disability and pain, somehow her innocence has been preserved. She and her siblings visited my husband in his final hours. I barely noticed Dipa gazing at him from the doorway of his room.

But in this moment of compassion, all the mists of mourning that surround me are dispelled by her belief and certainty.

Chapter 38

And suddenly I feel a tiny trace of life within the heart that I thought could not be revived. And through the grace that brings this young child into my world, a precious bond is formed. My grief has shattered any natural protection from the extremes of anguish and of pain. And yet as barriers dissolve, I realise that I have grown more sensitive to others' goodness and benevolence.

And thus, I understand at once the blessing that this young girl brings. For in this moment, Dipa teaches me that death is not the end of life and hope. And though the path ahead is to be strewn with sorrow and with challenges, throughout the days and years of desolation, I will cherish Dipa's words of faith and love.

39

THE SOLACE OF SIMPLE THINGS

2017

The narrow kitchen table wobbles as it always has done. It is a faithful and familiar friend, the centre of the life we knew. Here is the island where we loved to rest each night, sometimes exhausted from the tide of life we'd met that day. Sometimes we simply sat at ease as we revived within the silence that we shared. At times our words would tumble out. They were combative even – now and then. Behind our quiet eyes strong views would lurk. But mostly there was harmony.

It's over now, this interlude of closeness and companionship. And I must learn, once more, to face the strangers in this world.

The vicar, Martine, sits across the table from me now, thumbing through her bible, searching for a reading that reflects what thoughts of Alistair might bring to mind. I reject all that speak of powerful things and mightiness. But when the vicar offers the Beatitudes, I know at once that here are words with which I can identify.

Blessed are they that mourn, for they shall be comforted.

"The service will be yours to order," says Martine, thus giving me a focus and an energy that I had thought were lost to me. And in the days to come, I'll bring together words and music which will show the congregation something of the man my husband was. Not just a frail and frightened being struggling with the ignominies of illness and of age, but someone who once embraced life and love. And in return was loved.

And to remind myself that there is life ahead as well as in the past, my choices don't ignore those who just weeks ago were strangers in my life. And so it is that Dipa, in her wheelchair, sits before the chancel step and reads a simple prayer.

And I am comforted.

Ever Onwards

After the funeral, I struggle with my desolation and my grief. At night, I

Chapter 39

stare into the sky. Surely, I tell myself, Alistair is out there somewhere in that dark, remorseless, endless space. The placid moon reflects its pallor back. It also is subdued, as if in sympathy. I pray and plead: is there no moonbeam that will bring my husband back to me?

By day I stumble, and I falter as I force myself to walk and shop. I am so weary and each step I take reduces me.

Yet even now, I can take comfort from familiar things. Each day I pass the church. It also is a friend, a lodestone in my life. Edwardian turrets lend enchantment to this red-brick edifice which fronts the western corner of the street on which I live. Around the church a narrow garden lies and beckons temptingly to passers-by. Beside it, little children walk along the undulating wall, clutching confidently at their mother's hand. Older children clamber through the spreading branches of the gnarled magnolia. Neighbours of all generations gather here as they arrive to worship or to lend support. Others simply tread the well-worn path to make a shorter journey to the shops or pillar box. It matters not, for all are welcome in this place.

These scenes remain unchanged from day to day. Despite my grief, I marvel at the continuity of life.

Beyond the shrubbery, the heavy, studded door stands open to the passers-by. This darkened hollow seems to call to me. So many times in these last months I longed to enter here, just so that I might rest and pray. But I was always needed at my husband's side to ease the agitation that my absence seemed to bring. Respite was ever distant. There was no time then for myself.

But it is different now. And at this moment, words that I remember from the services that I attended through my childhood years echo in my mind.

Come unto me all that travail and are heavy laden and I will give you rest.

And as I glance towards the church, my gaze alights upon a tuft of celandines which pushes through the grass beside the porch. Despite inclement frosts and winter storms, this solitary clump endures as it returns each year. I love its stubborn bravery.

It calls to mind the hedgerow flowers that peeped through brambles on the roadside bank within the lee of Kinsley Wood. It brings a memory of long-gone childhood days when, sheltered from vicissitude, I seemed to live a life of endless joy.

I am in part restored by the remembrance of my childhood certainty and happiness and by the promise of renewal nature brings. And in this moment of relief, I lift myself and hug my recollected strength around me like some magic cloak that wards off all the evils of this world. But though at last I understand that there is light and life ahead, my healing is not yet complete. For now, my body is exhausted from the devastation of my grief. And yet, within me and despite it all, I can discern a tiny flicker of the incandescent flame of hope. And, as the tears of sorrow are at last released, I slowly drag myself into the church.

The Shaft of Light

Four months have passed. Throughout this time, I've sought in vain to find the perfect place where Alistair's remains might rest. Although it cannot matter to him now, it must be somewhere where I feel that he will be at peace. At times, my thoughts have turned to Switzerland where, in the mountains, we felt so at one with nature and the earth itself. The embassy assures me that my husband's ashes may be scattered there. But I am hesitant. It is so far away. And who will take me there to share his solitude?

He must stay closer to the life where memory of him endures.

Now finally I stand within a woodland glade not far from villages that Alistair once knew and loved. I also knew this gentle countryside. In springtime, I would gasp with joy as bluebells burst through moss and fern and carpeted the forest floor. And in our early married years, the two of us would roam the winding paths in harmony and peace.

Here in this tranquil setting, Alistair will surely be content.

Now, on this July day, the straggling burial party gathers here, drifting in twos and threes across the rough terrain.

Here between a beech tree and an oak, the ashes of my husband will at last be laid to rest within a grave that one day we will share. The quietness hangs heavy here. Only the scampering of woodland creatures and the rustle of the leaves will break this silence once the service is complete. Yet here, within this ancient greenwood, muffled sounds have no one to disturb. Birdsong will not bring my husband to a joyous wakening, as once it did.

We stand, unspeaking, as committal prayers are said. I shake with sorrow that I think will never pass. I cannot bring myself to say a last farewell. These final minutes trickle, unrelenting, like the sands of time, pushing me ever further from the past I loved.

Chapter 39

Too soon, the empty grave is filled. At last, I lay my purple freesias down. It's over now, I tell myself.

But I am wrong.

The sky is hidden from our view, beyond a canopy of trees. Although it's only afternoon, a deepening shadow falls. Unheeding of the other mourners, I am isolated and condemned to live within the bleakness and the emptiness of grief.

But then a miracle occurs. The darkness dissipates as suddenly there comes a shaft of radiant light. It filters through the tiny space between the intertwining trees. It seems to seek my husband's grave and, finding this, shines on the very spot on which my flowers are laid. We stand in awe, and no one speaks. This is a happening that is beyond our mortal grasp.

Subdued and overwhelmed, we silently depart. But I know this: Alistair is now at peace. And this I also understand: the path ahead, I will not tread alone.

The Dream

Next day I waken from the deepest sleep that I have had for many nights. It is a sleep in which there comes to me a dream so beautiful I set it down at once, lest I forget. It speaks to me from some now-distant place, surrounding me with memories of changeless watchfulness and love.

Within this dream, I travel through a house with many rooms. Alistair is with me. I cannot see him, but I feel his constant presence as the dream unfolds. From open windows, I look out onto the places where in our years together we found happiness.

The dream is filled with many colours. Music plays in every room.

Beyond the house, I sense that there is evil. Yet I have no fear, for with us is an unseen guide. I understand that nothing can disturb this harmony.

And as the dream draws to an end, the colours fade, the music stops. The rooms are bathed in radiant white. There is no place to rest, save for a ledge carved in a solid wall of rock, as in a sepulchre.

And at the end, when I awaken from this dream, I also am at peace.

40

LEARNING TO LIVE

2018

The Love of Strangers

It's Mother's Day. The house is full of energy. In the garden, children play, building hedgehog houses with the twigs that they have plundered from the plant they wrongly thought was dead. I smile and tell them how well they have done. In the affection and the playfulness these children show, I am reminded that life still has joy.

We have grown close, this family and I. They make me welcome in their home. With generosity, they share their lives with me. They carry out the promise Dipa made on their behalf, for they are always there for me, with kindness and with sensitivity. And when May senses that my mood is low, she brings her children to the phone.

"We love you, Lesley," they will chorus, banishing my melancholy and replacing it with joy.

Dipa is my godchild now. This formal title recognises both our need and bond. It also gives me easier access to the hospital where she is confined for weeks. I visit her most days. There's nowhere else that I prefer to be.

Unbelonging

My office has become a place of apprehension and of restlessness. There are changes that I cannot easily accept. In stepping back from seniority, I've opened up an opportunity for harsher management and practices which verge on bullying. And even though my life's work has been honoured with respect, in my diminished state of widowhood I find that I too am a victim of the changes that have taken place.

One day, just weeks after my husband's death, I am rebuked because my time sheet is not quite complete. I tell my critic that I know exactly what I've done. I have my notes. It won't be difficult for me to fill it in. Apparently, that is not good enough for him.

"You'll never get it right that way. If you aren't accurate, you'll be a fraud. You'll cheat the partnership. Or else you will defraud the clients you are here to serve," he says.

The accusation fells me, but there is more to come. The critic sees that I am shocked and that he has me in his power. As his diatribe continues, I shrink into myself. But I cannot escape his words.

"You ride a dangerous curve. The time is coming when you'll get your reckoning."

I can't believe what I am hearing but he speaks with such authority that in my lingering grief and lowered self-esteem, there is a part of me that thinks he must be right.

Inside my head the words collide in desperate dialogue. The bully's accusation that I am a fraud can't be dismissed. "A fraud". The words ring in my head. *A fraud? I cannot live if that is what I am. I cannot face the shame.* Then other thoughts pervade my mind. *You are a child of God. And you will live.* The inner conflict rages as the warring words re-echo in my brain. The bully cannot know the mortal struggle which his words have caused. But finally, this hector leaves the doorway where he'd blocked my path and left me trapped as if within a prison cell where I am guilty of some crime. For just an instant, I am paralysed. All certainty and self-belief have vanished with the bully's words.

And when, at last, I am myself again, I realise I have become a stranger in this place.

A Changing Role

Perhaps there is a world beyond the one in which I've flourished for these past decades. And though it is too early in my grief for me to understand, the truth is this: despite the devastation and the sorrows of my widowhood, I am now almost free of all constraint, save that of age and of my moral code.

I have a family of course. My sister and her children are all kind enough. But we have drifted as our busy lives took different paths. From time to time, they pay a visit. Now and then they ask me to their homes. They stand beside me when I mourn. But I am not essential to the lives they plan.

And that is not enough for me.

Though I don't realise it yet, I'm searching for a destiny that has so often been elusive or obscure. I'm reaching for a place where, though I've lost the anchor of my husband's love, I'll find fulfilment as I float within the freedom of acceptance of myself.

And through these days of change, as I adjust, it's Dipa's family who offer me the loving shelter that I need. Her younger siblings are just five and seven years old. Dipa's illness means their childhood can't be free from care, as mine once was. And yet their understanding of their sister's needs brings empathy, and this in turn augments the bond of love that outweighs any difficulty in their lives.

I'm struck by Kumar's sensitivity. He draws a picture for me and describes how he, at only seven years, has wept for "Mr Pendlebury". The youngest, Indu, loves to sleep in Dipa's arms upon her sister's bed. And when we visit Dipa in the hospital, her mother will not leave her stricken daughter's side. And thus, these precious two are often in my care.

Sometimes, when Dipa's agony can't be controlled, her howls of pain bring panic to the siblings that she loves. On one such day, I rush the children from the ward, and we take refuge in a playroom filled with toys that I hope may distract. But even here the screaming still intrudes.

"Is that Dipa?" asks her brother anxiously.

Suddenly I understand what I must do. It is for me to change the atmosphere and banish fearfulness. It is a challenge that I grasp. I long to lift these children from distress. And at this moment, my glance falls upon a toy guitar that lies abandoned on the playroom floor. Impulsively, I pick it up and strum a chord or two. And suddenly all semblance of decorum falls away as inhibitions melt before the overpowering certainty of deep protective love. For in this moment, I am Elvis, legs splayed outwards from my knees. My head is tossed from side to side as I gyrate. My shaken hair falls carelessly, obliterating my propriety. I cannot quite believe the spectacle that I, this creature of convention, now display. And yet the undiscovered self within me gasps with awe as I intone the words that once exploded on the 1950s world.

Don't you step on my blue suede shoes.
You can do anything but lay off of my blue suede shoes.

The magic works its spell. The children are entranced. Shoulders that were taut and rigid with anxiety now heave with laughter as they enter eagerly into the fantasy of make-believe.

Chapter 40

Hours later, when we have to part, the children leave reluctantly. And as we hug and break away and hug once more, I understand that God has given me another precious gift.

I have a part to play. I am alive.

41

A DIFFERENT WORLD

2018

As time goes by, I choose to spend increasing hours within the red-brick church in Elmwood Road. It's peaceful here and no one makes demands of me that I'm unready to fulfil. The congregation welcomes me with gentle smiles and nods. No one overwhelms me with a misplaced zeal. It is enough that I attend. They don't intrude. Yet they are ready to reach out to me. I am accepted here just as I am. They offer coffee but don't mind if I refuse. One Sunday, someone helps me find the place within the hymn book that I hold in trembling hands. There's always someone to provide the thing I lack.

And, as the months go by, within the quiet of the congregation, I learn to live again.

Beyond My Comfortable World

Sundays are now a day of hope. A day when I know I can rest and simply be. Yet unexpectedly, these days are also filled with strangers from the world beyond my comfortable married life – a world that I must navigate if I am to embrace the life that lies ahead.

And it's the driver of a minicab who offers me an outstretched hand to guide me through this new and strange environment.

In Alistair's last years the minicab became my friend. It saved me from the pressure of commuting by both train and bus. And in those years, I found the time spent in such cars en route to work was unique in the peace it brought. With Alistair's decline, the burden of responsibility lay heavy, both at home and in professional life, and while I gladly carried such a load, at times it seemed as if there was no respite anywhere.

They could not know it, but the kindly drivers changed all that. For just an hour or two each day, the driver was in charge. I was relieved and thankful then that, for a while, decisions would be made by someone other

Chapter 41

than myself. I could relax, at last freed from the raucous clamour of distress and anger that then overwhelmed my life.

Many of these drivers were once Afghan refugees. In their homeland some had been professional men. But trauma and the barrier of language condemned them to a lowlier form of work. They did it uncomplainingly, with courtesy and dignity. Sometimes, to my surprise, they turned to me for guidance and for help with bureaucratic problems they had struggled to resolve alone.

I answered with humility, grateful that these brave fugitives could reach to me, confident that there was help that I might give. They trusted me. They knew their questions would not be dismissed. With ease, I could provide the thing they lacked.

And in this way, these men showed me how easily most barriers can be dissolved – if we behave towards the strangers that we meet as we would like them to behave towards ourselves.

And now, to thank me for some simple help that I have given him, one driver invites me to a supper at his home. And on this evening, when I meet his children and his smiling wife, a page of life is turned. Impulsively, I offer that on Sundays I might help these children with the homework that their parents cannot always understand – and through this unexpected happenstance, my life is changed. I re-encounter eagerness and fun.

Sunday Afternoon

My empty house is silent, waiting for Karim and Razia. Everything is ready. The kitchen table has its cover on. The painted tin that once contained some garden tools now overflows with coloured pencils, Post-it notes and even glue. The cakes are in the tin marked 'Bread', but the children will know where to find them. They are familiar with the things I buy and where I keep my food.

Not everything delights. Karim is always worried by the bacon in the fridge. He has heard that anyone who eats this will burn in hell. I reassure him but I must not interfere.

Today I hear a rushing and a rattling at the door. The children tumble in. They hug their dad goodbye. Their father says that Maryam, his wife, has cooked today and she insists that I must eat with them tonight. It is a thank you for the lessons that I give. He calls me by the married name of which I am so proud. Only the drivers do that now. I smile and say I'll go.

Karim sets up his laptop. This takes him time but, though he rarely uses it, he is so proud of it. Razia, dainty Razia, is wearing a tiara on her head. She loves to try new looks. Once, she came in wearing her pink glasses over a piece of cloth with slits made for her eyes.

Karim pulls out his book. He is doing sums today. He does them quickly and I am relieved. I cannot help him understand the method, but I know when the answers are correct.

Razia is reluctant. Gently, I persuade her to read, but that's no fun for her. And so, we make a story – all of us. Karim is to begin, followed by Razia and then me. And so, an alien comes to land in a dragon's garden. Karim tells me that the dragon is angry because the alien has not asked permission to land on his lawn.

I think their parents might be pleased to have this story as a present. But not today, for Razia is bored and wants to go outside.

The garden is untended, but it is Razia's domain. And she is happy there to count the spiders' webs. She remembers the names of some of the flowers. I tell her others and encourage her to spell them back to me. From the vellum of the fallen magnolia, she will create a picture for her mother.

"Butterfly!" she shouts excitedly as it flutters by. A bee hovers. The children stiffen. I explain that the bee is only interested in flowers and pollen. Razia looks down at her dress, patterned with strawberries. "I hope the bee does not think that I'm a flower," she says.

My mind flies back to all the marvels of the natural world I knew in childhood long ago. I too was anxious at the bees which hovered near the woodland flowers that I longed to pick. And for a moment, I am young again.

We hurry back inside so that we will look busy when their father comes.

"Is there time for hide and seek?" they plead. "Just one?"

They scurry and I close my eyes. I know that I will find them behind the red velvet curtains or tucked beneath the campaign bed. The doorbell rings. Their father is now here. I tell him that they have been good.

They can't keep still. Is this – I ask – because the holidays are near?

"No," they tell me. "We are excited because you are coming to our house."

Chapter 41

Reflection

And so, I gradually learn that even on my own and without special skill, there's still a useful role for me to play. That even though I'm in my eighth decade and even though I have lost status as a wife, I can enhance the life of others and take comfort in the simple love they give to me.

I wonder why I spent so many years pursuing goals that were elusive, and which asked so much of me. At last, I realise that just to be myself may be enough. And as I start to feel at ease with the imperfect human being that I am, the love I feel extends to those around. And in the harmony that self-acceptance brings, I am empowered to offer hope and joy to those that I encounter on my path.

42

RAPPROCHEMENT

2018

Quietude

To my astonishment, my husband's death has consequences that I could not have foreseen. The new relationships that I have formed have carried me throughout the early months of desolation and of grief. And these relationships are somehow part of the new life that beckons me. It almost seems as if, in widowhood, there is a path marked out for me. And sometimes as I venture on this path, a tiny miracle or happenstance will guide me further on the road that I am called to tread.

Few weeks have passed without some sign of grace: the strangers who have reached to me to lead me forward or to ease my pain; the tiny celandines that point me to the church's open door; the shaft of light that shines upon my husband's grave.

Such reassurance eases my anxiety and my despair. And as I gradually calm and heal, from time to time some precious semblance of serenity descends upon my shattered world.

And at the heart of this new quietude is faith.

God and His church were in my childhood but my consciousness of these has sometimes faltered in the trauma and distractions of my adult life. But with my husband's suffering and through the new intensity of prayer, all that has changed. God's constant presence is made manifest. The wavering I felt from time to time has vanished now. All doubt has fled.

Somehow, I understand that it is not enough for me to keep this revelation to myself. And so it is that one November day within the red-brick church in Elmwood Road, I solemnly renew the vows that others made on my behalf when I was baptised more than seventy years ago.

I pledge that I will do my best to live and share the faith I have.

Chapter 42

Rapprochement

And side by side with spiritual renewal comes an unexpected opportunity to heal the wounds that are still open, borne of conflicts and confusions of the decades past.

My husband's early adulthood contained its share of trauma and of pain. That misery is dead. It died with Alistair. I won't revive it now. It is not mine to publicise and I won't judge my husband on his actions in a past I never knew and therefore could not understand. My memories of our marriage are untroubled, but I can't deny the buried pain my husband carried through our married life. A marriage must contain and bear each partner's history. With Alistair I could not overlook the silent sorrow that his earlier empty marriages and broken promises inevitably brought. I cannot know whose promise went unkept. I do not need to know who was at fault. Each one of us is flawed and no one, innocent or guilty, can escape the sadness that estrangement and regret must bring.

Yet now and then in life there comes a precious opportunity to move beyond the sadness of the past, to use our understanding and compassion to build harmony and hope.

And somehow in this time of miracles, my husband's daughter comes into my life.

Her given name is Hannah. Circumstance has meant she has been largely absent from her father's life and thus from mine. She is almost unknown to me. Yet here, I understand, is someone to whom customary childhood was denied. The inability of parents far too immature to take responsibility for the actions that they chose would lead to deprivation – for the two of them, but most especially, for their child.

Yet I will come to learn that from a past untrammelled by parental cosseting, a self-created woman has emerged with talent, fairness and humanity.

United through the stark formalities that govern death, inheritance and legal right, we are at first suspicious, awkward, and yet tentatively hopeful too. Our grief is raw, and it exposes feelings and emotions that are sometimes challenging. Anger is just one of these. The anger that I felt on learning that my husband was to die has dissipated with the love and the support I have received. But Hannah's anger is still unresolved and, thus, at times, I falter underneath the weight of this young woman's pain.

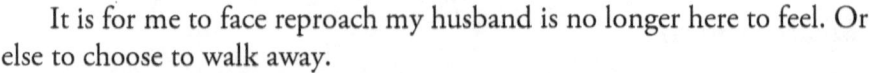

It is for me to face reproach my husband is no longer here to feel. Or else to choose to walk away.

I do not walk away.

And somehow in the frankness of the conversations and the letters that ensue, a pledge is made. Hannah and I agree that rancour must be set aside. We will not trespass on each other's memories. I understand that in this sensitivity, the greater generosity is hers. She knows, as I too recognise, that if we are to nurture this new bond, it must be sheltered from the lingering traces of all deep-remembered hurt. My husband can't defend himself. I will not hear one word against his name. With grace, his daughter honours this request. And in the months and years ahead, the confidence that comes with common longing and with honesty is to sustain the fragile flicker that will flourish – till, at last, our separate sadness is transformed within the wholeness of enduring love.

As months go by, we meet from time to time. Gradually, our stiffness softens as, behind the rigid mask that covers our uncertainty and fear, we each catch glimpses of the individuals that we are. It helps that we both love to write. Our written words provide an opportunity through which we can sometimes discern the things we lack the courage to reveal in speech. And as our e-mails flow, new confidences are exchanged; respect and trust are slowly built.

Despite my ever-present anxiousness in social situations that are strange to me, I sometimes go with Hannah to a concert to hear music that she loves. With eager fascination, I read reviews that she has penned. For her part, this new daughter trudges with me through the woodland cemetery. On Mothering Sunday, she sits quietly beside me in the redbrick church in Elmwood Road.

And months on from my husband's death, the boundaries of childless widowhood dissolve as Hannah turns to me and calmly says,

"I think it's time for you to meet my son."

Sam

Thus, on a crisp and sunny day in Elmwood Road, an unimagined gift arrives upon the doorstep of my home. I cannot quite believe the vision that I see. Sam is just twenty years of age. Before me is a youth whose dangling earring and whose nose stud mark him out as of a generation that is, as yet, almost unknown to me. Yet there is much in Sam that stirs

Chapter 42

my memories. I recognise the narrow hips that seem too slight to sustain all the energy this youth exudes. His wavy hair betrays the luscious waywardness that Alistair could not quite learn to tame. His slender hands are long and sensitive. They are musician's hands. And for a fleeting moment, I am sure that Alistair has come to life again.

I marvel at the mysteries of change and continuity that sweep us ever forward through the miracle of evolution, but which still retain the deep-felt comfort of enduring life and love.

My arms reach out to Sam, the grandchild that my husband never knew. And in the embrace that we share, I am revived.

43

ENDINGS AND BEGINNINGS

2018–2019

The Skin I Shed

Most weekdays I return with growing disillusion and distaste to join my fellow lawyers in the partnership that practices in Bedford Row.

Here in this Georgian building, it is hard to reconcile the present with the past. As I reflect on what once was, I recognise how I have prospered in this place. Here I was left alone to grow in knowledge and in confidence. Here, provided that I was no challenge to the status quo, I was allowed to be myself. And here, with time, I learned to speak for others, with authority, and shelter them till they could move beyond the current crisis in their lives.

Although traditions were conserved within this relic of the past, a liberal spirit was encouraged too – opposing traits that seemed to echo my own character. I understand how fortunate I was to be accepted here.

But more than thirty years have passed since I became a partner in this firm. The zeitgeist's different now. Even in Bedford Row, the mood has changed. The portraits of the founding fathers are no longer on display. The profession of which I was once so proud to be a part has been transformed. It has become a business enterprise. The god of profit now holds sway within these walls and those who do not worship at this shrine will not be welcome here.

The tiny innovations that I helped to make within this place have all been swept away. I fought so hard to help the poor as well as those who could afford to pay our fees. I dreamed that my advice and help would be accessible to all. No longer are such dreams indulged. The legal aid advertisement I placed within the corner of the window is long gone. Time that I once gave without restraint to meet my clients' needs must now be counted rigidly in intervals of minutes, all recorded so the correct price may be charged. The internal hierarchy that, now and then, I was allowed to shun has been replaced by a less human governance.

Chapter 43

And it is clear that this no longer is a place where I can serve my clients in the way that they deserve and need.

I realise at last that I must flee, for if I stay, my force will be snuffed out. I gather my few things. I take down the familiar paintings that have graced my office walls. Impulsively, I press them on a friend. I pack away the small blue box containing the smooth pebbles Aunty Florrie garnered from beside the River Teme. Though tears are close, I will not weep. I must leave quickly if I am to save my dignity.

The blinding light that streams down through the Georgian fanlight camouflages my distress. The black door opens to the world one final time. I linger, briefly, on the steps. All seems to be unchanged. How can this be when values that I clung to are now swept aside?

My gaze rests one last time upon the oval pillar box. Here it was, so many years ago, that I stood, so reluctant to despatch the application that would bring to an end my marriage to Robert.

My eyes alight upon the false acacia that adorns this corner of the street. Its lowest branch is bending earthwards, giving it a stooping shape. Here in this terrace, so symmetrical and straight, it's out of time and place. Perhaps that's why I've always loved it so. Suddenly, my eye is caught, for on this branch a note is pinned. Despite the urgency of my desire to leave this place, I am compelled to pause and read:

"This tree is dangerous. It is to be removed."

My heart stops as I contemplate this faithful friend. For almost thirty years this tree has been a witness to my life. Today it is companion to my grief. Now, beautiful as it still is, its time has come, and leave it must.

And yet I see that, spreading from its base, the tree has pushed up suckers, strong and vibrant green. Thus, even here and even on this day, I understand that nature will console and will revive. And though I know this is a last farewell, I comprehend that far beyond the sorrow of the present day, there is still life ahead.

A New Familiar

In my own neighbourhood, I realise that those who reached to me as strangers in the early days of grief are now familiar faces in my unfamiliar world.

Each Saturday I take the E3 bus. Most weeks I see the man who set aside his anger to console me in my wretchedness. He nods to me. I give small smiles. We learn to be almost polite. If I should miss a week, he later tells me that he was concerned. I reassure him I am fine and that I have been busy with some church work or a bookstall at a fete. In turn he tells me of a film that he is making. It is about life and survival.

One day I notice there are tears in his already bulbous eyes. I enquire, gently. He tells me that his partner's prostate cancer has returned.

"Things are looking bad. The prognosis is not good."

The words stutter with reluctance from his lips. It is my turn to rescue him.

He no longer notices the empty beer cans and the stale cigarettes. I no longer shudder at his approach.

It does not matter that I do not know his name.

The Written Word

"You should have been a writer." Hella cherishes my letter even as she chides. "Of course, you are a writer now – but you should write for other readers, not just me."

Our intermittent correspondence was a lifeline through the decades that have passed. Especially in our middle years, the time between our missives was irregular. Our lives were full then. There were few moments in which we took time to ponder and reflect. Caught up within the heady rhythm of our personal experience, we had no time to nurture all the fleeting friendships in our lives. And yet I always knew, with Hella, there would be another e-mail or a letter or perhaps a random gift. I always understood the ties that bound us would endure.

Once, there were anguished confidences born of teenage longing and uncertainty. Sketches, wit and humour featured in our letters too. Or else, when life was too demanding to find words, an offering would be received, perhaps a pill box made of pearl, or gaiters from Berlin.

It's different now, for so much of our lives is in the past. Our letters are a mélange of occasional new happenings, nostalgia and, at times, philosophy. We rarely contemplate what lies ahead.

Yet as I ponder on the message Hella sends, a tiny seed is planted in my mind.

Weeks on, perusing adverts in a Sunday supplement, I chance upon some lines which are to change my mood and life.

Posara, Italy – the ultimate workshop on how to write.

Chapter 43

Months pass until, as summer lingers to enfold us in its final sunlit hours, I sit in Tuscany within the garden of the Watermill. I have been asked to gaze around me and to notice what I see, so that the writing task that I am set will echo and reflect the things that are imprinted on my consciousness.

Perched on a bench, I glance at foliage that towers over me as, to my left, I see a multitude of early autumn berries. Hips that fall and cascade like a shower of amber rain. Behind them, rising like a host of golden suns, are flowers from the artichoke. Ahead, I see an ivy-covered barn. It looks neglected and my mind flies back to a French poem that I learned in school so many years ago: La Vigne et la Maison. I recollect the story and the words. The poet tells us that he has returned to see a house where once he was at peace within the harmony of family love. Those who once dwelled within this house have vanished. Most are dead. The house now stands deserted and devoid of joy. Vines grow without restraint, covering its emptiness.

Returned to the veranda, I cannot dispel the image that reminds me, cruelly, that days of laughter are behind me now and that I am and will remain alone.

But now there's work for me to do. I set about the task I have been set and I compose a poem from the thoughts that sear my mind. And, as I write, the words fall from my pen.

Am I deserted?
No! No! No!
All that is past, still is.
All that I felt, I feel.
All that was pain, still hurts.

I read aloud. The group is silent now. My voice breaks. Slowly a tear falls. Yet in the recollected pain that I express so openly and in the words that crowd my brain, I recognise that here, for me, a kind of solace lies.

44

THE GIFT FROM AFRICA

2019

Florence

Light filters through the stained-glass window in the chapel in which Morning Prayer is being said. Each day, a faithful few will gather here to read aloud the chosen scripture and familiar prayers. Then each of us is given space to speak in personal supplication or in thanks.

Such prayers are mostly held on weekdays. Thus, we rarely number more than two or three. But on this day, a stranger strides into our midst.

She's tall. Her dark skin gleams, unblemished and unlined. The woollen hat pulled down across her forehead can't disguise her striking features, nor the certainty of her intent. The slight hunch of her shoulders is at odds with both the grace and swiftness of her walk. It speaks to me of burdens borne with fortitude and faith.

We pause to greet her, and she tells us that her name is Florence. She says she seeks a church where she can worship as an Anglican. She is from Africa.

As she seats herself within the circle of the mismatched chairs, it is my turn to speak my personal prayer. And, in this instant, words I do not recognise fall from my usually cautious lips. Yet, as I speak, I realise that what I say is true.

"We welcome strangers in our midst. We welcome Florence and we welcome her with love."

And in this moment, I am certain that there is to be a bond between the two of us – that I must care for her and that she is to be my friend.

A New Routine

As months go by, I live a changed but ordinary life, composed of unfamiliar tasks with which I gradually come to feel at ease. I visit those who find themselves alone or who are overwhelmed by trauma or by grief. I give support to those who care for the disabled and infirm. I sponge the body of a dying man.

And in between all that, I write. And I record the memories that I cannot let go. I recollect the people who have made me what I am today. I reignite the vigour and excitement of my youth and energy. I live again the harshest moments of a life that was abundant in the opportunities it gave to share in sorrow and in pain. Slowly, I begin to see that if I only could reunite and reconcile the joy and pathos that I have experienced, I might receive a peerless blessing. I would be healed. I would be whole.

Beyond my yearning to relive and understand my past, I find that I am drawn to deeper study of the faith that now enfolds me in its wisdom and its grace. Though I'm still eager to avoid all formal gatherings, I overcome my hesitation, and I join a Christian study course. Despite the challenges of my irrational anxiety, I will not let it be a stumbling block. And though I cannot know it yet, in years to come I will find satisfaction as a chaplain to the students who embark on courses such as these. I'll stand beside them as they wrestle with the choices that they have. I'll help to guide them and sustain them as they contemplate the path that lies ahead.

The Grandma Shop

"My daughter wants a grandma," Florence sighs. "The other children at the nursery all have grandmas and Ruella now demands that she must have one too. She seems to think that I can buy one for her at a shop."

I smile, but sadly. For Ruella's grandma is in Africa. She has raised many children, but she'll never pick this grandchild up from school. She will not see this three-year-old engage with life. Yet this is not through any lack of love or care. It is the consequence of rootless lives of those who feel compelled to leave the country of their birth in search of safety and prosperity.

Ruella is not burdened with the gravity of missions and reflections such as this. She is a child and all she wants is to enjoy those things that other children have and do.

Days on, she and her mother visit as I hold a coffee morning for my friends. Beside me, on the sofa that is clothed in amethyst, another widow sits. Ruella makes a beeline for the two of us and flings herself between us until, suddenly, her head inclines onto my lap. She is beside herself with unimagined glee.

As she wriggles with excitement, my thoughts return to her predicament. I glance at Florence, and I say, "Perhaps Ruella thinks you've brought her to that grandma shop of which you spoke!"

Ruella's eyes grow larger, and a hopeful smile transforms her face. Her mother looks at me with questioning eyes and in this moment of decisiveness, I tell myself I will accept the role this child holds out to me.

From this day on, Ruella is a joyful presence in my life. She visits me in search of chocolate. She loves to help me as I water flowers in my garden, even though she squeals and shrieks each time she sees a spider or a snail. Each week in church, she will come late and, though the vicar may be speaking, she will rush to me, a flower in her hand. She will have picked the flower from the wayside. It will be her treasured offering to me.

Ruella has a child's single-mindedness and does not know that other human beings will build barriers of race or class or faith.

She is a precious gift from Heaven.

Ruella is, as yet, untainted. She is love.

45

CATACLYSM

2020

Solitude

In Elmwood Road, I sit alone within the house that holds so many memories. Outside, the world is strange and still. The street is silent and beyond the laurel hedge, the noise of traffic is subdued. The azure skies are empty, for the planes are grounded now.

It is lockdown. I am here in isolation, sheltering from the cruel virus that has swept across our world. I learn about so many deaths and so much grief. I can't absorb this cataclysm, for it seems so far away. It is a frozen picture on a television screen. It's hard to understand that this is real.

Until I slowly realise the impact this will have on my own life. Until I understand that I can't see the people that I love.

I can't see Dipa, even if her pain grows worse. I can't see Kumar, even though we have a bond that's rare. I cannot watch as Indu grows into an adolescent. Although they need me, I cannot be there.

But I remember my life as it used to be. The memories are all around. The house will prompt me if I should forget.

I see, once more, the children at the kitchen table, scrabbling for coloured pens and looking in the painted tin for glue. I see them holding up, for me, their homework and designs.

I see them rushing to the fridge because they know that somewhere in there is a cola or a juice, and they are sure that I won't stop them having one, although their father might say no if he were here.

I remember how Ruella used to race to me along the road from church in search of chocolate and fun. Ruella's rarely still. Her long legs carry her at speed. I miss her childlike eagerness and energy. One night I dreamed that she was running down a hill. I waited for her at the bottom, arms outstretched. She ran straight past me just as if I was invisible to her. And when I woke, I thought that now she had perhaps forgotten me.

And I remember Razia and Karim, rushing to my door and rattling at the bell. They loved to hide themselves, just out of sight, and then to leap and startle me. They always understood that they came first with me. That nothing could usurp their place within my world. That they were free to be themselves.

None of them has freedom now.

I recall the children's made-up words and fantasies. I gaze upon the mantelpiece that Kumar always called a mantelshelf because he'd never seen a proper fireplace before. I still can see the bush next door that Indu told me was a dinosaur.

Remembrance is my consolation. Although the children may not visit me for months or even years, they are alive within my head. They still enchant me, and they still compel my joy.

But in the many hours that I can't dream, joy is suppressed. I am bewildered, frightened and confused. How can the sun still shine upon a world that is perhaps forever damned? Why has the sky not fallen in on us, bringing our suffering to an end? Where are the tears of Heaven that we know as rain?

I am desolate. The world I knew has changed forever, so it seems. I marvel at the quietude. Yet in my heart, I am afraid.

Until I hear the birds.

Birds – ungainly pigeons, long-tailed tits and drab, familiar sparrows – have been ever-present in the untamed garden that I love. From time to time, I used to see a robin perch upon the wooden seat my husband loved so much. But when these shy birds sang, they made a slight and subtle sound that mingled with the muffled hum of traffic which flowed eastward, towards the morning sun. Yet now the birdsong takes its proper place. Each piercing call is confident, unchallenged till another songbird flutters down or swoops to reclaim its domain in what was once our human territory. A tiny wren alights upon the wires of the birdbath hanging from the smoke bush branch. A common blackbird perches on the fence.

And suddenly, I hear a perfect symphony that drowns the silence of my solitude. And even though I'm told that death is everywhere, I know this is untrue. I see the life beyond my windows, and I give thanks for this new, recreated world.

Chapter 45

Companions in the Loneliness

Days pass and slowly I adjust as I discover ways and means by which I may survive the exile that's imposed on me.

I am fortunate, for even now that I am banished from the world I used to know, I need not be deprived of human touch. For we are told by powerful men that those who live alone may form a 'bubble' with another family. Thus, it is natural that, within days, I welcome Florence to my home again. Her spartan high-rise is no place in which a child of four should be confined. Ruella needs the space and freedom that my garden gives, and I need respite from my loneliness. With Florence, I take courage, for together with the optimistic, caring hearts we share, we'll see this through. Ruella's innocence and ignorance distract us. They remind us of our adult duty to create security and calm. Thus, Florence watches, smiling, as Ruella hides and calls to me, insisting I must seek her out. And as I dance beside this child, to songs of pirate tales, the sound of laughter blots out my despair and fear.

On other days I am amazed to learn about technology as my computer screen becomes a window on a distant world that I may never see. It serves to reunite me with my friends, as well as other students on the Christian studies course I take.

But, more than that, it shrinks the world and brings it to my home. To those who care to look beyond the edges of once inward-looking lives, it opens up the richness and diversity of human life. The other writers in the Wednesday Circle that I join are based in distant countries, some of which I scarcely know. Each week we write at speed as thoughts fall from our pens. The trigger word or phrase that we are given propels us to a store of memories that otherwise might lie forgotten in our minds. And as we share our inmost thoughts, new bonds are forged and boundaries dissolve.

Strange Consolation

Despite these innovations and discoveries, this time is sobering. I mourn the faithful friend who died in the first days of this harsh new regime. She was my friend for decades and a constant comforter in my own grief. But though I love her, I can't honour her in death or stand beside her stricken family. All I can do is place a card upon the altar in the church.

Throughout this cruel lockdown it will stand in recognition of her as it raises her to God.

But from an unexpected source comes consolation of a deep, enduring kind. For Hannah, in her sensitivity, sends videos of music that she hopes might comfort me. The solemn strains of Handel's *Jephtha* now pervade the home I love, and I am moved by images of mortals borne by angels through celestial skies.

This almost-daughter pledges that for every day that I must spend in lockdown, she will send me music for my consolation and delight. And as the weeks extend and Hannah fills my home with other offerings of care, in music and in letters that she writes, I realise that, even in this time of isolation and despair, I have been blessed.

46

REFLECTION

2024

It's hard to realise that eight decades of life have almost passed. It seems impossible. Yet time does not stand still. Time rushes forward to a future that I cannot see. I try to hold it, but it slips and slides away like sifted sand. I face the transience of earthly life. Here in the evening hour, I will not look ahead. I choose instead to contemplate the past that nurtured me and shaped the path on which I walk today.

As I reflect, I see again the child that I once was. I see again the Knighton of my early childhood years. And from the window of the house where I was born, I see once more the sheep that graze within the field beyond the grey stone wall. Beyond the field, the willow trees of yellow green still grace the riverbank. Once more, I walk, reluctantly, with Mummy to the Knighton church. I feel again the tautness of her grip, which always challenged my recalcitrance. I feel again the fierce ferocity of our conflicting wills.

I realise how much my mother's sense of right and wrong lives on in me. For even now it is so hard for me to shun the rules she set. Yet gradually, with time and hurt and with experience, I've come to realise that I must also listen to the voice that is my own. And though in adult life I often cared too much what others thought of me, increasingly, my sense of self prevails.

This was the constant conflict of my life. I could not always be the person others wanted me to be. I longed to please and satisfy the ones for whom I deeply cared. I always tried. I often knew that I would disappoint. And when I failed, as frequently I did, I could not love myself. It took so long for me to understand that I would never be at peace until I could accept myself with all the kindness and forgiveness that I try to show to every other human being.

At other times, I was impetuous and rashly gave my trust when it had not been earned. This led to misery and woe. I think of Johnny and the perfect joy of our togetherness. I was too much in love to spurn the union he had no right to offer me. I was too weak and overwhelmed to turn away. Yet, somehow, even in this time of heightened anguish and despair, I learned so much of the complexities of human life. And though I'm shamed and saddened by the hurt I've caused, I give thanks for the love I knew.

The months in Bethlem showed me that we cannot look to others for a remedy for what we see as imperfections of the psyche or the soul. The answer lies within ourselves. Yet I found lasting inspiration in the care and the compassion of the fellow travellers who shared my isolation and distress. They gave me courage to believe that when we reach out and support each other, we begin to heal ourselves.

In other hospitals, I faced the agony that was to lead to certain childlessness. But there I learned that suffering that's shared and understood can lead to bonds that outlast any mortal pain.

In times of sadness and in grief, I was uplifted by the constant beauty of the natural world. I stood in awe before the reassurance of the shaft of light that shone upon my husband's grave.

Yet sometimes, in the moments of my positivity, I faced bewilderment when natural instinct led me to cross barriers that many others saw and would not move beyond. I did not need to learn the value of diversity. Why could not every mortal understand the joy that comes from walking with our fellow human beings on a road that's free of barriers of race or class or creed? Why could so many never share the openness of heart that was my natural gift? A gift that drew me to attempt to build a tiny private universe where no one is an 'other' and where every stranger may aspire to share a communality of love.

So much of life is unpredictable. My life brought me within reach of those whose lives were vastly different from my own. Chance, masquerading as misfortune, took me into hospitals of body and of mind, where I would live a life of suffering beside the sick. Chance took me to a place in Notting Hill, where I could glimpse and, for a fleeting moment, share the lives of aliens and immigrants. And, in my thirties, chance, together with a stranger's generosity and trust, guided me to a career in law which was to anchor me and hold me fast in a position from which I could grow. And shelter others in the crises of their lives.

I am amazed and grateful for the chance encounters with those strangers who discerned potential and ability that lay unrecognised within

Chapter 46

myself. And I am thankful for the energy, resilience and curiosity that helped me to take up the challenges they offered me.

Now in the early evening of my life, I see how much of this was shaped by God. For He was there in the encounters through which I learned that, timid as I often was, I could stand up for others and the justice they deserved. God guided me to the experiences through which I slowly garnered seeds of self-respect.

I realised, much later than I might have done, I did not need to change and try to fit the image others might project on me. I learned that it was possible to love myself.

And, strangely, it was often in life's harshest hours that I would learn to tread a path that in time's fullness was to lead to joy.

The years of love I knew with Alistair led in the end to loss and grief. Yet with my grief came renewed faith and hope. My husband could not be replaced, but somehow in the sorrow that I felt and feel, more barriers dissolved as strangers came into my life. Although their stories are not mine to tell, these people, too, had needs that were then unfulfilled. And through the extra sensitivity that comes with loss, we recognised our common lack. We held each other in the hope our mutual pain would wither and dissolve.

Years on, these spiritual daughters, sons and children populate my life. They bring me worry and they bring me hope. Our needs have dovetailed. God has ensured that this is so. The pain of childlessness I carried for so long has been assuaged.

My life is rich. My spiritual children grace my days. They illustrate the fulfilled promise of redemption and enduring love. With God, the bleakest emptiness is coloured in with joy. Love given out or taken from us is replenished, if in unexpected ways.

And now I see that every setback is as nothing when I measure it against the things I have. I realise that all my childhood visions and my early life experience have lingered on within the woman that I have become. I understand that, since there is no turning back in life, each one of us must harness all the love and beauty that we can, for only these sustain us when the past is gone.

And since I've learned to carry these within and sought to share them with the ones I met along my path, I see there is another miracle.

The love I share shines back at me and, in acceptance of myself, I add to all the generosity that life has shown, the gift of peace.

Epilogue

Behind me is the contemplation of the life I've lived for eighty years. My task is almost done. I've come to understand so much about myself. I hope that others, too, will learn from my account of happenings and challenges that may have touched their lives as well as mine.

From this reflection I have been able to assess my life, excluding almost nothing that has mattered to me. I have been able to contemplate with clarity the frailties I had – but finally I have developed a more rational understanding of my weaknesses and faults. I have been able to appreciate more fully the kindness and the help that I've been given. And I have recognised the strengths I had and have. I came to see that, with time and pain and with experience, I gradually became a true reflection of the self I was.

Finally, I have learned that, just as I am, I too have worth.

Now in the seventh year of widowhood, my career behind me, I am finally released from the burden of others' expectations. My path ahead is mine to choose.

And in these last few years, I have received the precious gifts of new relationships and close enduring bonds. For those who grace these final chapters, those I call my spiritual daughters, sons and grandchildren, have welcomed and accepted me with simple, undemanding love.

The love I share shines back at me. At last, I can float freely in acceptance of myself.

I am at peace.

Yet other lives have impacted upon my hesitant, emergent self. And if the reader wonders what has happened to the characters who graced my early life, I can tell something, if not all.

Most if not all the characters from my first forty years are dead. But in this age of internet, some snatches of their later lives have been recorded for posterity.

I know that George became the father of the sons for which he longed. Charles died last year, but in his life, he knew prestige and honour for his wisdom and humility. Childless though he was, his eulogy declared he was a father to the many who he mentored and advised.

Of those who shared my life in Bethlem, I have traced only one. It has been heartening to learn that one of those for whom I cared became, in adulthood, a woman of compassion and a counsellor to those whose frailties she understood. I'm full of joy to learn that someone other than myself survived and thrived. And that she, Rosamund, has dedicated her life's work to those who suffer still.

And what of Johnny, who for so long dominated every thought I had? Throughout my forties, fifties, and sixties I worried for him and what life held for him after I removed my presence from his life. Then one night, in my seventies, I searched the internet and chanced upon a photograph. And in it there he sat, with daughter Dee behind his chair. And at his side, despite it all, was Emmeline. Her arm stretched out protectively and rested on her husband's arm. And something in her gaze alerted me. Instinctively I understood that this man for whom each of us had cared was gravely ill. And although I was shocked and saddened by this understanding of his plight, my heart was gladdened that he had his family's care.

As Alistair had mine.

A few years on I learned that Johnny, claimed by Parkinson's disease, had died.

The fate of Barbara alone eluded me. Our bond was deep. Throughout the years, we met from time to time. Each of us was an eager witness to the other's life. We shared each other's failures and success. Until one day, in 1985 or thereabouts, we met outside a private bank at Charing Cross. I gazed upon her careworn countenance one final time. And as she looked at me, she whispered wistfully, "You look so young."

Epilogue

I knew then that our paths would never cross again.

These people touched my life, as perhaps I touched theirs. The memories they leave me are their gift to me.

And beyond these few names, I give thanks to all who grace this record of my life. Of those who may feel slighted or impugned by what I write of them, I ask forgiveness, understanding and compassion too. My gratitude to them is equally sincere. For they brought richness to the world I knew, and they too helped to shape a life with which at last I am at peace.

HOW TO LIVE

Embrace the wonders of the universe.
Marvel at the Natural World.
Greet each day as if it is the first.

Linger as you savour every moment.
Create memories to cherish.
Gather love to ward against calamity.

Cultivate an open heart and open eyes.
Notice everything.
Seek the soul beneath the dressed-up skin.

Welcome strangers. Turn them into friends.
Understand there's something good in everyone.
Be prepared to love the one you're wary of.

Nurture children. Venerate the frail and elderly.
Listen to their confidences.
Heal the wounds and inspire hope.

Count the miracles and share the blessings.
Even those that looked at first like pain.
Hold the suffering in your arms until they're whole again.

Share the wisdom God has given you.
Share your life.
Share love.

Acknowledgements

I would like to acknowledge that no achievement in life is possible without help and encouragement. Producing this memoir is no exception, and it would be impossible to name all those who have contributed to the personal satisfaction that I have gained in completing this record of my life.

Whilst I hope that this book may prove of interest to others, especially those who may face similar challenges to those that marked my life, the writing of it has brought to me a sense of peace and, at times, of joy. A day that I write is a day when I am happy and, beyond that, these reflections have helped me to make sense of a life that, in the living, was often challenging and sometimes turbulent.

My gratitude goes out to those who gave support, in particular the members of the Writers' Circle to which I have belonged for the past five years. Thank you to Rhoda Bangerter, Cécile Desmarest, Isabelle Min, Caron Moran, Vivien Moss, and Charmaine Saw.

Jo Parfitt was the link that brought us all together. More than that, it was at her workshop in Tuscany that I first understood that writing would change my life. I thank you, Jo, for your constant mentoring and friendship. And for the way your introductions have opened up my world.

Samantha Marcussen took on the heavy labour of critiquing my manuscript, particularly the second half. Her editorial skills were applied relentlessly in the finessing of my craft. Thank you, Samantha, for your energy and generosity. And thank you also that you never tried to change the way I knew that I must write or the direction that my writing took.

Lastly, I record my special thanks to Hella Ernsting Hermanns. At age thirteen Hella and I were assigned to one another by our schools as pen friends. Despite the natural gaps that opened up at times in our separate and busy lives – led countries and sometimes continents apart – our unwavering friendship has survived for more than sixty-five years. Through

Acknowledgements

that time Hella has been an exemplar of constancy, punctuated by a sense of adventure or inquiry which she has always encouraged me to share.

And Hella it was who, shortly after my husband's death, first suggested that, as well as my contribution to letters that continued to flow between us, I might write for other people too. Thank you, Hella, for planting in my mind the seed of creativity, for reading everything that I have written. And for giving me, at a low point in my life, the confidence to be myself.

About the Author

Born on the borders of England and Wales in 1943, Lesley was, from an early age, led by a burgeoning passion for the underdog, the unfortunate and the displaced. She took a social science degree at Birmingham University, specialising in the African diaspora. Moving to North London's trendy Crouch End in the late sixties, rather than embrace the excitement of the age, she looked on from the sidelines, a dreamer, deep in thought. The roads to life, love and career were blighted by an unexplained anxiety that led her to admit herself to the once notorious Bethlem mental hospital for several months. Despite being denied the treatment for which she had hoped, it was here that Lesley began her metamorphosis into the strong, capable woman she remains, still in demand in a range of voluntary mentoring and legal roles, despite being in her eighties. Her highly successful professional life began almost by accident when a day's work as a temporary typist turned into a career in general litigation, eventually specialising in family law, and as a partner in a Holborn law firm. Whilst family has always been important to her, Lesley was, sadly, unable to have children. Today, widowed for seven years after a happy twenty-three-year marriage to Alistair, she lives in leafy Chiswick, loved and supported by children, friends and people who regard her as family and to whom she is Mummy, Mum or Grandma. Coming to creative writing in recent years, she now spends many hours each week involved in online classes, writing poetry and reflective essays.

The church is an important part of her life, and she has become course chaplain for The Diocese of London Christian Studies course.

www.ingramcontent.com/pod-product-compliance
Lightning Source LLC
Chambersburg PA
CBHW030256100526
44590CB00012B/414